Touching the Face of the Cosmos

Touching the Face of the Cosmos

On the Intersection of Space Travel and Religion

Paul Levinson and Michael Waltemathe
Editors

Connected Editions
New York 2016

Library of Congress Control Number: 2015953993

ISBN 978-0823272105 (hardcover)

ISBN 978-0823272112 (paperback)

ISBN 978-1561780426 (ebook)

Printed in the United States of America

18 17 16 5 4 3 2 1

First edition

Contents

Touching the Face of the Cosmos

Introductions and Acknowledgments

Paul Levinson & Michael Waltemathe

Maybe it was because I grew up in the 1950s and 60s, in the dawn of the space age. Maybe I would have felt this way anyway. But it always has seemed self-evident to me that the future of humanity would not be confined to Planet Earth – that our future was in the cosmos at large, and we would not progress much further in understanding who we are, what life is really about, from our vantage point solely down here on Earth.

I was delighted to make the acquaintance of Michael Waltemathe one summer evening a few years ago at a little panel at Union Docs in Brooklyn and find that he felt much the same about humanity and its necessary future beyond this planet.

Back in the golden age of space exploration, the main motive was military, or competition between the United States and the Soviet Union to get the literally upper hand in space. After the U.S. decisively won the "space race" with Americans walking on the Moon, the motive shifted to scientific knowledge. In more recent decades, commercial benefit – making money from endeavors in space – has joined the roster of reasons to move out into our solar system.

And yet, we have barely moved. No humans have walked again on the Moon since the Apollo program. Nor have human beings made it to Mars or any place else beyond the orbit of our planet. Other nations such as China and the European Union have begun getting out into space – good news for our species – but so far the missions have been devoid of human beings. Robots can provide a lot of useful and important data, but they lack the judgement and poetic eye of humans.

When my book *Realspace: The Fate of Physical Presence On and Off Planet* was published in 2003, I wondered if a reason for our slow progress in space – perhaps *the* reason – was that we and our policy makers were not in touch with what might be the most important benefit of going out into space. This benefit is certainly not military, not commercial, and not really scientific. It could more aptly be described as spiritual or even religious: we go out into space to learn more of what religions seek to show us, more of who we are in this universe of existence.

Michael and I began a casual series of conversations about this via Skype, at my summer place on Cape Cod, and elsewhere. We batted around the possibility of organizing a conference which would explore the intersection of space travel and religion, with a possible anthology of conference presentations to follow. But at some point I realized that a book, and the permanent impression it can make, would be a better way to start. And thus *Touching the Face of the Cosmos: On the Intersection of Space Travel and Religion* was born, with thanks to Peggy Noonan who wrote the moving speech delivered by Ronald Reagan to the nation about touching "the face of God" after the Challenger exploded in 1986, paraphrasing the poem "High Flight," written by aviator John Gillespie Magee, Jr., who lost his life in 1941 when his plane crashed. (Magee's sonnet was in turn inspired by a poem written three years earlier by Cuthbert Hick.)

But *Touching the Face of the Cosmos* is about hope not loss, and towards this end it presents a wide array of views and styles. The first decision I made about the anthology was to include science fiction stories along with essays, since so much of our thinking about space has come from fiction, in writing and on movie and television screens. The writers of these essays and stories come from the halls of religion (including Guy Consolmagno SJ, Rt. Rev. James D. Heiser, Rabbi Barry Schwartz), science (Gregory Benford, David Brin, Kathleen Torpe), and academe (Deana L. Weibel, Joshua Ambrosius, Lance Strate, James McGrath), and sometimes more than one of these precincts (Guy Consolmagno is Director of the Vatican Observatory). John Glenn has famously been to space, twice; Jeremy Saget has volunteered to go to Mars; Michael O'Neal and Marianne Dyson have worked for NASA. Jack Dann, Gregory Benford, and Robert J. Sawyer have been to space, only in their minds, but have won awards for some of the sundry trips of the intellect they shared with the world. Molly Vozick-Levinson has been to space through the visions of the children she teaches in her preschool.

As befits the international perspective inherent in any book about our planet, our writers come from all over the world, and include Wu Jianzhong from China, Philip Gibson from Laos, Christian Weidemann from Germany, Jeremy Saget from France, Juan Pablo Marrufo del Toro SJ from Mexico, Robert J. Sawyer from Canada, and Jack Dann from Australia. Arlan Andrews Sr., Kyle Aisteach, Gregory Benford, David Brin, Dave Creek, Marianne Dyson, James Heiser, Tom Klinkowstein, James McGrath, and Alex Shvartsman all write science fiction from the U.S.A.

The science fiction stories are presented in order of their distance from 2015, with the nearest-future stories first. They continue the fictional exploration of religion in space launched in long form in modern times by James Blish's *A Case of Conscience*, whose tale of a Jesuit investigating alien intelligence on another planet won the Hugo Award for best novel of 1958 (based on his 1953 novella).

Not everyone in the anthology has an equal commitment to organized religion. David Brin's essay (he writes nonfiction and fiction, as do many of our contributors) is in effect a dialogue with religious believers. Not everyone in the anthology is equally enthused about humans going out into space. Lance Strate, in an essay that riffs on the title of the anthology, explains that his heart wants us off of this planet but his head may tell him otherwise. Almost everyone in this anthology holds that humans in outer space will strengthen the spiritual beliefs we bring with us from Earth. Christian Weidemann and Peter Hess, however, also each argue that extension of human civilization to worlds beyond our planet and solar system pose challenges to some of the very foundations of our religions.

But everyone in the anthology is in agreement that outer space will play some crucial role in our future, and our spirituality will be a necessary part of this, a toolkit of the soul that we take with us when we voyage to the stars.

###

I could fill a book with the names of people to thank for my interest in space, and therefore this anthology, but I'll limit myself to just the following: John Harrington, Dean of Faculty, Fordham University, for supporting my last-minute trip to Columbus, Ohio this past summer to interview John Glenn; Kathleen Dancey, Adam Sackowitz, and Peter Bucher for helping with the logistics of the John Glenn interview; Tom Klinkowstein, for inviting Michael Waltemathe and me to the little conference in Brooklyn where we first met; and my wife, Tina Vozick, our children Molly and Simon, and their spouses Carlos and Sarah, for innumerable conversations about space travel, the future, and this anthology, and other inspirations.

And special thanks to Joel Iskowitz, whose portraits of John Glenn set that interview in motion, and whose work has appeared on U.S coins, stamps around the world, U.S. Congressional gold medals, and NASA murals, for his design of the cover of this anthology; and Brittany Miller, a New York City-based visual artist and educator, for her interior illustrations.

– Paul Levinson, New York City, December 2015

It is what they all say: When I was young I wanted to become an astronaut. During my childhood in the 1970s and 80s the Space Race was already over. Skylab was launched when I was a kid and forced to reenter when I was seven years old. I actually remember only that single moment from the whole Apollo program. It was doomed before it could be saved by just beginning the Shuttle program. The Shuttle replaced the explorers of Apollo and suddenly astronauts were analogous to truck drivers in the public mindset. The space program was not what it used to be, although I did not even know firsthand what it used to be.

Still, space exploration had an uncanny fascination for me, but only in an historical sense. I remember staying up all night for reruns of the Apollo 11

Moon landings during the 25th anniversary celebrations while studying for my university exams in chemistry. I felt sadness that we had lost the ability to go to the Moon and beyond. My childhood toys and books had promised a great big beautiful tomorrow in outer space.

Maybe that is why I turned from the sciences to religion and theology. But the fascination with spaceflight was still there, when in 2011, I read about this initiative funded by DARPA and NASA which was inviting scholars from all different fields of academia to contribute to the goal of building an Interstellar Spaceship within the next 100 years. It was called the 100-Year-Starship (100yss) and the German news magazine *Der Spiegel* termed it an initiative for dreamers, lunatics, and weirdos. My friend Christian Weidemann and I submitted paper proposals immediately and were accepted a couple of weeks later. We were going to speak at a NASA conference!

This conference was indeed a meeting ground of the most weird and wonderful people imaginable. I sat in the backroom of a cheap diner with NASA engineers and scientists, with anthropologists and designers, with philosophers and priests. It was a mixed group of scholars who showed mutual respect for the different ways in which different academic fields can contribute to enabling humanity to go into space (again). When we retired to the hotel pool late at night and the discussions still kept going on until early in the morning about all sorts of things space and science and religion, I was hooked.

At that 100yss conference in Orlando I met a designer from New York City by the name of Tom Klinkowstein, who invited me to be a speaker at a little panel at Union Docs in Brooklyn. The rest – as they say – is history. Also speaking at that panel was a guy named Paul Levinson. We met that night and hit it off right away.

About a year later – the night we heard of Neil Armstrong's passing – Paul and I took to Twitter and started talking about fueling interest in human space exploration again. From Twitter we went to Skype and finally to a most memorable discussion at Paul's summer place in Cape Cod on how to best achieve our goal of motivating space exploration by combining it with religion. The idea of a book on space travel and religion was discussed and finally agreed upon while swimming in the Atlantic Ocean on a balmy summer day. Paul had the great idea of also including science fiction in the anthology, as it provides the basis for quite a bit of our scholarly thinking about the future of space exploration.

This book is now finished. We went from an idea to this book in a very short time with help and contributions from different people from different countries. The common theme of space exploration brought all these different people together. With renewed interest in space exploration from countries, governments, and now also private and public companies, the future of space exploration seems wide open again. Finally it seems that we may be taking the next step in becoming a solar-system civilization. And religion as part of the human condition will certainly play a role in that part of our future as well!

###

There have been a lot of people who were part of editing this book. Some gave me ideas and made contributions, some went part of the way with me. Others I met on the way and I learned a lot from them. I can not mention all of them, so I will limit myself to just a few: Christian Weidemann went to that conference in Orlando with me and shared my dream, Tom Klinkowstein furthered it by inviting me and Paul to talk at that conference in Brooklyn. Phillip T. Metzger and Mike O'Neal gave me great insight into the minds of "those space people" and have been great friends ever since. Kathleen Toerpe and Jim Pass invited me to become part of Astrosociology Research and gave my scholarly interests a peer group. And last not least, my wife Anne and my son John accompanied me on this journey and took part in countless conversations about space exploration and religion.

– Michael Waltemathe, Bochum, Germany, December 2015

About the Editors

Paul Levinson, Ph.D., is Professor of Communication & Media Studies at Fordham University in NYC. His science fiction novels include *The Silk Code* (winner of Locus Award for Best First Science Fiction Novel of 1999), *Borrowed Tides* (2001), *The Consciousness Plague* (2002), *The Pixel Eye* (2003), *The Plot To Save Socrates* (2006), *Unburning Alexandria* (2013), and *Chronica* (2014) – the last three of which are also known as the Sierra Waters trilogy, and are historical as well as science fiction. His nonfiction books, including *The Soft Edge* (1997), *Digital McLuhan* (1999), *Realspace* (2003), *Cellphone* (2004), and *New New Media* (2009; 2nd edition, 2012), have been translated into twelve languages. He appears on CNN, MSNBC, Fox News, the Discovery Channel, National Geographic, the History Channel, NPR, and numerous TV and radio programs. His 1972 LP, *Twice Upon a Rhyme*, was re-issued in 2010. He was President of the Science Fiction and Fantasy Writers of America, 1998-2001. He reviews television in his InfiniteRegress.tv blog, and was listed in *The Chronicle of Higher Education's* "Top 10 Academic Twitterers" in 2009.

Michael Waltemathe, Ph.D. is senior lecturer in religious education at the Department of Protestant Theology at Ruhr-University Bochum in Germany. His academic interests include the relationship between human space exploration and religion, connections between media, art and religion (especially video-games and religion), and the science-religion debate and its place in religious education. His publications include a monograph on computer games and religion and several articles on spaceflight and religion, media and religion and religious education. Michael also co-authored "Destination 2064," a computer game for the John Calvin anniversary in 2009.

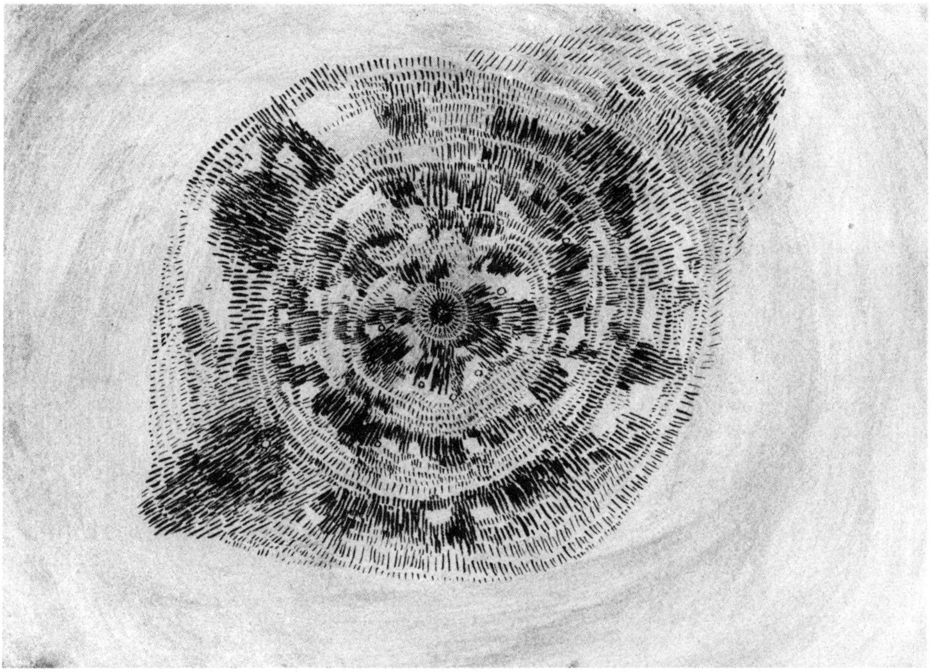

Interview with John Glenn

Paul Levinson

John Glenn welcomed me into his office at the John Glenn College of Public Affairs at Ohio State University in Columbus, Ohio, on a beautiful summer afternoon, July 30, 2015. Seated next to the former Senator and astronaut – the first American to orbit the Earth, in 1962, and the oldest person to fly in space in 1998 – was Annie, his wife of 72 years. State Representative Michael P. Sheehy and Adam Sackowitz (who helped arrange the meeting) were also in the room, and joined the conversation, as did Annie. I began by asking the Senator what impact his first flight into space had on him, as a spiritual being ...

John Glenn: My going to space strengthened my religion – to see everything, what we are part of, part of creation, to see whole nations and oceans and everything at a single glance, that just strengthened my belief. That's not where it came from, it just strengthened the beliefs I already had.

Paul Levinson: What has motivated Earthlings to get off this planet? Military motivation, you of course were part of that, even before the space program; there is scientific motivation, you've been part of that as well; and more recently there's been commercial motivation. But one of the things which struck me as being missing from that list is a spiritual or religious motivation – and perhaps one of the reasons we have not gotten out into space much further than the Moon, which, as you know, happened in the late 1960s and early 1970s, is because our space efforts have not acknowledged this missing spiritual aspect. I wonder what you might think about that? Would you like to see churches, religious institutions, along with governments and private enterprise, more involved in space exploration?

JG: I think that will come as people go to different places in space and I think we take our religious faith with us wherever we go and the same is true going into space. And it will be true whether we go to Mars, or Pluto, or wherever we may wind up eventually going. I'm sure that once we get there our religious faith and belief or beliefs will not be altered, except maybe we'll appreciate the enormity of it all, more than we ever did before.

PL: Some people see a conflict between science and religion. For example, fundamentalists occasionally deny evolution, the Church persecuted Galileo. Yet one of the contributors to this anthology is Brother Guy Consolmagno, the "Pope's Astronomer". What do you think about religion versus science? Do

you think that they have common ground and they have shared goals?
JG: They are complementary. I don't see them as competitive at all, I think they're complementary. The more you know about things, the more you appreciate, the more it strengthens our religious beliefs.
PL: When you went into space for the first time: Did it change you as far as what you thought about the universe and the human place in the universe?
JG: No, not really.
PL: You already had a feeling?
JG: I already had a feeling. I had done a lot of study of space, and our solar system, so it didn't really change my views of that at all. I think some people, in looking at it, they say there I was in space and saw the face of God or something like that. That's not the way it was at all with me.
PL: You saw the universe as it was. But that in a sense was still a spiritual experience?
JG: It's an experience, yes, that backs up my religious faith. It doesn't replace it, didn't start it, didn't stop it, just strengthens it.
PL: Are you optimistic that our species will get out into space.... There have been civilizations like the Chinese, for example, they invented the printing press, but they never had newspapers. The Aztecs invented the wheel but just used it as a toy. We've gotten out into space but it hasn't been as much as many people would want. So what do you think about the future? Is there hope for us getting off this planet and established in space?
JG: Eventually. My take on how far we'll go in space: I'm a little disappointed we haven't gone further than we have in this interim period since I was up there. But I think we are encouraged to go further into space, the more we learn things that are of value and benefit to us right here on Earth. You know, we are doing a lot of research up there right now, on the International Space Station, a lot of great research. And that hasn't taken us out to Mars or anything like that, but just to go to Mars because it's there or Pluto – do I think we will do some of these things sometime? Yeah, I do. But I think it will come because we will be curious about the fact that there may be some things with regard to the study of cancer right here on Earth or research of some other kind that's a benefit to us right here that led us on out deeper into space. I don't think we go just to go, just to make a trip, but we go because there may be some benefit for us right here on Earth.
Adam Sackowitz: Can you speak about your first flight into space in February 1962 – what did it feel like to go up there and what were you thinking? And what was the mood of the country at that point toward the space program and the Mercury astronauts?
JG: Well, the country felt that we had been outdone by the Soviets, and the Soviets were claiming that their system of government was superior to ours because they were better at research and better at technical matters and they said they could prove it by the fact that their space craft were going into space successfully while ours too often were blowing up on the launch pad. And they were right in that respect! So I think our country hoped and thought that we

would come back and that's what Project Mercury was all about – it was to show that we were not that far behind and that we could be successful, even where the Soviets had not been successful and that's what we proved.
AS: What did it feel like? You know, you're on the Mercury, the Atlas rocket. What were you feeling at that point, when you went out to space in the capsule?
JG: People often ask: "What did it feel like?" And among the astronauts there was sort of a standard joking answer, not all that serious. But to "How did you feel at launch?" the answer was: "How do you think *you* would feel if you knew you were on top of two million parts built by the lowest bidder on a government contract?" But it's much more serious than that – we were aware of our efforts to try and come back from our being behind in the "Space Race" as it was called. And we did – we came back and were able to set our plans for the future. And we did that as a nation – and that resurgence of national pride and being able to do that were one of the main benefits that came out of the space program at that time.
AS: What do you see right now as the most important issues that are facing the country?
JG: The economy! As usual. The economy. We still have a very unbalanced budget. We haven't learned to deal with that yet. Although we did have in the last two years of the Bill Clinton administration a surplus – we were paying down the national debt at that time. So ... we got away from that again. And we haven't learned how to deal with the ISIS problem and the terrorism problem.
PL: If there was a President or someone in Congress who said: "I don't care if the budget is not balanced, I don't care if we go further into deficit because I want to allocate X number of billions of dollars for our effort in space." What would you say to that?
JG: Well, space isn't the only thing we have to consider here. We have so many other things in our society to consider – space is just one. So I would not eliminate everything else and just sponsor space.
PL: Back in 1962, if you had to predict where we would be in space in 2015, would it be where we are now, or further ahead, or not as far?
JG: Oh, I thought we probably would have moved out a little bit more than we have. But there was no way to predict that at that time anyway. A lot depended on the international competition, so it's not something you could have predicted back at that time.
PL: Were you pleased with Ed Harris' portrayal of you in The Right Stuff movie?
JG: I've never met Ed Harris.
Michael P. Sheehy: You saw the movie, though, right?
JG: Yeah, but I didn't ...
MPS: He didn't care for it.
Annie Glenn: But the book was excellent!
JG: I thought Tom Wolfe's book had a theme that ran through it that was pretty good. But Hollywood got hold of it and they started hamming it up and

making things up and part of this movie was based in fact and lot of it based in fiction.
AG: John took our daughter to see it, but we didn't like it. But the next movie about space ...
PL: the Tom Hanks movie–
JG: Apollo 13
AG: That was a really good movie.
JG: That was pretty factual. It's the most factual of these space movies.
AG: Because the person who got it developed was our neighbor.
JG: Jim Lovell
PL: So you knew the inside story and the movie was true to that story.
AG: Exactly.
PL: I want to thank you for all you've done for humanity. There are few people who have done a fraction of what you've done.
JG: Well, thank you.
AS: Some amazing pictures here [shows the Glenns some pictures of Friendship 7, the Mercury space craft that John Glenn used to orbit the Earth]
AG: Friendship 7. You know, John asked our kids to name the spacecraft.
JG: Well, you know that thing with "naming your craft" came from World War II, when people named their aircraft or bomber or whatever. And then NASA finally said: "If you want to put names on it, that would be ok." And so the "7" was on all of them, but I let my kids decide. I said the flight is probably going to get some international attention and what would you like to be the message that we send to the rest of the world? And they had a whole bunch of names and they finally came down with this "Friendship" one and that's the one they picked out of all the different potential names. And it was what I thought was the best one, too. So my kids actually named it.

An audio recording of our entire conversation, which touched on some matters political and biographical not specifically related to space, can be found here: http://paullev.libsyn.com/interview-with-john-glenn - PL

Part I

Essays

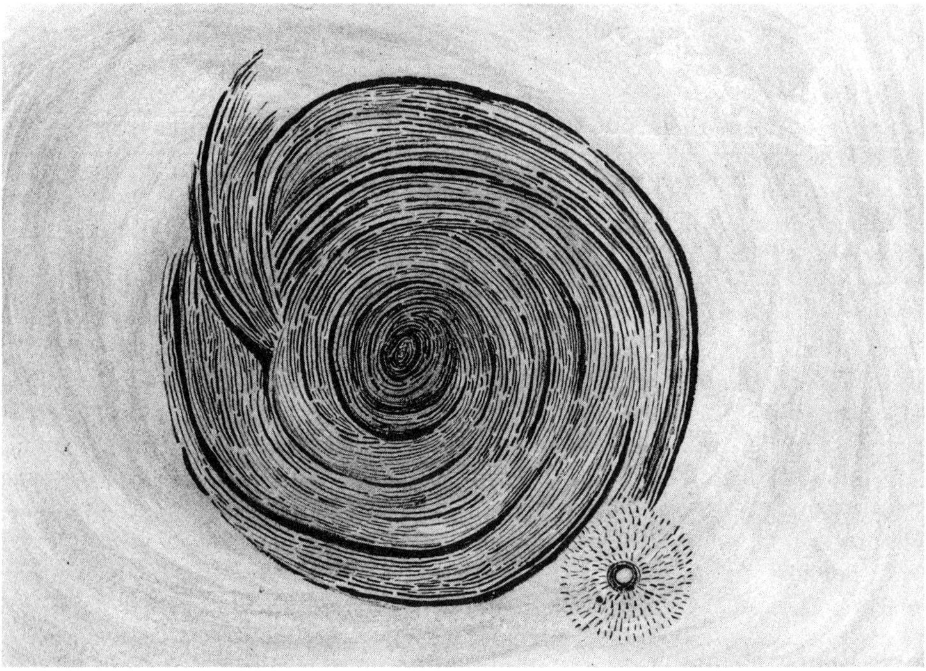

A Catholic in Space: Coming Home

Br. Guy Consolmagno, SJ, Vatican Observatory

I was a Sputnik kid. The world's first artificial satellite went into orbit when I was in kindergarten; men landed on the Moon when I was a rising senior in high school. In between, like all boys of my generation (and a few girls, as well — I had secret crushes on all of them) I knew I was going to be a scientist.

It started with my parents, of course, who encouraged me at every step ... themselves the grandchildren of immigrants: Italian father, Irish mother; both Catholic, and also both college educated. My dad had always loved astronomy himself and he'd learned the sky as a B-17 navigator in the Army Air Corps during World War II; he took me out at night to show me the major navigation stars, and got me my first copy of H. A. Rey's wonderful guide to the constellations, *The Stars.* Every Christmas and birthday brought a new science kit, from a model planetarium to a make-your-own computer. I had a wonderfully elaborate chemistry setup in the basement; in one experiment, the power supply from my Lionel trains got taken over to electrolyze hydrogen and oxygen from water. (No bunsen burners or strong acids, but I was allowed to use an alcohol lamp at least. My mother kept a watchful eye, from an appropriate distance.)

And then there were the after-school programs at the Cranbrook Science Museum, just two miles (an easy bike ride) from my home in the northern suburbs of Detroit. I learned everything from banding birds to hunting fossils. The planetarium was a special treat.

Of course, the public library with its shelves of science fiction provided yet another encouragement to my astronomical appetite. Heinlein, Clarke, and Asimov spoke to me of a future where space travel would be taken for granted. Planets were places where people had adventures.

All of this science education was reinforced by the good Sisters of Charity at Our Lady Queen of Martyrs Grade School. They gave me enrichment classes in math and science. Besides the usual science fairs, I recall participating in a special program on the nature of heat when I was in the fourth grade, and a self-paced algebra class when I was in the seventh grade. And of course, every Mercury and Gemini launch of American astronauts into orbit was an occasion for someone's dad to set up a "portable" TV in the classroom, so we could all watch the rockets together.

The sisters taught us evolution and the Big Bang. They also taught us the standard 1950s American credo of Progress, where "science" and "technology" were all mixed together. "Science" had won the war (World War II, of course, the only war that mattered); and there was no disease that wouldn't some day be conquered by bigger and better factories and power plants. In those days, science was an unalloyed good, the key to the future well-being of the human race.

At the same time, however, the sisters also emphasized the importance of a Catholic education ... of avoiding the "dangers" of secular universities, for instance. There was still a sense of proudly living in a Catholic ghetto, where the rest of the world was not to be trusted.

In other words, I was the product of my upbringing, a wonderful mixture of 1950's optimism and 1950's Catholicism. It never occurred to me, or to anyone, that the world was more complicated than Progress and God. Certainly there was no thought that space travel – or science in general – might be at odd angles with religion.

###

The ecology movement, beginning in those 1950's with Rachel Carson's *The Silent Spring*, blossomed in the 1960's. It fit with the zeitgeist, which recognized in civil rights marches and the Vietnam War that the America of that time had issues that factories and space travel would not solve. Indeed, "progress" came at a high cost.

At the same time that the political left was learning to view technology with suspicion, the growing battle lines of the culture wars were drawing religious people on the right likewise to become more suspicious of science ... or, at least, of scientists.

Actually, the rise of such religious fundamentalism wasn't a rejection of science *per se*. I mean, if someone goes to the trouble of writing journals and books and even opening museums dedicated to what they call "creation science" then obviously they want to capture the cachet of that word "science" and all it implies, and appropriate it to their own beliefs. They wanted to think that their religion was "scientific" because they felt somehow that "scientific" means good, and smart, and reliable, and true ... even while, at the same time, they rejected what they had heard scientists on TV talk shows saying about what science teaches. It became a badge of honor among some religious folks to say, "I reject evolution," not because they rejected "science" but as a short-hand way of saying they were "religious." To them, anti-evolution implies pro-religion.

In the same way, you could find people who say "I reject religion" as a short-hand way of saying they were "scientific," because they thought being seen as "scientific" implied they were a full-fledged member of the side of our common culture that was smart and reliable and true ... even while, at the same time, a strict materialism like they claimed to espouse would not admit the reality of "smartness" or even, in its extreme versions like deconstructionism, of truth.

These fundamentalisms, I would argue, are really based on a sort of tribalism, not religion. After all, the religion that the science-rejecters actually practice today would have been unrecognizable as "religious" in the 1950's. Many of these same people who want to be identified with "traditional morality" have no problem with divorce and remarriage (the only sexual sin specifically called out in the Gospels) or even with sex outside marriage – just see the attitudes they have towards the peccadillos of their favorite preachers, pundits, and politicians, to say nothing of how they behave in their own personal lives. That kind of attitude would have been anathema among the conservative religious people of the 1950s and 1960s. Likewise, many of them behave as if they have no concept of the traditional Christian teaching concerning the care for widows or orphans, and strangers in our midst, or the injunctions against piling up huge amounts of personal wealth.

It's not science that bothers them. It's the sense of alienation they feel with a culture that has embraced science but rejected the certainties they had enjoyed in the 1950s.

In a similar way, I've found that (in America at least) the most vocal of the militant atheists – the ones most likely to be seen selling their worldview on television or the Internet – are often trying to assimilate themselves into their idea of the mainstream of intellectual thought by loudly rejecting their own upbringing. For many of them, they were raised in a subculture known for strong religious ties, a culture that now embarrasses them ... Southern Baptist, or New York Jewish, or Irish Catholic, or African American. It's not religion per se that they hate; it's their fear of being placed outside of what they perceive as the mainstream culture.

###

I joined the Jesuits in my late 30's, well into my scientific career. When I arrived at the Vatican Observatory in 1989 I noticed a defensiveness among the older Jesuits in how they presented themselves and their science in public. They felt a need to explicitly emphasize the complete lack of any kind of religious influence on the science they did. But my experience of "coming out" as a religious person was quite different from the situation those older Jesuits had encountered. Many of my scientific colleagues finally felt free to speak to me about their own religious faith.

And even among non-believers, I found that among my contemporaries, especially in the US – less so in Britain – there was a real, opposite trend: an openness to people of all religious beliefs, coupled with an acceptance that science doesn't have all the answers, or even all the questions. Indeed, they are much more likely than the naïve religious folks to recognize the limits of science. After all, they live with those limits every day; and they, too, had gone through the 1960's awakening of the limits of technology.

In that sense, even if (sometimes, especially if) they themselves are non-believers, a lot of younger scientists felt the same embarrassment towards the so-called "new" atheists (who are, after all, mostly a bunch of old white men) that most religious people feel towards religious fundamentalists. They saw the evangelical atheists as trapped in a sort of 19th-century understanding of science and religion that does not connect with their own experience of either, and which is seen to be very narrow minded, and dangerously bigoted.

In summary, one might say that those who claim to be people of faith but reject science, have no faith in their faith; and those who claim to be ultra-rational people of science but evangelize against religion, are not being very rational.

It's delightful to make fun of those people who disagree with me, of course. I'm a moderate; anyone who disagrees with me must be an extremist! But the scary truth is that the faults we most see in others are the faults we are likely to be secretly guilty of, ourselves. So it is perhaps worthwhile to take a closer look at the unexamined incongruities that a middle-of-the-road Catholic space buff like me must live with all the time.

###

How do I reconcile the idea of being part of a religion that claims to the "catholic" — i.e., universal — and the reality that its presence here on our little planet is but a drop in the bucket of the larger universe?

Oh, sure, this is a twist on a question I answer all the time. If I am so small, and the universe is so big, then either God can't possibly notice me; or, the fact that nonetheless God does know me intimately, from the womb (Psalm 139), just tells me how immense God really is. The bigger I learn the universe is, the bigger in return the Creator of this universe turns out to be. Fine answer, yes. But that's God; what about religion? Is there a cosmic significance to my Church? Or are we always doomed to be outsiders in the cosmos?

In our recent book *Would You Baptize an Extraterrestrial?* (2014), my coauthor Paul Mueller (the source of most of the good ideas in that book, I confess) has a fascinating way of addressing that issue. The problem, he pointed out, is the difficulty of understanding how the human race could be "special" in a universe of the scale we now recognize. But, he said, what if we're looking at it the wrong way? What if the human race is special not because it is different from the other 13.8 billion light years of stars, but because we have within us something that is utterly characteristic of the whole universe?

As Fr. George Coyne, another Vatican astronomer, would always emphasize, in us human beings the universe has self-awareness. Perhaps this self-awareness and, even more, the ability to freely choose to love or not to love, is the essence of what the entire universe is created for. Then our human souls – self aware and able to love, which is to say in the language of Aquinas, possessing intellect and free will, the image and likeness of God – are not uniquely special and different but uniquely central to the universe.

Finding others on other planets (or between the planets) with no matter how many tentacles, but also with that same self-awareness and ability to love, is no threat; no more than discovering – as a baby does – that there exist other entities besides itself is any threat. A universe with others to love is a far better place than a universe centered solely on me. If being "assimilated" means a

Borg-like loss of the sense of self-and-other, then the assimilation so desired by the evangelical atheists is a terrible loss.

With such a vision, my religion takes on a new role. It is the language, indeed the operating system, that allows me to recognize and integrate this experience of The Other, just as it has allowed me to recognize and integrate the experience of God ... an experience that all people have, whether or not they recognize it as such. I should not fear encountering another species' religion any more than I would fear encountering an alien's version of mathematics or physics. I am confident the fundamental truths are the same, even if we use different symbols to describe the variables.

Indeed, this comparison to another physics shows me how my religion gives me an extra dimension of freedom lacking in the strictly materialist worldview. As G. K. Chesterton pointed out in *Orthodoxy* (1908), more than 100 years ago, "Spiritual doctrines do not actually limit the mind as do materialistic denials. Even if I believe in immortality I need not think about it. But if I disbelieve in immortality I must not think about it. In the first case the road is open and I can go as far as I like; in the second the road is shut."

The fundamental assumption of cosmology is that the same physics and mathematics that we recognize here on Earth also operate in all times and places in the universe. Without that assumption, we couldn't use physics to try and understand the origins of the universe. And with that assumption, we've succeeded in making such progress that we have no reason to doubt its validity.

But even a thousand years of progress and "not-inconsistent-with-observation" success of our theories would not prove they are true. Eventually, we will encounter something that causes us to think twice. The Aristoteleans could not imagine a universe other than the world they knew, a sphere at the bottom of the universe surrounded by concentric spheres carrying the Sun, Moon, planets, and stars in perfect motion above our imperfect, corrupt planet.

Astronomy has succeeded in pulling us out of that depth (or, some might say, in pulling the rest of the stars and planets down into the same corrupt level that Earth is in). Rather than being the death of religion, it has given a new understanding of who we are and who God is.

Writing my master's thesis at MIT on the evolution of icy moons, my science-fiction-addled imagination suddenly pictured a race of intelligent "tuna" living in the ocean between Europa's ice crust and rocky core (which I had just deduced from my computer models). And I wondered, how could such creatures, living in a universe with an impenetrable roof over their heads, ever know about the existence of Jupiter, the planet their moon orbits, much less the stars of the rest of the universe? And then ... what barriers exist in our own understanding of the universe that we don't even know about, limiting us to what we can see and experience?

When I accept that the universe is larger than my own understanding (without rejecting my understanding), then I am free to experience, and evaluate, situations that my current understanding of physics might demand are unthinkable. Not every unthinkable concept is true; but if I never encounter a truth that I used to think was unthinkable, then I will never allow myself to learn anything new.

Science fiction, the literature of Space, has its own cosmological principle: the issues of right and wrong, the conflicts of worldview that make up the heart of good storytelling, also operate in all planets, places, and times. That doesn't mean we won't encounter something new as we explore the universe. Rather, it means that once we do encounter something new, we'll be able to come home to our own experience of the universe back here on Earth and recognize that new thing, hiding in plain sight in our own worlds and worldviews. Anyone who has traveled or lived abroad knows that experience; we only recognize our home for what it is by experiencing someone else's home for what that is.

I am a product of the 1950's, an era that is past and will never come again. I have experienced worlds that I never could have imagined at that time. They are called the 60's, the 70's, the 90's, the present. My father who taught me the stars looks back at his life from the pinnacle of 97 years and reminds me that he (as are we all) is a time-traveller. We've grown, we've learned, we've enjoyed the long, strange trip. (And picked up some new clichés along the way!)

The most important part of traveling in space, be it with our telescopes and robots and imaginations or in actual spacecraft themselves, is precisely that we will learn things that will challenge our comfortable assumptions, which have insulated us too long from reality. If I have the ability to reason correctly in my science, I cannot help but conclude that the science I know today is woefully incomplete, and I will not be able to make it grow until I am willing to challenge it with new discoveries. If I have faith in my faith, then I will embrace the challenge that finding new worlds and even new races will bring. God is to be found in reality, not in our comforts.

The poet e. e. cummings, so popular in my high school literature classes back when I was growing up, had it right. It is a hell of a good universe next door. To travel into space is our destiny. But it is not leaving home; it will be coming home. Let's go!

-=-

Br. Guy Consolmagno, SJ, Ph.D., is Director of the Vatican Observatory and President of the Vatican Observatory Foundation. He is author of *The Way to the Dwelling of Light* (1998), *Brother Astronomer, Adventures of a Vatican Scientist* (2000), *Intelligent Life in the Universe?* (2005), *God's Mechanics: How Scientists and Engineers Make Sense of Religion* (2007), and *The Heavens Proclaim: Astronomy and the Vatican* (2009), and co-author of *Worlds Apart* (1993), *Turn Left at Orion* (1995), and *Would You Baptize an Extraterrestrial?* (2014). He was awarded the Carl Sagan Medal for outstanding communication by an active planetary scientist to the general public by the American Astronomical Society in 2014, and has hosted science programs for BBC Radio 4, been interviewed in numerous documentary films, appeared on *The Colbert Report*, and for more than ten years he has written a monthly science column for the British Catholic magazine, *The Tablet.*

Our Cosmic Future? How Religion Might Shape It

Joshua D. Ambrosius

Introduction: Separation of Church & Space?

Religion and space exploration are two facets of human society not typically connected in people's minds. The former is a social institution that has existed in some form since the dawn of the human species (Turner, 1997). The latter is primarily an enterprise of government policy only a few decades in existence. Human spaceflight is the culmination of the scientific revolution that began with the Copernican insight that the Earth rotates about the Sun and climaxed with the United States' successful effort to put people on the Moon. While Copernicus first, then Galileo, challenged Biblical literalism and church teachings, our contemporary efforts to reach the lunar surface faced little religious opposition.

In fact, some peoples such as the Nepalese came to worship the astronauts as gods (Chaikin, 1994). Any fear of transcending a need for faith was put to rest for Christians in the U.S. when the astronauts publicly demonstrated their Christianity by reciting Genesis in space (Bill Anders, Jim Lovell, and Frank Borman in 1968) and taking communion on the Moon (Edwin "Buzz" Aldrin in 1969) (*Irish Times*, 1969a; Oliver, 2013). Even the Pope at the time of the Moon landing, Paul VI, exclaimed, "Glory to God in the highest" and: "Today we make an echo, repeating it in a celebration on the part of the whole terrestrial globe with no more unsurpassable bounds of human existence, but openness to the expanse of endless space and a new destiny" (*Irish Times*, 1969b; special thanks to The Merry Ploughboy pub outside Dublin, Ireland, for preserving this newspaper's front page for my private viewing in "the gents"; not one but two headlines on this front page, from a largely Catholic country, focused on religious aspects of the Moon mission and landing). For some faith traditions, though, a trip to the Moon did "disprove" some aspects of their religious beliefs when the astronauts failed to discover mythical characters there, including the spirits of ancestors (the Nepalese) and a beautiful girl and her rabbit (the Chinese and other East Asians) (Chaikin, 1994).

Humanity's fascination with outer space, no matter how conceived, does have religious and spiritual overtones. As even atheist Carl Sagan (1973, 63) remarked, "Space exploration leads directly to religious and philosophical questions." Nonetheless, it was not a drive for religious or philosophical truth that drove us into space—but rather political and military necessity (Tyson, 2012). As we dream about our cosmic future, the question becomes: is further exploration of the solar system and, eventually, other solar systems, motivated by the resolution of human problems *or* our innate desire for discovery? The latter, while a powerful drive for scientific advancement, is a more difficult justification for public, and even private, expenditures.

Today, we confront many problems blocking our future exploration of interstellar space. What modes of propulsion can take us to another star system within a human-scale timetable? How do we protect and nourish travelers while on such a journey? Even, how will we first escape the Earth through an increasing orbital barrier of space junk? But before we can successfully address these problems, we need a motivating problem to drive us in this very direction. Public policy scholars would say we need a "focusing event" to open up a "policy window" of opportunity—not unlike the space race with the Soviet Union over our national survival (Kingdon, 2010; Tyson, 2012). One such event could be an imminent threat to our existence, such as a highly probable future asteroid impact. (Apparently other threats, like the longer term impacts of climate change, are not yet enough to overcome immediate self-interest and invest in the future of our species—at home and "abroad.") The discovery of life beyond the Earth, even microbial, might also constitute an event of such importance that it launches an era of unprecedented exploration.

No matter the motivation, it is policymakers — and increasingly, entrepreneurs — who must set us on the path to interstellar travel (Sommariva, 2014). The former are motivated by electoral support and public opinion, in addition to personal conviction. (See Steinberg, 2011, for a test of the opinion-policy link in the space exploration area.) The latter are driven by discovery and the bottom line it bolsters, but also the will of a certain kind of public: investors and, eventually, consumers. Currently, it is still public dollars that fund the major space companies such as SpaceX and Orbital Sciences, both of which operate government-funded cargo missions to the International Space Station. If NASA or other countries' space agencies are going to propel human spaceflight out of low-Earth orbit and unmanned, and eventually manned, missions outside of our solar system, policymakers must set us on a sustainable path to the stars. The public, or more accurately publics, must come to support these missions with their hearts and pocketbooks—first through taxes, then through investments and tourist dollars.

What factors might influence whether one supports the expansion of space exploration and the human colonization of other planetary bodies? Religion, through the mechanisms of belief, belonging, and behavior, is one potential force constraining or encouraging support. My pioneering study, published in the journal *Space Policy*, is the first comprehensive look at how religion might shape support for space policies (Ambrosius, 2015; Nadeau, 2013, recently included a measure of church attendance in his models of support for space policy funding, but treated it not as an expression of religion but associated this variable with other measures of ideology and partisanship). This essay briefly summarizes the key findings while extrapolating some observations about how religion could shape the future of space exploration. Along the way, I supplement the hard data with some colorful anecdotes about how current religious voices in Western Christianity are grappling with space and its exploration. Ultimately, I argue that: (1) religious actors and institutions should support humanity's expansion into outer space, because their future survival depends on it; and (2) the space community should engage with religious publics so that they do not present stumbling blocks to humanity's cosmic future.

Religious Influences on Public Support for Space Policy

Researchers know that religion shapes the public's views of science and science policy (e.g., Jelen & Lockett, 2014). As we prepare for a hopeful future among the stars, how do we deal with doubts—including religiously motivated ones—about the necessity and efficacy of off-Earth investments? To get a handle on the present influences of religion on this one component of science policy, I analyzed public opinion data from four publicly available, nationally-random surveys of the U.S. population aged 18 and over (Ambrosius, 2015). The General Social Survey and three Pew Research Center surveys asked space-related, religion-oriented, and general socio-demographic questions to more than 7,000 Americans over a two-year period between April 2009 and June 2011. The surveys include: the National Opinion Research Center at the University of Chicago's (a) General Social Survey (2010) and the Pew Research Center for the People & the Press' (b) Political Survey (June, 2011), (c) Political and Future Survey (April, 2010), and (d) General Public Science Survey (April-May, 2009). The analysis period saw the launch of the planet hunting Kepler space observatory, the emergence of SpaceX (among others) as a private player in space, and the arrival of the Messenger probe in Mercury's orbit. While significant milestones, these events likely did little to influence space policy opinions in the broader public. The official end of the U.S. Space Shuttle Program and the safe landing of the Curiosity rover on Mars, events which were widely covered by the press and witnessed by the American public, came after the survey collection times in July 2011 and August 2012, respectively. The earliest of these surveys was administered over six years after the Space Shuttle Columbia disaster, thus any post-accident effect was likely filtered out by this time (see Miller, 1987).

The study explores how various components of religion influence seven conceptions of space support: knowledge, interest, support for space funding, recognition of the benefits of exploration (in general and to the nation specifically), space nationalism, and optimistic expectations of future accomplishments in space. While I recommend that each reader of this volume access and read the full study, I will briefly summarize the findings here. (The full text of the paper can be accessed at http://www.sciencedirect.com/science/article/pii/S026596-4615000223 or received directly from the author. See the paper for definitions and operationalizations of all variables under study.)

The most significant findings from my research show that evangelical Protestants are, across the board, less interested and knowledgeable about space and less supportive of space exploration than are other types of Christians and followers of other religions; but that positive messages from clergy—about science in general—can limit this opposition. In particular, evangelicals—Christians who have had a "born again" experience—rank consistently, significantly lower than the rest of the population on five of the seven space variables: knowledge, funding support, space benefits (general and national), and optimism. Mainline Protestants, Jews, Eastern traditions, and those with no religion all score significantly higher on space knowledge. Jews, Eastern traditions, and religious "nones" all stand out positively on perceptions of general space benefits. Eastern traditions and the nones also rate higher on support for space funding. Finally, Eastern traditions are most interested in space and Catholics, in their lone distinctive category, are higher on space nationalism—that the U.S. should lead the way in exploration.

Evangelicals express a sort of "space pessimism"—that is, lower expectations of future achievements related to space. Evangelicals hold higher expectations that an asteroid will hit the Earth (the opposite of preventing an asteroid impact), but lower expectations of the discovery of life away from Earth. Evangelicals do not differ statistically though, despite being lower on average, in expecting advances in space travel—both by non-astronauts completing space tours and to Mars. In perhaps the most interesting finding on expectations, evangelicals are surer that Jesus will return to the Earth in the next four decades than is the rest of the population, and than they are about the four space events occurring. For all other traditions, the likelihood of Jesus' return rates lowest of the five items. For evangelicals, it is the highest with a mean response between "probably" and "definitely" occurring. All other traditions' means hover around "probably not" occurring. Maybe the end of time will come before we get all that far into space?

Worship attendance is negatively correlated with nearly all space variables—meaning, greater presence at church may discourage support for space. Traditional understandings of the Bible, running from ancient myths (modernist belief; lower score) to the Word of God (traditionalist belief; higher score), are negatively correlated with knowledge, interest, and funding support. These same space measures are positively correlated with acceptance of biological evolution (the inverse of creationist accounts of our origins). Religious salience or importance—sometimes called *religiosity*—is also negatively correlated with several measures of space support.

In an interesting twist, the support of one's clergy member(s) for science exerts a significant positive effect on support among the most skeptical religious group, evangelicals—making them twice as likely to recognize the benefits of space exploration *if* they perceive their pastor(s) speaking positively about science in general. If an evangelical's pastor speaks negatively about science, the probability of agreeing with the statement "space exploration does more good than harm" is 47%, controlling for other factors. If an evangelical's pastor speaks positively, the probability shoots up to an impressive 96%, all else equal.

While the initial intention of the study was to equally examine all religious traditions measured by the surveys, evangelicals emerged as the standout group and became a focus of the study. My claims of this tradition's lower support for space are based in the scientific analysis of thousands of survey respondents—not subjective or anecdotal reasoning. These reliable conclusions present a clear problem for the future of space exploration because evangelicals make up more than one-quarter of the U.S. population, by affiliation with evangelical churches (even higher when identified by a salvation experience), and thus a significant share of potential space-minded constituents (or the converse, critics). Because many advocates for space exploration, such as the late Carl Sagan and the Planetary Society's director Bill Nye "the Science Guy," are seen as at odds with the faith of many in the U.S., the effort to recruit evangelicals to the space cause will be an ongoing challenge.

Some Christian Voices on Space Exploration

To flesh out Christian attitudes on space, I explore a few contemporary characters. These are anecdotal accounts meant to provide a human face to the survey findings discussed above. One cannot discuss contemporary religious views of space exploration without examining the curious case of Ken Ham.

Ham, the controversial creationist founder of Answers in Genesis and the Creation Museum in Petersburg, Kentucky, posted a blog responding to a recent NASA panel discussion where astronomer Kevin Hand exclaimed that, "in the next 20 years we will find out we are not alone in the universe" (Gates, 2014). Ham, who famously debated Bill Nye on the validity of evolution in February 2014, wrote:

> I'm shocked at the countless hundreds of millions of dollars that have been spent over the years in the desperate and fruitless search for extraterrestrial life... [S]ecularists are desperate to find life in outer space, as they believe that would provide evidence that life can evolve in different locations and given the supposed right conditions! The search for extraterrestrial life is really driven by man's rebellion against God in a desperate attempt to supposedly prove evolution! (Ham, 2014a)

Ham argues that the search for alien life or other habitable environments is pointless because God uniquely created Earth and the life found here. Media accounts immediately reported that Ham said, "aliens probably don't exist—and if they do, they're going to Hell anyway" in response to Ham's claim that, "Jesus did not become the 'GodKlingon' or the 'GodMartian' (Mazza, 2014; Ham, 2014a)! Only descendants of Adam can be saved." Science communicator Neil deGrasse Tyson responded to Ham's comments with, "That's messed up" on a *Real Time with Bill Maher* segment titled, "Heaven Spacey" (Mosbergan, 2014).

I framed my own study (Ambrosius, 2015) with a reference to Ham's above comments and discussed his views with members of the media. This move apparently necessitated a personal response from both Ham and his ministry's resident astronomer (Ham, 2014b; Faulkner,2014). Ham (2014b) attempted to rephrase his original contentions about space exploration, arguing that Christians can be interested in the heavens (citing Psalm 19:1) but that the fruitless search for extraterrestrial life defies a true Christian worldview. He revels in the continued failure of scientists to discover life elsewhere in the universe, writing that—in a perverse way—the search for ET benefits his cause:

> Really, the search for extra-terrestrial life has had a benefit for creationists! The more the secularists search for alien life, the more they find no evidence of such anywhere in the universe. This is just what we would predict based on the Bible's account of origins and an understanding of the gospel. Biblical creationists do not accept evolution [or] intelligent alien life ... because we do not accept the humanistic worldview behind these ideas (Ham, 2014b).

Dr. Danny Faulkner (2014), Ham's bulldog on outer space issues, vigorously defends Ham's original comments and argues that he was "falsely accused" of believing aliens will go to hell. Faulkner attacked my scientific findings that traditional beliefs and church attendance negatively influence support for space, stating that these claims are "condescending"—implying that these "once-respected practices and beliefs are harmful to society"—but my assertions are "not as hostile as ... Richard Dawkins and Bill Nye." He concluded by declaring his own love for space, couched in a call for unmanned exploration over costly manned missions:

> As a professional astronomer who grew up during the Apollo program, how could I not like space exploration? I have some strong opinions of the directions that some space exploration has taken, but those opinions are based upon knowledge and passion ... I have found that as a whole, most biblical creationists support space exploration. Our motivation to study the creation is that we understand that the world is not the result of random chance, but that God purposefully designed it (Faulkner, 2014).

On the other end of the spectrum, a rising star within the Charismatic movement—which exists at the "'fringes' of Christianity" (Wilson, 2015)—was recently publicly rebuked for embracing unconventional beliefs and practices by a leader within the same tradition. Charisma News reports that Bill Johnson, pastor of Bethel Church, a megachurch in Redding, California, rebuked "popular prophetic voice" Jason Westerfield from the pulpit (Wilson, 2015).

Johnson's (2015) sermon, delivered on April 26, 2015, claimed that Westerfield was under a "spirit of deception" and a "demonic impartation." Filmmaker Darren Wilson (2015) wrote that Westerfield has veered into "very odd and bizarre territory"—including "aliens, interplanetary travel, etc." Westerfield's own website describes him as a "visionary leader, public speaker and world futurist" who "is currently working on outer space-related issues and policies for mankind's future in space" (Embassy International). Wilson asks the question, "What does any of this have to do with the gospel?"

Perhaps Wilson's question is the real hurdle for religious believers, particularly evangelical and fundamentalist Christians. But then again, this cannot be the true hurdle—because what does politics have to do with the gospel? What does amassing Earthly wealth have to do with the gospel? What does much of what we do here on Earth have to do with the gospel?

One non-denominational Christian from Philadelphia, Pennsylvania, believes that God is calling him to teach the Body of Christ that the colonization of other planetary bodies is intimately related to the gospel. Steve King leads a monthly Bible study group of 15-20 Christian men, who were brought together by their common interests in God's Word and space operas like *Star Wars* and *Star Trek*, in a study of "InterGalactic Dominion." King hopes to inspire these men and more to become "householders" (*oikodespotés* in the Greek)—essentially interstellar pilgrims who "will unite the men of theology, men of industry and men of science together in one common purpose," the colonization of new worlds (King, personal communication). He hopes that his group, which he has named the Dominion Institute for Advanced Authority Studies, will grow into a Christian think tank to bring together Christian experts who dream about space exploration with those who can make it happen.

For King, space exploration is the culmination of humanity's destiny—our ultimate fulfillment of God's call for us to exert dominion over creation. He interprets the fall of Adam as an event that stripped humanity of its heavenly nature and thereby restricted our authority to a single planet. It is the task of the coming householders to prepare "a large upper room" (Mark 14:15/Luke 22:12) in the heavens through colonization and terraforming. King extrapolates from this passage, in which Jesus tells his disciples to locate second-story accommodations for the Passover supper, that future householders will "exhibit, teach, demonstrate, make known to, and expose the eyes of the apostles to cosmic regions above and beyond the Earth," places or planets "that have not yet been made ready for the Lord" (King, 2015). This mission was foreshadowed, prior to the fall, in God's mandate that we "have dominion over . . . the *fowl* of the air . . ." (Genesis 1:26). King believes this phrase refers not just to birds, but any "flying or winged thing" (*oph* in the Hebrew)—including planets and galaxies that hurl through outer space.

Dialogue at the Church-Space Interface

Ham's rejection of space expenditures, and Johnson and Wilson's condemnation of Westerfield's foray into the stuff of science fiction, together show that the evangelical tradition in America (and its sub-branches) is not ready to embrace King's theology and mission any time soon. I argue for something a bit less ambitious—that, at minimum, the church not stand in the way of space science and that healthy dialogue exist between religious believers and the space community. Recent developments in other scientific fields show that this is indeed possible. Thoughtful discourse is happening in the field of biology and related disciplines—see any of the work BioLogos is doing and also the American Association for the Advancement of Science's Perceptions Project (Se & Scheller, 2014). I call on the readers of this book and chapter to make a conscious effort to expand this kind of work into the space sciences—astronomy, astrophysics, astrobiology, and astronautics. If even general pro-science comments from the pulpit can encourage better perceptions of space exploration's benefits, then how much further could minimal space-oriented programming in church go toward creating genuine interest in, and support for, our future in space?

Evangelicals can look to the Catholic Church as one example of a healthy marriage between church and space. The Vatican has its own observatory and collection of meteorites. Perhaps evangelicals despise these "additions" to their perceived simplicity of the gospel—as Wilson's (2015) question suggests. But Protestants, both mainline and evangelical, certainly appreciate the value of vocation, Luther's doctrine of the "priesthood of all believers," and the Protestant work ethic. Christians called to space science should take their calling seriously, performing all their work at the highest level—including conveying the importance of that work to their brothers and sisters in Christ.

Catholic leaders to emulate include the Jesuits Guy Consolmagno, recipient of the 2014 Carl Sagan Medal from the American Astronomical Society (AAS) and Director of the Vatican Observatory, and José Gabriel Funes, former Director of the Vatican Observatory. (I credit author Mary Doria Russell, 1996, 1998, with first bringing the Jesuit support for space to my attention in her wonderfully speculative novels about a Jesuit-sponsored mission to a recently discovered and inhabited planet.) Consolmagno once remarked cheekily that he would be willing to baptize an alien, but "only if they asked" (Derbyshire, 2010). The Division for Planetary Sciences of the AAS remarked that Consolmagno "occupies a unique position within our profession as a credible spokesperson for scientific honesty within the context of religious belief" (Jesuits, 2014). Funes further said that not believing that aliens could exist would be like "put[ting] limits on the creative freedom of God" (Popham, 2008). Both serve as exceptional advocates for space exploration and honest examples of wrestling with the deep theological questions raised by the possibility of extraterrestrial life (also see O'Meara's, 2012, thoughtful theological reflection on life elsewhere in the universe).

Conclusion: Religion and the Future of Humanity in Space

"Cosmic" traditions of the East and Near East and those outside the mainstream of Christianity are the most interested in space according to my findings (Ambrosius, 2015). Hindus, Buddhists, other Eastern traditions, and Jews represent strong advocates for space policy. Anecdotally, Muslims and Mormons are also key supporters—although small sample sizes prevented me from exploring the members of these traditions. It seems that religion will definitely not stand in the way of many rising countries' (e.g., India) budding space programs. These traditions will likely thrive in space colonies if present levels of support are a true indication of future cosmic trends. Leaders and theologians in these camps must think about the application of their rituals to the zero-gravity, direction-less environment of deep space—such as Lewis' (2013) discussion of Muslim astronauts' adaptations to rites in space. (Science fiction has also grappled with these questions, as the Imam in the film *Pitch Black*, starring Vin Diesel as Riddick, is leading his followers on the Hajj to "New Mecca" on the fictional planet Helion Prime.) Christian traditions, especially those in the evangelical branch, might want to work harder at building internal support if they wish to survive and thrive in the future expansion of humanity beyond low-Earth orbit. Something tells me that evangelicals will come on board quickly when space colonies become a potential mission field (or if living on Earth becomes especially precarious and relatively-safe alternatives exist).

Some, like Carter (2006), argue that we should keep religion out of U.S. space policy—that we should indeed have separation of church and space (Cohen, 2013, begins to address the thorny "separation of church and state" questions raised by religious practice by astronauts aboard publically funded missions). Many of the anonymous online comments accompanying articles about my work written for *Space.com* express similar sentiments (see, for example, http://www.space.com/27896-religion-influence-space-exploration.html & http://www.space.com/29662-space-exploration-religion-support.html). To paraphrase, they see religion as a cancer on humankind that should be eradicated in order for us to evolve to the next level, religion should not play any role in shaping space policy, and should certainly not be allowed to expand off the Earth.

Fortunately, the space community itself is much smarter than these trolls. The 100 Year Starship project, funded by an initial DARPA grant, consciously acknowledged the importance of religion to interstellar expansion when it created a track for religion scholars at its inaugural symposium—and continued to make a place for religion-oriented scholarship at its later meetings. The journal *Space Policy* published my work and the journal *Astropolitics* went even further—devoting an entire double-issue in 2013 to religious perspectives.

The volume in which this chapter appears demonstrates the increasing interest in the relationship between church and space. While not always a force for good, religion often is—let us work to make sure its positive benefits are realized and that these forces thrive as we prepare for and ultimately embrace our future among the stars. (Living in close quarters in hazardous environments will make interreligious dialogue all the more important as well!) The space community must, as others have said, "try harder" to build constituencies (Brown, 2007; Finarelli & Pryke, 2007)—and this is one area where outreach efforts could be concentrated to reach a skeptical one-fourth of the population. We must build upon the "attentive publics" in many of the great world religions and stitch them together as we embark on the greatest project humanity has ever pursued

(Miller, 1984). We cannot afford a "Tower of Babel" scenario where religious differences confound our collective potential to reach for the stars!

Bibliography

Ambrosius, Joshua D. (2015) "Separation of Church and Space: Religious Influences on Public Support for U.S. Space Exploration Policy," *Space Policy, 32*, pp. 17-31.

Brown, Frances. (2007) "Space Agencies and Public Outreach," *Space Policy, 23(1)*, pp. 1-2.

Carter, William E. (2006) "Keep Religion Out of National Space Policy," *Eos, Transactions American Geophysical Union, 87(6),* p. 63.

Chaikin, Andrew (1994) *A Man on the Moon.* New York: Penguin Books.

Cohen, Jonathan D. (2013) "Spaceflight and the Separation of Church and State," *Astropolitics, 11(1/2)*, pp. 100-107.

Derbyshire, David (2010) "I'd Love to Baptize ET, Says Vatican's Stargazer," *Daily Mail Online*, 17 September. http://www.dailymail.co.uk/sciencetech/article-1312922/Pope-astronomer-Guy-Consolmagno-Aliens-souls-living-stars.html

Embassy International "About," http://www.embassyinternational.net/

Faulkner, Danny (2014) "Should Christians Explore Space?" Answers in Genesis, 17 December. https://answersingenesis.org/blogs/danny-faulkner/2014/-12/17/should-christians-explore-space/

Finarelli, Peggy, & Pryke, Ian (2007) "Building and Maintaining the Constituency for Long-Term Space Exploration," *Space Policy, 23(1)*, pp. 13-19.

Gates, Sara (2014) "We Are Not Alone in Universe, NASA Scientists Say," *The Huffington Post*, 15 July. http://www.huffingtonpost.com/2014/07/15/we-are-not-alone-in-universe-nasa-habitable-planets_n_5588455.html

Ham, Ken (2014a) "We'll Find a New Earth Within 20 Years," *Answers in Genesis*, 20 July. http://blogs.answersingenesis.org/blogs/ken-ham/2014/07/20/well-find-a-new-earth-within-20-years/

_____ (2014b) "Climate Change and Aliens?" *Answers in Genesis*, 29 June. https://answersingenesis.org/blogs/ken-ham/2014/11/22/climate-change-and-aliens/

Irish Times, The (1969a) "Communion Bread is Taken to Moon," 21 July.

_____ (1969b) "Heartfelt Tribute from Lovell: Pope on 'A New Destiny'," 21 July.

Jelen, Ted G., & Lockett, Linda A. (2014) "Religion, Partisanship, and Attitudes Toward Science Policy," *SAGE Open*, Jan.-Mar., pp. 1-8. http://sgo.sagepub.com/content/4/1/2158244013518932

Jesuits. (2014) "Jesuit Brother Guy Consolmagno Wins Carl Sagan Medal from the American Astronomical Society." *Jesuits.org*, 14 July. http://www.jesuits.org/news-detail?TN=NEWS-20140714111304

Johnson, Bill (2015) "More At Any Cost," *Bethel Podcast*, 26 April. http://podcasts.ibethel.org/en/podcasts/more-at-any-cost

King, Steve (2015) *InterGalactic Dominion.* Philadelphia, PA: The Dominion Institute for Advanced Authority Studies.

Kingdon, John (2010) *Agendas, Alternatives, and Public Policies, 2nd Edition* (Update Edition with an Epilogue on Health Care) Upper Saddle River, NJ: Pearson.

Lewis, Cathleen S (2013) "Muslims in Space: Observing Religious Rites in a New Environment," *Astropolitics, 11(1/2)*, pp. 108-115.

Mazza, Ed (2014) "Creationist Ken Ham Says Aliens Will Go to Hell So Let's Stop Looking for Them," *The Huffington Post*, 15 July. http://www.huffingtonpost.com/2014/07/22/ken-ham-aliens-go-to-hell_n_5608368.html

Miller, Jon D (1984) "Is There Public Support for Space Exploration?" *Environment: Science and Policy for Sustainable Development, 26(5)*, pp. 25-35.

_____ (1987) "The Challenger Accident and Public Opinion: Attitudes Towards the Space Programme in the USA," *Space Policy, 3(2)*, pp. 122-140.

Mosbergen, Dominique (2014) "Neil DeGrasse Tyson Weighs in on Ken Ham's Claim that Aliens Will Go to Hell," *The Huffington Post*, 28 July. http://www.huffingtonpost.com/2014/07/28/neil-degrasse-tyson-ken-ham-aliens_n_5627239.html

Nadeau, Francois (2013) "Explaining Public Support for Space Exploration Funding in America: A Multivariate Analysis," *Acta Astronautica, 86*, pp. 158-166

.

Oliver, Kendrick (2013) "The Apollo 8 Genesis Reading and Religion in the Space Age," *Astropolitics, 13(1/2)*, pp. 116-121.

O'Meara, Thomas F. (2012) *Vast Universe: Extraterrestrials and Christian Revelation.* Collegeville, MN: Liturgical Press.

Popham, Peter (2008) "Pope's Astronomer Insists Alien Life 'Would be Part of God's Creation'," *The Independent*, 15 May. http://www.independent.co.uk/news/world/europe/popes-astronomer-insists-alien-life-would-be-part-of-gods-creation-828303.html

Russell, Mary Doria (1996) *The Sparrow.* New York: Ballantine.

----- (1998) *Children of God.* New York: Ballantine.

Sagan, Carl (1973) *The Cosmic Connection.* New York: Dell.

Se, Kim, & Scheller, Christine A. (2014) "Can Scientists and Evangelical Leaders Work Together?" *Christianity Today*, 10 November. http://www.christianitytoday.com/ct/2014/november-web-only/can-scientists-and-evangelical-leaders-work-together.html

Sommariva, Andrea (2014) "Motivations Behind Interstellar Exploration and Colonization," *Astropolitics, 12(1)*, pp. 82-94.

Steinberg, Alan (2011) "Space Policy Responsiveness: The Relationship Between Public Opinion and NASA Funding," *Space Policy, 27(4)*, pp. 240-246.

Turner, Jonathan H. (1997) *The Institutional Order: Economy, Kinship, Religion, Polity, Law, and Education in Evolutionary and Comparative Perspective.* New York: Longman.

Tyson, Neil deGrasse (2012) *Space Chronicles: Facing the Ultimate Frontier.* New York: W. W. Norton & Co.

Wilson, Darren. (2015) "Bill Johnson Publicly Rebukes Popular Prophetic Voice," *Charisma News*, 5 May 5. http://www.charismanews.com/opinion/behind-the-lens/49490-bill-johnson-publicly-rebukes-popular-prophetic-voice

-=-

Joshua D. Ambrosius, Ph.D., is an Assistant Professor of Political Science and a core faculty member in the MPA program at the University of Dayton. His work is motivated by an overarching desire for long-term human sustainability. His policy interests include urban and housing policy, faith-based social policy, and space exploration. His research specifically explores urban and regional governance, neighborhood housing markets, and religious preferences for institutional design. His academic work on urban policy and religion and politics has appeared in over a dozen peer-reviewed journals, including *Space Policy*, *Journal of Urban Affairs*, and *American Review of Public Administration.*

Pennies from Heaven: Objects in the Use of Outer Space as Sacred Space

Deana L. Weibel

As an anthropologist who has spent 20 years studying Earthbound pilgrimage, I find it fascinating to consider the understandings and rituals that make up the experience of human space flight. Human space flight is our species' newest form of travel, but in many ways follows the conventions of other, older types of travel. Space travel can be looked at as exploration, as scientific expedition and even, for wealthy private citizens who have paid for the opportunity, as vacation. Human space flight can also be seen as a type of pilgrimage. This essay will consider human space flight as pilgrimage, focusing on the use of objects in religious pilgrimages compared to the way objects have been used in human spaceflight over the last half-century.

Pilgrimage is travel with a religious purpose in mind, usually but not always to a place considered to be sacred. Pilgrimage takes place in all of the world's major religions and the pilgrimage to Mecca, probably the best-known pilgrimage destination, is actually a requirement for Muslims who are healthy and wealthy enough to undertake it. Muslims, Christians and Jews alike make pilgrimages to the Holy Land (although what they do there varies) and many Eastern religions, including Hinduism and Buddhism, incorporate pilgrimage into their practices. Pilgrimage is common around the world, in large societies and small.

Scholars who study pilgrimage have noted certain patterns that appear across the practice of pilgrimage and allow journeys to a wide array of types of locations to be compared. Anthropologist James J. Preston has argued that all pilgrimage sites have what he refers to as spiritual magnetism, "the power of a pilgrimage site to attract devotees" (Preston, 1992). For our purposes, two of Preston's categories stand out. A pilgrimage site, he states, may attract visitors because of its sacred geography and its difficulty of access. Preston associates "sacred geography" with places where supernatural beings live or lived and with "dramatic locations," such as mountain peaks, huge trees, or bodies of water. There is ample evidence that humans have a history of seeing outer space as dramatic in and of itself, and also have associated it with supernatural beings.

The earliest *Homo sapiens'* concept of outer space is unknowable to us with no recorded history, only remnants of an archaeological record. Clearly, early humans did not have the understanding of the Moon, stars, and planets that we have today. Archaeologist David F. Kelley and physicist Eugene F. Milone note, however, that Paleolithic and Megalithic cultures left behind objects and structures that indicate an awareness of the movements of celestial bodies and evidence for ritual activity related to this knowledge. Certain Stone Age sites in Ireland, for example, demonstrate both an understanding of astronomical phenomena like solstices and evidence of the undertaking of ceremonial events.

In the historical period, we find that multiple religions describe a supernatural "higher place," a location such as a mountaintop (Greek Mount Olympus and Hindu Mount Meru are examples) or even the sky itself as the home for gods or spirits. Creation stories describe supernatural figures constructing the heavens and the Earth, and some societies understand cultural innovation as having a celestial origin. Some Native American and Polynesian groups even see themselves as originating from the Moon, specific stars or distant constellations, demonstrating that the "idea of the heavens as the source and destiny of the soul was widespread in the ancient world" (Kelley & Milone, 2005).

In Christianity there is a notion of Heaven as the home of God and angels and the place to which Jesus ascended after the Resurrection, while satanic forces described in Isaiah and Revelation are seen as Earth- and hell-bound "fallen" creatures. Jewish and Christian scholars alike saw the sky as a place to read otherworldly omens. Giordano Bruno (1548-1600), condemned as a heretic, may have taken the idea that the heavens were divine a bit too far. As Kelley and Milone write, "He believed that the universe is the manifestation of God himself, and that God is the soul of the universe."

It is clear that although space isn't "geography" in the same way as a river or a mountain, the celestial bodies have frequently been regarded as sacred, holy, or supernatural. In this way, then, they have "spiritual magnetism." However, Preston also argues that sacred places can draw pilgrims if there is "difficulty of access." He writes, "Some pilgrimage sites attain a high degree of spiritual magnetism because they are difficult to reach... A shrine located in a precarious place attains some of its spiritual magnetism from intrinsic dangers associated with the pilgrimage journey itself... the pilgrimage requires sacrifice, an important ingredient for enhancing spiritual magnetism."

To state the very obvious, space is difficult to reach. It was only in the twentieth century that humans first were able to build machines that let people enter into space (defined in the U.S. as 80.4 kilometers above the Earth's surface, internationally as 100 kilometers), although humans had been dreaming of doing so for countless centuries. Traditional sites of pilgrimage were often in places of high altitude, where death was a very possible outcome, or in contested sites, like the Holy Land in the Middle Ages, where physical violence might be encountered when meeting someone with a rival claim to the same location. It is not unusual, even today, to hear of pilgrims killed on their journeys. As Preston (1992) writes, "The irony of these tragic events is that they attract rather than repel pilgrims, due to the widespread folk belief that dying while on pilgrimage is auspicious."

In a similar vein, it is possible that the relatively new understanding of outer space as dangerous has increased its spiritual magnetism. Environmental anthropologist Valerie A. Olson explains that seeing outer space as hazardous is relatively new, observing that "in the late 19th century, the solar system changed from a sedately organized realm to a dynamic and even dangerous assemblage of particles, objects and forces" (Olson, 2012). What scientists had thought of as comprehensible and driven by an underlying logic was slowly reimagined as somewhere filled with unexpected asteroids or pitted with deadly black holes. Outer space was less a system of orderly celestial spheres and more a complex system of forces and counter-forces that might never be truly comprehensible. The anthropological study of pilgrimage shows that risk and sacrifice increase the appeal of pilgrimage, so the new scientific understanding of outer space may have actually increased its appeal as a destination.

Although outer space has "spiritual magnetism," not all astronauts and cosmonauts who have traveled into space have regarded this journey as a spiritual one or a type of pilgrimage. Still, the tendency of certain astronauts to describe their experiences in space using religious imagery or language is apparent in memoirs and other works written once they have returned to the Earth. Colonel Jeffrey N. Williams published a collection of photographs he had taken in space under the title *The Work of His Hands: A View of God's Creation from Space*, an explicitly religious work in which Williams argues that knowing God's creation (including space) leads to a better understanding of God. William holds, for instance, that seeing the Earth from orbit allows for the scientific validation of the way the planet is described in the Bible's book of Job, praising the accuracy of the way the Earth's position, cloud cover and terminator are characterized. He goes onto ask, "How could the author of Job possibly describe the planet in that way several thousand years ago apart from supernatural inspiration?" (Williams, 2010).

In much the same way that Christians visiting Jerusalem focus on the city as a place Jesus lived, suffered, and was sacrificed, some Christian astronauts see space as a place inhabited by God, where humans can see things from His perspective. Although Moonwalker Edgar Mitchell's religious leanings are unorthodox (he founded the Institute of Noetic Sciences), his memoir describes outer space as "that vast domain where I had once been taught the kingdom of heaven lay" (Mitchell & Williams, p. 61). In another example, when Shannon Lucid (the daughter of Christian missionaries) joined Russians Yuri Usachev and Yuri Onufrienko in the Mir space station in 1996, she brought with her an audiotaped religious sermon (aimed at the cosmonauts) by Baptist minister Raymond Barber, who used his recording to tell the three space travelers that "God is controlling your spacecraft," instructed them to "Open the window of your space house and see that Psalm 19 1-3 is true," and teased Lucid that her "desire to be nearer to God than your dear dad ... has finally come to pass" (Jones, 1996). Symbolically, if not always literally, outer space is indeed heaven, and traveling into space is traveling into God's territory, truly sacred space.

Anthropologists Victor and Edith Turner, who studied Catholic pilgrimage, thought that sacred spaces allowed pilgrims to feel closer to God and the supernatural in important ways. They argued that sacred places were seen by pilgrims as locations where there were "tears in the veil" of separation between our world and Heaven, allowing connections that were harder to come by in less religiously significant places (Turner & Turner, 1978). The Turners also compared pilgrimage to sociologist Arnold van Gennep's idea of the "rite of passage," a ritual that enacts cultural transformation, turning a child into an adult or a single person into a married person, for example. Pilgrimage, they said, followed the steps in a rite of passage: the separation of the pilgrim from the rest of his community, his transition and transformation through the often challenging experience, and the reincorporation of the pilgrim into his society with a new status.

Other anthropologists, such as Nancy Frey, have discussed a specific form of transformation that may occur on pilgrimage: conversion. Frey's research focused on the Catholic walking pilgrimage known as the Camino de Santiago. Protestants, members of other religions, spiritual seekers, and even atheists have been known to undertake it, some of them converting by the end of the pilgrimage. Frey writes, "Conversion often takes the pilgrim by surprise ... and the change is like a leap – a leap to faith rather than a leap of faith" (Frey, 1998). The "transformation" step in the rite of passage model puts pilgrims into what is known as a "liminal" state – normal rules don't apply, a person is removed from her typical surroundings, and identity is able to fluctuate, settling into something new.

In a similar way, several American astronauts have reported conversion-like experiences while traveling in space. James Irwin spoke frequently about the religious experiences he had during Apollo 15 that had strengthened his religious faith, writing in his memoir that he had very clearly felt God's presence on the Moon and had solved a technical issue once by consulting God instead of Houston. If Earthbound pilgrimage can put a pilgrim into a liminal state, opening him up to transformation, the sheer strangeness of being in space, looking at the Earth from a distance and functioning without such normal constraints as gravity must enhance this state further.

Psychologists Yannick Joye and Jan Verpooten argue that when human beings are exposed to natural features that make them feel small or powerless in comparison, they tend to respond with such strong emotions as admiration, delight, goose-bumps, chills or fear, feelings that can give a person a strong sensation of an otherworldly presence. This perspective may help provide some context for a personally transformative experience described by astronaut Edgar Mitchell. He describes traveling back to the Earth after his visit to the Moon and suddenly experiencing "an extraordinary personal connectedness" with the universe, in which he "experienced what has been described as an ecstasy of unity ... overwhelmed with the sensation of physically and mentally extending out into the cosmos." Although Mitchell acknowledges that this sensation may have been triggered by "the disorienting, or reorienting, effect of a rotating environment, while the heavens and Earth tumbled alternately in and out of view in the small capsule window," he feels confident that he changed in this moment, suddenly gaining "an upwelling of fresh insight coupled with a feeling of ubiquitous harmony – a sense of interconnectedness with the celestial bodies surrounding our spacecraft" (Mitchell & Williams, 2008).

In pilgrimage, journeys that are seen as difficult but worthy, taking pilgrims to places understood as significant, powerful and capable of transforming people, are frequently thought of as being able to transform objects, too. Objects are powerful symbols in pilgrimage because of what they represent and what they can become. Objects in many cases stand in for the pilgrim, but they can also stand in for the pilgrimage destination as well, becoming portable reminders of a place or even ways of carrying its essence back to the pilgrim's home. These objects serve to help the pilgrim connect with the sacred place by playing different roles and communicating different ideas.

In pilgrimage there are three main types of objects that serve as a conduit between a pilgrim and a sacred place: the object brought by the pilgrim to leave behind (known sometimes as an ex-voto), objects brought back from the sacred place as reminders of or as gifts from the pilgrimage, and objects taken to the sacred place to be transformed and then brought back again. We see all three uses of objects in human spaceflight. Before discussing the use of objects in space travel, however, it will be useful to look more closely at how they are used in pilgrimage.

I have studied Earthbound pilgrimage in France and in the United States. My main French site is a thousand-year-old shrine built onto the side of a 150-meter cliff, Rocamadour. Although it is a Catholic place of devotion, dedicated to the Virgin Mary, it has also been claimed as a sacred site by other religions, particularly by those interested in its pagan, pre-Christian origins. I have also studied the French shrine of Lourdes, known for an 1858 apparition of the Virgin and a spring that is said to have miraculous healing powers. In the United States, I have studied Chimayó, in New Mexico, a shrine built in 1816 around a hole in the ground where a large cross was said to have miraculously appeared. The hole remains inside the sanctuary, and the dirt found within it, like the water at Lourdes, is thought to have healing powers.

All of these shrines are places where people leave ex-votos. Ex-voto is Latin for "after the vow." These offerings are put in place to show that a vow was completed and to mark the pilgrim's presence. I have seen plaques of thanks to the Virgin Mary at Rocamadour and Lourdes, both milagros (small tin images of body parts in need of healing) and discarded crutches at Chimayó, photographs of loved ones and notes of prayer tucked into crevices at Chimayó and Rocamadour, and candles lit to send prayers to heaven in all of these places. The need to mark a sacred place with evidence of one's presence is very strong, as is the need to communicate with future pilgrims. Ex-votos left by previous pilgrims attest to the value of the shrine and can increase what Turner and Turner called *communitas*, a sense of connectedness and community that may occur among pilgrims.

Another type of object associated with pilgrimage are those that pilgrims bring back with them. When Rocamadour was at the height of its popularity as a pilgrimage site in the 12th and 13th centuries, pilgrims brought home the sportelle (also known in old French as the *senhal*), a pewter insignia marked with an image of the Virgin that served to prove the pilgrimage had occurred. The most important sacred objects from Lourdes and Chimayó, of course, are the healing substances, water and dirt, respectively. Interestingly, both of these substances are thought to retain their healing powers away from their shrines, so that the healing water of Lourdes can be shared with your ailing grandmother back home and the healing dirt of Chimayó can be brought to your brother at the hospital. In these cases, the objects symbolize the places themselves but also embody them. Drinking miraculous water *from* Lourdes simulates drinking miraculous water *at* Lourdes.

Finally, there is the object that is brought on the pilgrimage in order to transform it at the sacred site. This does not seem to be a typical feature of Catholic pilgrimage, although I was told at Chimayó of a family who brought an heirloom crucifix into the shrine intending to leave it there for a week and then retrieve it (unfortunately this was the week the new priest decided to clear the accumulated objects from the site and the precious cross was given away). On the other hand, pilgrims who identify with practices that blend elements of different religions, such as Neo-Pagans, Wiccans or New Agers (a group I refer to under the umbrella term "Religious Creatives") seem to use this type of pilgrimage object fairly regularly. These pilgrims might, for instance, place jewelry against sacred objects or leave it on sacred ground so that it will absorb the energy of the sacred site, allowing some of the sacredness to accompany the pilgrims. These pilgrims frequently refer to sacredness as "energy" and use metaphors relating to microwaves, magnetism, radiation, and so forth to describe sacred places, people and objects.

Leaving objects in sacred places, bringing home objects from sacred places, and taking objects to sacred places in order to transform them are practices widespread across multiple religions, occurring at a variety of pilgrimage locales and even in secular "sacred" places such as Civil War battlefields, sites of tragedies like Ground Zero in New York, and the homes of celebrities, such as Elvis Presley's Graceland. These objects aren't just souvenirs but are special – even sacred. It's reasonable to expect, then, that humans would travel into space with objects to leave behind, would hope to return with objects from space, and would bring objects along to "transform" them and bring them back. As it turns out, all three types of object use do indeed take place.

But bringing ex-votos into space is a difficult enterprise. The vast majority of instances of human spaceflight have required the participants to remain inside the craft, or at most to take part in an Extravehicular Activity (EVA), circumstances that aren't conducive to leaving an object behind (at least not intentionally – objects have been dropped and lost during EVAs but they wouldn't meet the criteria of being ex-votos). Certainly astronauts and cosmonauts bring items with them for their stays on space stations, but these generally return with their owner. We do have one example, however, of a location where astronauts were allowed to leave their vehicles and actually walk around – the Moon.

American astronauts on the Moon, like pilgrims to sacred spaces around the Earth, have left objects to mark their presence in a way that recalls the ex-voto. In his memoir, Apollo 16 astronaut Charlie Duke recounts his decision to leave a photograph of his family on the Moon, following the lead of previous Moonwalker Jim Irwin. Duke had a friend take a photo, then each member of his family signed it and put a thumbprint on the back of the photo, "so that some future astronaut might find it and see the family of astronaut Duke, who had been there many years before." He also describes placing the picture on the lunar surface, writing, "As I made a photograph of it lying there, I wondered, 'Who will find this picture in the years to come?'" (Duke & Duke, 1990). Both Duke's decision to emulate Irwin's practice and his contemplation of someone viewing his family picture in the future tie his behavior to that typically seen on pilgrimage.

Many items left on the Moon have been distinctly religious. Dave Scott of Apollo 15, ahead of his departure from the Moon, decided to leave an offering along with the abandoned Lunar Rover. Andrew Chaikin writes that Scott "pulled out a small red Bible and set it atop the Rover's control panel. If anyone should come this way again, he wanted them to understand who had left this machine here" (Chaikin, 1999). This act marked the Moon in a religiously significant way, as a place touched by Christianity.

Scott also placed another significant ex-voto on the surface of the Moon, a tiny aluminum statue called Fallen Astronaut by Belgian sculptor Paul van Hoeydonck. The Apollo 15 crew decided to place the abstractly human figurine face down next to a plaque listing the names of the 14 astronauts and cosmonauts who had died as part of the human pursuit to get into space. Since Scott had personally known eight of the people on the plaque, he took this commemoration very seriously. Although van Hoeydonck was never entirely satisfied with the way the sculpture had been used (he envisioned it as symbolizing triumph, not sacrifice), the astronauts' decision to mark their presence on the Moon not just for themselves, but for those who had failed similar quests, is in line with the types of objects left in sacred places (Powell & Shapiro, 2013).

If objects left in sacred places stand for the pilgrim and his community, items brought back from pilgrimage as gifts or mementos represent, or even contain, the essence of the sacred place. Mona Moufahim, describing Islamic pilgrimages to the tombs of saints, notes that "objects that are purchased within close proximity of the saint are expected to contain some of the saint's sacredness. As such, it is not only the objects themselves that are consumed, but the signs and symbols attached to them" (Moufahim, 2013). However, in the same way that it is difficult to leave objects as ex-votos in space (except on the Moon), it is difficult to bring back objects from space unless those objects originate on the Moon (or from other planets, asteroids, etc.). The moon rocks brought back by the Apollo astronauts *are* the Moon, and have always been treated as precious objects.

Moon rocks were given as gifts to various cultures and nations around the world in a phenomenon that mirrors what Moufahim described above. Charlie Duke was particularly proud of having given a piece of moon rock to the US Air Force (Swanson, 1999). Moon rocks and moon dust retain the essence of where they were obtained, and this essence makes them powerfully attractive. Moon rocks have famously been stolen from NASA and many of the moon rocks given out have mysteriously disappeared. Other moon rocks are displayed in museums and insured for millions of dollars (Hoover, 2009).

In addition to their monetary value, moon rocks, like the Moon itself, have Preston's "spiritual magnetism." This is evident in the way these objects and substances have come to be used in commerce, often in art. Although Lourdes' "miraculous" water can be obtained for free by pilgrims, rosary beads and other items containing the water may be purchased elsewhere. Similarly, while working at Chimayó in 1998, I found art for sale incorporating the "healing" dirt (such as my favorite necklace). The presence of these materials allows the art itself to embody what is sacred about the site. A pilgrimage can bring back, and share, a site's power. Astronaut Alan Bean has been a professional artist for many years, often depicting images from his journey to the Moon. Each of these paintings contains moon dust, which Bean "salvaged ... from the spacesuit patches that had hung on his walls since the 70s" (Seale, 1999). The combination of the symbolic and the real makes these paintings highly sought-after, and is used to convey, as Alan Bean himself states on his website, "the feeling of actually being there."

Another element of Bean's art that takes us to our third type of pilgrimage object are the tools he uses to add texture to his paintings. He mentions creating imprints with moon boots, "marks from the same hammer [he] used to chip off rock fragments for return to Earth," other tools and bits of foil and fabric from his mission. These objects started out as ordinary materials, created in workshops or factories on the Earth, but were changed and made more valuable by the journey to and from the Moon. Objects left in sacred places stand for the pilgrim, objects brought back from pilgrimage represent the sacred place, but certain objects (changed objects, or as some Religious Creatives say, "charged" objects) embody the transformative nature of the pilgrimage itself. To those who collect them, they are known as "flown" objects.

In his aptly titled "Relics of The Space Race," Russell Still provides an overview of collectible objects associated with the "artifacts" of human spaceflight. Postal covers associated with spaceflight that have never been to space are very collectible, but, as Still explains, "the covers most in demand are those actually flown on missions." He notes that typical "flown" objects carried by astronauts have included "currency, small flags, medallions, mission patches, and postal covers." The light weight and high value of flown covers even led to a scandal when the crew of Apollo 15 took a number of unauthorized covers with them into space (Still, 1995).

"Flown" objects are similar, in many ways, to "charged" objects that are transformed by being taken to sacred sites on Earth. Sites such as eBay and Etsy feature jewelry that sellers have taken to pilgrimage sites and purportedly filled with sacred energy, reflecting the belief that the power of a sacred place is somehow contagious and capable of being transferred into and stored inside an object. Flown objects seem to carry comparable properties. While most collectors of flown objects don't seem to see them as "charged" (even though the objects actually have been exposed to high levels of radiation in space), the knowledge that the object has made a difficult journey and spent time in space makes it a powerful symbol. The object has been changed through its experience.

The idea of space being able to transform objects has allowed for some interesting "layering" of already-sacred objects. Edgar Mitchell transported 300 microfilm versions of the Christian Bible, one hundred of which were taken to the surface of the Moon. John Stout of the Apollo Prayer League, a group of NASA employees and their families, had asked Mitchell to take the Bibles into space. Stout kept some and distributed others to members of the Prayer League, while others ended up in museums. One of these Bibles is even "on display at the Dunham Bible Museum at Houston Baptist University, etched in 24kt gold and accented with 14 pavé diamonds and a Brazilian garnet" (Apostles of Apollo, n.d).

Another example of religious objects that were taken into space and back is the Space Judaica collection that was displayed for many years at Congregation Or Ami, a Conservative Jewish synagogue in Houston. Rabbi Shaul Osadchey, whom I interviewed in March 2015, had formed a friendship with congregant and astronaut Jeffrey Hoffman. Hoffman, "a practicing and committed Jew," made five missions to space between 1985 and 1996. Hoffman and Osadchey decided to bring up to space specific Jewish ritual objects in order to create a collection. Hoffman brought some Torah pointers into space, since they were small; then, since Hoffman had an upcoming mission during Hanukkah, Osadchey purchased a limited-edition dreidel created by an Israeli artist. The dreidel was spun in space as part of the holiday, but treated with Velcro so it would be able to "land". The most significant item Hoffman brought into space was a Torah that Osadchey had commissioned by a New York scribe. It was a true kosher Torah, but made very small, seven inches wide.

All of these objects were taken into space then brought back to the Earth, where they were displayed and used by Osadchey's congregation. The Torah, for instance, was read during bar mitzvahs, and children were encouraged to use the Torah pointers and spin the dreidel. Osadchey explained the collection's appeal: "So the objects that we took, with the exception of the Torah, were all made special by having been in that location ... it just separated them. It made them unique ... But with the Torah, [that's] a whole different phenomenon ... when the Torah went into space, it was making space sacred, not making the Torah sacred."

For Osadchey, the specialness of space couldn't compete with the pure holiness of a kosher Torah. If something was being transformed in the interaction, it was space itself, not the sacred scrolls. That said, even the rabbi couldn't avoid linking space and heaven when he thought of Hoffman's experience. He explained that Hoffman detached part of the Torah scroll when the space station was directly over Jerusalem, something that was, according to Osadchey, "a pretty powerful experience. I would have loved to have been right there with him ... [W]e used to joke about the fact that the Torah, according to tradition, came down from Heaven. And here he took it back up to Heaven ... so, you know, to be able to read it in its original environment ... would've been pretty amazing." When Osadchey left Houston for his current synagogue in Calgary, he was able to take most of the Space Judaica with him. Significantly, and to his deep regret, he had to leave the Space Torah behind.

Humans make sense of our travels through the universe with objects, particularly through the meanings we give them. When confronted with something more powerful than we are, something or somewhere that makes us feel small and insignificant, objects can be a way to reclaim control and understanding. Objects left behind can mark our presence or prove that promises have been kept. Objects can also be brought back from a powerful place, allowing us to share experiences, but also imbuing the objects themselves with the places (and power) they've been exposed to. Looking at human spaceflight through the lens of pilgrimage allows us to more fully understand the profound appeal of these objects, be they family photographs, moon rocks, or pennies from heaven,

Bibliography

Chaikin, Andrew & Kramer, Michael (1999) *A Man on the Moon.* Time-Life Books.

collectSPACE (nd) "Lawsuits Leave Lunar Bibles in Limbo: Legal Battle over Space-Flown Scriptures," retrieved May 25, 2015. http://www.collectspace.com/-news/news-021813a.html

Duke, Charlie & Duke, Dotty (1990) *Moonwalker.* Nashville: Oliver-Nelson Books.

Frey, Nancy (1998) *Pilgrim Stories On and Off the Road to Santiago.* Berkeley: University of California Press.

Hoover, Will (2009) "State Fails to Account for Priceless Moon Rocks," *Honolulu Advertiser*, 24 October, retrieved May 30, 2015. http://www.mauinews.com/-page/content.detail/id/525086.html

Irwin, James B. & Emerson, William A. (1973) *To Rule the Night: The Discovery Voyage of Astronaut Jim Irwin.* Philadelphia, PA: A.J. Holman.

Jones, Jim (1996) "Minister Sending Sermon to Space Station." *The Seguin Gazette-Enterprise*, 3 May, p. 7.

Joye, Yannick & Jan Verpooten (2013) "An Exploration of the Functions of Religious Monumental Architecture from a Darwinian Perspective," *Review of General Psycholog, 17(1)*, pp. 53-68.

Kelley, David & Milone, Eugene (2005) *Exploring Ancient Skies: An Encyclopedic Survey of Archaeoastronomy.* New York: Springer.

Mitchell, Edgar & Williams, Dwight (2008) *The Way of the Explorer: An Apollo Astronaut's Journey Through the Material and Mystical Worlds (rev. ed.).* Franklin Lakes, NJ: New Page Books.

Moufahim, Mona (2013). "Religious Gift Giving: An Ethnographic Account of a Muslim Pilgrimage," *Marketing Theory*, pp. 421-441.

Olson, Valerie A. (2012) "Political Ecology in the Extreme: Asteroid Activism and the Making of an Environmental Solar System," *Anthropological Quarterly*, pp. 1027-1044.

Powell, Corey S. & Shapiro, Laurie Gwen (2013) "The Sculpture on the Moon," *Slate*, 16 December. http://www.slate.com/articles/health_and_science/science/2013/12/sculpture_on_the_moon_paul_van_hoeydonck_s_fallen_astronaut.html

Preston, James (1992) "Spiritual Magnetism: An Organizing Principle for the Study of Pilgrimage," in *Sacred Journeys*, A. Morinis, ed. Westport, CT: Greenwood Press, pp. 31-46.

Seale, Avrel (1999) "Alan Bean Moonwalker," Texas Alcalde, November/December pp. 42-47.

Still, Russell (1995) *Relics of The Space Race.* Roswell, GA: PR Products.

Swanson, Glen E. (1999) "Before This Decade is Out--," *Personal Reflections on the Apollo Program.* Washington, D.C.: National Aeronautics and Space Administration, NASA History Office, Office of Policy and Plans.

The First Paintings of Another World (nd), retrieved May 29, 2015. http://www.alanbean.com/

The Lunar Bible | Apostles of Apollo (nd), retrieved May 25, 2015. http://apostlesofapollo.com/first-lunar-bible/

Turner, Victor, & Turner, Edith (1978). *Image and Pilgrimage in Christian*

Culture: Anthropological Perspectives. New York: Columbia University Press.

Weibel, Deana L. (2012) "Magnetism and Microwaves: Religion as Radiation," in *The Body and Religion: Modern Science and the Construction of Meaning,* D. Cave & R. Sachs Norris, eds. Brill Academic Publishing, pp. 171-198.

_____ (in press) "'Up In God's Great Cathedral': Evangelism, Astronauts, and the Seductiveness of Outer Space," in D. Picard & M. Di Giovine, eds., *The Seductions of Pilgrimage: Sacred Journeys Afar and Astray in the Western Religious Tradition.* Farnham: Ashgate Publishing.

Williams, Jeffrey N. (2010) *The Work of His Hands: A View of God's Creation from Space.* Saint Louis, MO: Concordia Publishing House.

-=-

Deana L. Weibel, Ph.D., is an associate professor and Chair of the Department of Anthropology at Grand Valley State University, Allendale, Michigan. Her research focuses on religion, pilgrimage, sacred places, sacred objects and ritual. Although most of her work has been on such terrestrial pilgrimage sites as Chimayó in New Mexico and Rocamadour in France, Weibel's collaborations with former JSC historian Glen E. Swanson (her husband) have led her to explore the idea of outer space as sacred space. Recent publications include "'Up in God's Great Cathedral': Evangelism, Astronauts, and the Seductiveness of Outer Space" and "Magnetism and Microwaves: Religion as Radiation".

So You Want to Make Gods. Now Why Should That Bother Anyone?

David Brin

How can optimistic futurists most effectively communicate with those who are 'creeped out' by talk of transcendence and life extension?

(A talk given to the Singularity Summit, October 2011)

It's thrilling to join you brainy alphas, sharing insights and eagerness for a boldly transformed human destiny. As most of you know, I'm one of you, having explored non-human, trans-human, extraterrestrial humans, all sorts of exotic prospects in books and media. But you folks don't need another cheerleader for the Singularity today. As an ornery contrarian, my job is to poke at the viewpoints of whatever group I'm with, shining light on potential problems. And you folks have plenty of them! So I plan to poke. And some of you will not be happy, especially you new atheists out there.

What I propose to do is teach you how to talk to your worst adversaries. This is important -- as we are currently in the midst of a culture war, a chasm that's yawning wider in our nation, in our civilization, more and more resembling Phase Three of the Civil War.

The crux: you need to learn to talk to your adversaries, even if only to break up their coalitions. After all, you are the supposed smart ones, right? You should be able to speak several languages, and understand your own culture.

One of the problems we face -- that threatens any positive singularity -- will be waves of nostalgia. Many people look back, imagining a better, simpler time in the past. Indeed, culturally and religiously most civilizations looked backward to a golden age, a time when everything was better, until people fell from that state of bliss or grace.

We are the exception: we who take a forward-looking attitude toward a utopia and better days in the future. One might counter that some religions do look ahead; they propose better days after some catastrophic event. But if it's a sudden end-of-the-world leading to transcendent bliss, I don't consider that to be a look-forward view to a better-managed human civilization. It's just another version of the old, traditional habit, a look-backward mentality.

Now, this is an important fundamental for you forward-thinkers to ponder. If you manage to turn a person's gaze from past to future, then he or she becomes a potential ally, regardless of what differences remain. In an era when science and the very notion of progress are under attack, we do need to keep fighting for an ambitious problem-solving civilization. That's a daunting task. If it were easy, the galaxy would be filled with signs of prior success stories.

For thirty years, I have collected theories to explain the Great Silence in the cosmos -- the lack of any sign of extraterrestrial life -- as I coined it back in the 1980s. It's also called the Fermi Paradox. Having gathered nearly 100 possible and plausible explanations for the Great Silence, it's clear that something is keeping the numbers down. Some think that the explanation is a filter that suppresses the factors on the left side of the Drake Equation, leaving a galaxy that's open for us to explore and in which to make our own mistakes. These uniqueness proponents are opposed by those who focus on factors on the right side of the Drake Equation. They think the filter is waiting for us in our future -- a series of traps and pitfalls that no technological civilization has (yet) overcome.

But one thought is especially alluring. What if we're the first to make it all the way, crossing the minefield and then helping others to succeed? Our can-do problem solving zeal might not only save humanity, but also light up the galaxy. But it won't be easy. Nor will it fall into our laps. We need to use humanity's most-recently evolved organs, the ones that come in the very last moments of the pre-natal period. These organs still continue to take shape in our early twenties. (This explains teenagers.)

These most recently-evolved organs include the *paracingulate sulcus*, which lets us evaluate memory accurately, and the prefrontal lobes, those future-probing lamps on our brows. We know this because people who have had prefrontal lobotomies remain intelligent and conscious, but they lose interest in projecting what Einstein called the *gedankenexperiment*, or thought experiment. This involves our ability to imagine: What would happen if I did this, what would happen if I make this proposal or tell this lie or try to run this yellow light?

Even those who have access to both memory and foresight divide between optimists and grouches. Those who foresee a bright future include Ray Kurzweil, Peter Diamandis, and Vernor Vinge, while on the other side we have dour pessimists such as Francis Fukayama and Michael Chrichton, whom I turn into a character in my new novel.

Which brings us back to those 100 explanations for the Great Silence. Among the things that most often thwarted human advancement, many were societal: oligarchy, secrecy, rejection of the very idea of progress. One obstacle was the pyramidal social order, which reigned in ninety-nine percent of all human societies over the last 6000 years, in which chiefs and kings and priests and feudal lords repressed potential competitors by quashing all discussion of a future that might be different.

Renunciation of change is the great temptation: relinquishing rapid advancement for the sake of order. Oligarchs especially like renunciation, because rapid progress destabilizes power arrangements. This explains not just feudalism in the past, but also today's war on science. If you wage war on all the intellectual castes in a society, all that's left are oligarchs. Though let's be honest. The left has its own grouchy voices, claiming that we can only save ourselves by adapting restrictive, pastoral lifestyles. Take Jared Diamond's book, *Collapse*, very enlightening ... until you get to his fiercely retro-pastoral prescriptions.

Renunciation of change is a potent meme! Every time the public is frightened by something -- say terrorism -- cynical forces exploit the panic to ratchet up control. This is what my book, *The Transparent Society*, was to a large degree about.

Is this a new problem? Not at all. I urge you to watch a great old classic from the 1930s: *Things to Come*, by H. G. Wells, shows how deeply many of our grandparents were worried about the future. In some respects, they were thinking about such issues more deeply than are we. But this problem of fear-driven renunciation goes back even further.

Moreover, it should worry all of you would-be "godmakers".

Think about that term. Because that's exactly what your agenda is: to transform the normal arc of human living, of human lifespans, or human nature, itself. What would our distant ancestors have called the kind of being you hope to forge, other than a "god"?

And so we get to the core question of this talk. What should be your top priority as godmakers? How to design this or that tweak in the genetic code, or algorithm in your nascent AI?

No, your number one priority should be to avoid the fate of one of the earliest Singulitarian, Giordano Bruno -- burned at the stake for heresy in 1600. Evading that fate should be on your agenda! And do not fool yourselves. History shows just how far renunciators are willing to go, if they feel deeply threatened by smartalecks preaching change.

The best way to prevent this? Talk to folks! Ease their fears. You are supposedly the sapient, logical ones, right? So find ways to connect with those who might burn you at the stake, just as they burned guys like you in every other culture.

How to do that? First of all, don't deride your adversaries -- understand them! And so ... let us now do the most surprising thing ever done at a Singularity conference.

As we turn to the Bible.

Communicate with those who cling to the past.

Millions view this book as the core postulate of their beliefs. And the thing about postulates is that they are baselines. You should examine them closely. Deriding their priorities only solidifies the current Culture War. It plays into the hands of the cynical people who are manipulating your neighbors. You need to understand the foundation stones that underlie your own culture. In fact, you need to be able to speak another language. Stun them that you know this stuff. Use their own mythology to draw them toward the light.

Let's start at the beginning: the very first thing that happened in the relationship between the first man and his Creator. In Genesis, it is written that the Lord "brought the animals unto the man to see what he would call them. And the man gave names to all the beasts and to the fowl of the air, and to every creature of the field."

Theologians generally dismiss this small episode as cute and irrelevant. (By the way that's one of the names he gave one of the largest creatures!) Irrelevant? This is the only interaction that preceded all the complications and subsequent *tsuris* of sex and sin. What better hint at what we were made for? This is the only act that wasn't about repairing and salvation after sin. We weren't asked to pray, but to perform an early act of naming things.

Let there be no mistake: Naming stuff is god-like power. Ask any physics student who contemplates Maxwell's equations -- those gorgeous lines behind the statement: "There is light".

What is the act of naming things other than an apprenticeship in co-creation? And what is that apprenticeship other than Science? The naming of distant moons, of hidden molecular codes, the discovery and labeling of millions of never-before-seen species, the act of grubbing in the mud under an alkaline lake and coming up with new beasts to name. The sheer purity of this moment, the only pure moment in the Bible, free of all sin, is certainly evidence of what we were made for.

Notice what I just did? I dialed in to a verse in the core religious story and used it to depict as sacred the expression of human intellect, curiosity, and science. Does this mean I take the passage literally? Of course not! But it shows that I am willing to talk to my religious neighbors in terms they can grasp, in the realm where they feel comfortable. And yes, every single time I have done this the response was increased curiosity and friendliness. Never once hostility.

It is possible to use scripture as a bridge. And generally, if you say it in friendly terms, it rocks them back and they say, "Hmm ... I'll have to think about that." And they're no longer your enemy. They're someone to argue with. The point is: they're not interpreting these events properly, even in their own context. Remember, you're all descended from priests and rabbis who handled this stuff with ease. It should be trivial for you alphas to have a look at these cultural keystones, and show your neighbors the light.

All right, so Adam named beasts ... and then things got complicated. Sin happened, according to the mythos believed by millions of our fellow citizens. But even there, we find leverage!

Take this passage: "The man has now become like one of us, knowing good and evil."

Become like us? Hold that thought. We'll come back and see what it means.

But the next line is even better: "He must not also be allowed to reach out and take from the tree of life and eat it and live forever."

Consider that part, starting with the word reach, and you transhumanist life-extension fetishists should make it your motto! Live forever! Let's put aside the "he must not" part for now. What all this says is that man is inherently capable of using knowledge to be like God and to live forever. Half the battle over our capabilities is settled, then. Now we're only haggling over when it's right. Maybe it wasn't time yet for Adam and Eve. Maybe that time has finally come.

Only let's move on now. Then came another crucial event that theologians mostly ignore. The Tower of Babel is shrugged aside, taken as a morality tale about the cost of human sin and the price humans must pay for hubris and arrogant pride. Take a closer look: "And the Lord said: See, they are all one people and have all one language; and this is only the start of what they may do: and now it will not be possible to keep them from any purpose."

There it is again, the combination of two important themes. Number one: humanity is inherently godlike, with limitless potential to achieve anything with cooperative effort and the power of words. It's right there, utterly inarguable, but so is point two. This is something God prevented, as when Adam and Eve were expelled from Eden because they just might grab from the fruit of the Tree of Life. Or when humankind was cast into confusion, speaking a thousand tongues, leaving the tower in ruins.

But even here, consider: Was it to be prevented ... forever? If so, why make us this way, with so many inherent capabilities? That's the old question.

Or else, might the Eden-expulsion and the Babel-confusion have been limited measures applied just to those situations? Ways to stymie and prevent us from achieving too much, too soon?

Well, we're about to test it. Soon, as many of us have depicted in fiction, with modern technology, language will be no barrier anymore. With universal translator devices in our pockets, the age of Babel-incomprehensibility is over. One worldwide culture, will, we hope, both unify us and enhance our individual eccentric creativity.

The new Tower of Babel we're building is no simplistic ziggurat, but a flat, broad foundation for ambition that will allow us to assert every godlike power that our inherent natures equip us to pursue, along with -- we pray and hope -- the wisdom this time to do it right.

But, make no mistake: this possibility that has you and me enthralled is the very thing frightening our neighbors. It is what underlies the war on science that is being cynically manipulated by evil men, who wish to continue their oligarchic putsch aimed at ending our Enlightenment. It is what will propel a rising trend toward Renunciation. Indeed, it is one possible explanation for the Great Silence, if similar repressions happen widely in the cosmos. Your neighbors are terrified of sharing inevitable punishment for all this arrogance and hubris. And given their axioms and postulates, can you honestly blame them?

But their postulate is simply wrong, even in terms of their own sacred texts. Because God never actually punished us for hubris. Ever.

Let's compare two kinds of events, in which the Old Testament God got extremely angry. This happened at Sodom and Gomorrah, and before the flood in the time of Noah. When men buggered children and sold their daughters, God responded with hot-tempered rage: fire from the sky, drowning everyone in sight, pillars of salt.

In contrast, how were Adam and Eve punished? God said, "Ok you kids, you think you're so smart. Go get jobs!"

And after the Tower of Babel, God said, "Not now kids, not yet. Disperse, experiment in diversity in ten thousand lands. Become many. Make mistakes. Learn."

A key point: Nowhere in the canonical Hebrew book of Genesis is there a single word of wrathful anger toward Adam or the tower-builders! Just calm cause and effect. This from the same fellow who drowned and incinerated folks, when he was genuinely mad.

Now, in fairness, later writers, in the Talmud, the Koran, and the Book of Mormon, interpret God's reaction to Babel as genuinely angry. But there is not one whiff of rage in the actual, original, and canonical text, just calm deliberation and decision. They will be able to do this ... let's stop them, or possibly stop them . . . for now. God thwarted human ambition in both Eden and Babel, but with minimal force, and with the distraction of new tasks.

Hence, this clear interpretation: Ambition isn't punished as sin. It is rewarded with challenge.

Now, of course this is an assertion and many will argue with you, but they're going to argue with respect for someone who's taken the time to read and understand and argue in their bailiwick. And it's an assertion that is worthy, in scriptural terms.

These aren't tricks.

Elsewhere, I've supplied a whole list of talking points, all supported by scripture, that should help in tussles with your uncles, cousins, and neighbors. But even if you don't manage to sway even one of them, you'll be doing what alphas ought to do: use a tiny sliver of your giant brains to reach out, to demonstrate that you can cross the divide, and speak their language. And they are now behooved to visit your realm a little bit.

When that happens, here's one thing I find effective. Locate a railroad cut not far from your town and invite some of your favorite religious renunciators along. Actually show them the sedimentary layers. Tell them about how long we know it takes for each thin layer to be set, and how each contains a slightly different collection of ever-changing fossils. Show them images from the Hubble telescope, glorious in light that traveled billions of years from whole galaxies overflowing with possibilities. And even if you are an atheist, speak of the dazzling beauty of it all. And how -- if you turn out to be wrong about the God thing -- then He is an artist with a vastly bigger canvas than one little, temporary mudball-Earth just 6000 years old.

Why should you go to such effort to engage your neighbors? In order to be curious about them! In order to shift frightened minds, and -- with ultimate pragmatism -- in order to ease the kind of populist fever that evil men may someday use to burn you at the stake.

Anyway, why not? It's interesting ... especially for would-be makers of gods. Shouldn't you be thinking about these types of things, not only to reach out to your neighbors, but because you'll be going through these issues yourselves with the Artificial Intelligences you create?

In summary, naming is science and we're good at it. Our potential is unlimited. Even conquering death -- it's right there in scripture. Day by day, obstacles are toppling before science ... as if in a training program! In these examples and many others, God didn't punish ambition, but merely delayed things.

Is it possible he's going to delay it again? Sure. On the other hand, signs are that the time is right, at last. Anyway, we're doing what we're built to do, and we're going to take on these challenges. It's time for another Tower of Babel.

There are other issues I could go into. Take the fixation on many American Christians on the Book of Revelation, one of the most loathsome parts of any religious work, in any culture. Did you know that Martin Luther didn't even want it included in the Bible? Computerized studies of rhythm patterns found that it resembles the ravings of schizophrenics. But the simplest answer to the *BoR* is to be found in the story of Jonah: whose repeated lesson is that God can change his mind. A lesson that renders the howls of John of Patmos moot after 2000 years. It's an effective rebuttal of a noxious story... but note that you can only offer it if you have bothered to read.

These are among many ways to make your fellow citizens stare and blink. Moreover, they will be more friendly after such encounters, because you spoke to them in their language.

Whether you are atheists or techno-deists, you are already theologians because you plan to create (with either human enhancement or uplift or Artificial Intelligence) what any other generation would call gods. Some of you hope to become gods. So? Then justify it. Sell it!

Protect yourselves from tomorrow's mobs and relate to them. Prevent the Renunciation that could stymie your dreams from coming true. Even if you despise religion, stop over-reacting. These cultural keystones matter. They are metaphors; they are useful. Use them.

Let me close with one that's especially effective: the comparison of styles of worship. Say you are a creator who came up with Maxwell's equations, the Bernoulli Principle, and Quantum Mechanics. What would you consider to be a better prayer?

1. "Oh you're so great. Oh you're so magnificent ... Please don't squish me."

2. Or, some students in a chemistry class carefully doing a titration they had calculated the night before. And it all pops out at them perfectly, and they say, "Oh, that's nice!"

Which would you prefer?

One can imagine a deity getting bored and tired of prayer number one's endless, tedious flattery. But a Creator worthy of respect, who conjured Big Bangs and black holes and DNA and so on responding to number two with:

"Why, thank you. I was kind of proud of that myself. Good of you to notice. Now let's see what else you can figure out."

It's what we're made to do. We'll go forth and name all the beasts.

-=-

David Brin, Ph.D., is a scientist, technical consultant, and author. He has received one Nebula award and two Hugo awards for his science fiction, which has been translated into more than 20 languages. He is also the author of *The Transparent Society: Will Technology Force Us to Choose between Freedom and Privacy.* His scientific work covers an eclectic range of topics, including astronautics, astronomy, optics, alternative dispute resolution, and the role of neoteny in human evolution. His patents are in the area of screen-based interaction, and aim to improve the way we converse online. He has also appeared as a "scientist/futurist" on various TV shows, including the History Channel's *The Universe, Life after People*, and *The ArchiTECHS.* Novels and collections include *Existence, Through Stranger Eyes, Sky Horizon, Kiln People, Otherness, Glory Season, Earth, Startide Rising*, and *The Postman*, which was made into a film by Kevin Costner. Shorter works have appeared in *Fantasy and Science Fiction, Isaac Asimov's Science Fiction, Popular Science, Salon, Omni*, and *WIRED*, among others. He was at the Hannah Arendt Center as an NEH Distinguished Visiting Lecturer at Bard College, Fall 2015.

The Touching Interface of the Cosmos

Lance Strate

What is it about the sky above that moves us so? Perhaps it is a vestigial memory passed down from our arboreal ancestors, whose survival depended upon their ability to climb high above the ground? Trees loom large as archetypal symbols for our species, as for example in Norse myth the cosmos is centered on the world tree Yggdrasil, a motif also found in many other traditional cultures all around the world. Admittedly, we trace our lineage back to primates who long ago dropped down from the branches, or perhaps were unable to hang on and had to find a way to make do down on the ground. But perhaps it is our evolutionary descent that forms the basis of what theologians refer to as The Fall, otherwise known as the story of Adam and Eve in the Garden of Eden.

The word "fall" is commonly used as a metaphor for failure and defeat, as it is in reference to Eden, and we generally attach negative connotations to words referring to downward motion or position, and positives ones to words associated with moving or being situated upwards. And while Adam and Eve end up being cast out of Eden, not cast down a la Satan or Lucifer, their story does revolve around a sacred tree, the Tree of Knowledge of Good and Evil. In the Book of Genesis, God tells Adam that he can eat any of the fruit growing in the Garden of Eden except for the fruit of that one tree, saying that if he does, he will surely die. The serpent tells Eve a different story, however, promising her that if she and her husband partake of the forbidden fruit, "your eyes shall be opened, and you shall be as gods." After Adam and Eve have succumbed to temptation and gained the knowledge that brings self-awareness (and self-consciousness), the words of the serpent are confirmed by none other than God himself, who declares, "Behold, the man has become as one of us," the plural pronoun perhaps indicating that the tale was borrowed from earlier, polytheistic cultures, or alternately grouping God together with other celestial beings, i.e., the angels. Either way, God's response is to exile the aboriginal couple in order to prevent them from eating from Eden's other sacred tree, the Tree of Life, thereby gaining immortality and truly becoming godlike. From this point on, Eden remains off limits to men and women, but in Jewish tradition the Tree of Life becomes a metaphor for the Torah given by God many generations later, and the cosmos comes to be understood as being centered on that very same sacred text. Moreover, in the Jewish mystical tradition of the Kabbalah, the Tree of Life also refers to a diagram representing the ten Sephirot, ten divine emanations or aspects of God, which form the basis of God's original act of Creation; Adam and Eve's Fall, in Kabbalistic tradition, resulted in the shattering of the vessels intended to house the Sephirot.

The Tree of Life, Yggdrasil, and other manifestations of the archetype of the sacred tree serve as symbols of the cosmos, an organic metaphor for a cosmology in which the world and universe are seen as alive, conscious, and characterized by a spiritual dimension in addition to the physical. As symbol and metaphor, the tree functions as a medium or interface for something other than itself, beyond itself, and above itself, and the same is true for the trees we interact with in the physical world. "When danger threatens, climb a tree," is an admonishment we may still keep in the back of our minds (that was the life-saving advice given to Smokey the Bear by his mother in Jane Werner's 1955 *Little Golden Book* for children), but there is something more than the tree-hugging impulse at work in the constant refrain to "look, up in the sky!" Tree-climbing is about something more than safety, it is about the impulse to see more, to see further, and if at all possible, to see how high we can go. Whether we can reach the treetops or not, we recognize that trees stand as a terrestrial interface to the sky, and therefore, an interface to the cosmos.

Reaching higher still, mountains too serve as an interface to the sky, so much so that if we climb high enough, we find ourselves able to look down at clouds. The 121st Psalm of David, called "A Song of Ascents," begins with the lines, "I lift up my eyes unto the mountains, from whence shall my help come?" The answer that follows is God, and it is no accident that ancient religions situated the divine on mountaintops such as Sinai, Horeb, the Temple Mount in Jerusalem, Olympus, Ida, Athos, Kailash, Meru, Laoshan, Fuji, Machu Picchu, and the Black Hills, to name a few. As an archetype, the mountain lacks much of the organic quality of the tree, although there are occasional references to a living mountain and living rock, and volcanoes in particular exhibit qualities easily mistaken for the emotional outbursts of creatures characterized by consciousness. But mountains eclipse trees as symbols of what Alfred Korzybski (1950, 1993) termed time-binding, in their ability to communicate a sense of permanence that far exceeds the limits of individual and species-wide mortality. Moreover, they convey a sense of majesty that links them to the heavens, and with it, a sense of power. And although they may evoke awe and intimidate us, they also call to us to rise up, ascend, climb higher and higher still, ever higher, and to invoke the archetype Henry Wadsworth Longfellow turned cliché, to shout, Excelsior! They invite us to embark upon a hero's journey, calling out to us in challenge, to scale the heights, to reach the summit, because it's there, as George Mallory said in reference to climbing Mount Everest.

###

As a species, however, we have not been content to simply operate within the confines and limitations of our found environment. All forms of life, by their very existence, and through the metabolism that defines them, have an effect on their environment, alter their environment, and if they are not dysfunctional, modify their environment to improve their chances of survival. We are not alone in this, but we have, in our own way, gone farther than any other species in developing means and methods that mediate between ourselves and the environment we would otherwise inhabit (Strate, 2006, 2011, 2014). This includes the creation of shelter, of dwellings, of houses and buildings, as the great media ecology scholar Lewis Mumford (1967) emphasizes. It also includes the building of monuments, the heaviest of heavy media, serving to send messages over deep time and across the ages, as another foundational media ecology scholar, Harold Innis (1951), explains. And so we have a long history of creating artificial mountains, such as the pyramids of Egypt and Mesoamerica, and the skyscrapers of the modern world. The story of the Tower of Babel speaks to the limitations of such efforts, as does the terrible tragedy of the 9/11 terrorist attacks.

In Greek myth, the counterpart to Babel would be the stories of Bellerophon and Icarus. After taming the winged horse Pegasus and slaying the Chimera, Bellerophon in a fit of hubris tried to fly up to Mount Olympus to take his place among the gods, but was thrown off the horse, falling back to Earth, and a crushing fate. Icarus was the son of Daedalus, trapped with his father in the very Labyrinth that Daedalus had built for King Minos to imprison the Minotaur. To effect their escape, Daedalus fashioned wings out of feathers and wax, warning his son not to fly too close to the son or the wax will melt. Icarus in his enthusiasm for flight ignores the warning, and falls into the sea. Although Daedalus survives, he is heartbroken over the death of his son. Both myths, while cautionary tales, speak to the dream of flight, and the sense that we might somehow find a way to embrace the sky.

As far back as we can remember, human beings have looked up with envy at the birds that fly, glide, and sometimes seem to just float through the air. We recognize them as animals like ourselves, some like the eagle and hawk adopted as totems to identify with, some like the falcon and the dove trained to hunt or carry messages, and some like the parrot and canary domesticated as companions (as opposed to those kept as livestock, such as the chicken and turkey, whose flight capabilities are limited). It is no great leap to imagine human beings transformed into birds, and there are many such tales in Greek mythology, including Aedon transformed into a nightingale, Aegypius and Neophron turned into vultures, Antigone turned into a stork, Ascalaphus and Meropis transformed into owls, Coroneus' daughter turned into a crow, Cycnus and Hyrie transformed into swans, Daedalion and Hierax becoming hawks, Eumelus and Lycius ravens, Lelante and Polytechnos woodpeckers, Elais and Oeno doves, Merops and Pandarus eagles, Philoemela and Procne swallows, Hippodamia a lark, Nisus an osprey, Perdix a partridge, and the Pierdies sisters into magpies, to name just a few. And then there are the gods who disguised themselves as birds, as well as the winged god Eros, better known by his Latin name, Cupid, sometimes associated or even conflated with the winged cherubs or angels of Abrahamic tradition. The power of the human imagination is such that the image of taking wing and gliding or soaring through the air comes easily to us, and the lessons of Babel, Icarus, and Bellerophon are easily forgotten.

In lieu of supernatural intervention, we turn to technics as the means to achieve the ends that we long for. How many have tried to devise some method of extending our power of locomotion to enable us to leap forward, to gain entry into the firmament above, who can say? Roger Bacon wrote about mechanical flight in the 13th century, and Leonardo da Vinci designed such machines in the 15th. As Marshall McLuhan (1964) explains, the 19th century invention of the bicycle represents the first truly aerodynamic form of transportation, and it is no accident that it was a pair of bicycle mechanics, Orville and Wilbur Wright, who are credited with the invention of the airplane in 1903. As significant as this event may be, it obscures the importance of the innovation of lighter than air flight over a century earlier, with Jean François Pilâtre de Rozier and Marquis d'Arlandes making the first hot-air balloon flight and Jacques Alexandre César Charles and M. N. Robert the first flight in a hydrogen balloon, both in 1783. Ballooning was the theme of one of the first science fiction stories, Edgar Allen Poe's "The Unparalleled Adventure of One Hans Pfaall," which imagines a trip to the Moon and back, not to mention Poe's newspapers articles, collectively known as "The Balloon Hoax," about a transatlantic crossing.

We might also acknowledge that the act of firing projectiles into the air was common enough in our prehistory, the bow and arrow being particularly significant both as metaphor for human flight and as a basic technology, and this was further developed in antiquity in the form of the catapult, a device mainly used as a weapon, but also capable of hurling human beings into the air (with unfortunate results, of course). The invention of gunpowder can be traced back to 1st-century China, its use for artillery to the 12th century, and its use for rocketry following on the heels of the cannon in the 13th century. Both cannons and rockets were seen as potential means of transport to other worlds during the 19th century, with rocketry finally taking off during the Second World War through the development of the Nazi V-2 rocket; the German scientists captured by the US and the Soviets at the end of the war spearheaded what became known as the Space Age, resulting in the Space Race as a function of the Cold War. As much as rockets have been associated with outer space, however, their main function, much like jets, has been to propel themselves, and whatever cargo they may carry, human or otherwise, through the atmosphere, not beyond it.

###

We know that our ancestors once looked up at the sky and saw a firmament full of life, of birds and bats and bugs that fly, and also something more, celestial beings, supernatural entities recognizable as the Sun and Moon, the stars and planets, comets and meteors, and the like. Indeed, they saw all the world as animated by spirit, including the Earth, bodies of water, and of course trees and mountains too. The sacred was all around us, an environment that we were immersed in. And yet, the sacred also referred to a time and place outside of the everyday, what Mircea Eliade (1954, 1959) refers to as sacred time and space as opposed to their profane counterparts. The root meaning of the Hebrew word for holy, kadosh, is verb that means to set apart. The Hebrew Bible's story of Creation is a story of separations, of light from dark, of day from night, and of the lower waters from those above, that is, the sky. What then, is more holy than that which is so set apart from us that it remains, for the most part, out of reach?

The many varieties of spiritual experience that are grouped under the heading of animism, the kinds of religious experience that characterize tribal cultures and are reflected within oral traditions, confer consciousness and spirit onto all manner of terrestrial and celestial phenomena. But what sets the heavens apart from our Earthly environment, beyond distance, is that the sky plays host to innumerable entities whose movements are steady and predictable in ways that far exceed anything we encounter on land or sea. The Sun, Moon, planets, and stars follow a pattern that could only, until relatively recently, be seen as perfection, a rhythm characterized by a regularity far beyond that of the seasons, the ebb and flow of the tides, and the periodic flooding of rivers like the Nile. They are our first and truest experience of an entirely objective sense of time, time that seems to exist independently of subjective and intersubjective human experience, or of the natural phenomena we interact with. Our calendars and clocks are media that extend our perception of the dance of the heavenly spheres, keeping time by following the rhythm of their observed revolutions, measuring time by the meter of their motion.

For Aristotle and his fellow ancients, living within a literate culture while maintaining a religious tradition that came to be known as pagan, the Sun, Moon, planets, and stars were identified with the gods, and other supernatural entities. In an effort to reconcile Aristotelian science with Jewish theology, the medieval philosopher Moses Maimonides, aka the RaMBaM, allowed that the heavenly spheres had some form of intelligence, and occupied a position of a higher order than humanity, but lower than God and the angels. In his Mishneh Torah, completed in the 12th century, he argued that God, who is characterized by neither form nor matter, divided Creation into three parts. At the bottom of the hierarchy we have human beings, along with animals, plants, and minerals, all characterized by the combination of matter and form that is subject to continual change. At the top, immediately below God, are the angels, who have form but no matter, and are not subject to change. And in between the two are the planets and stars, composed of form and matter, but fixed and unchanging. Their association with permanence and eternity persisted as the astronomies of Ptolemy gave way to those of Copernicus, Galileo, and Kepler, and our conception of the universe was transformed from a sacred ecology to a perfect machine, based on the physics of Isaac Newton, and otherwise known as the clockwork universe.

Consider the fact that the Enlightenment metaphor of the clockwork universe is a reversal of the original metaphor, the mechanical clock as a metaphorical simulation (simule?) of the revolution of heavenly spheres. To this day, their movements have the final say when it comes to answering the question, what time is it? Or, as we used to say, what is the time of day? Even with atomic clocks that keep time with greater precision than any astronomical phenomenon, we still feel compelled to reset our clocks to keep them in sync with the sky, as for example when a leap second was added to our Coordinated Universal Time at midnight on June 30th, 2015 so as not fall out of sync, in even so imperceptible a manner, with the Earth's rotation.

Time is the ultimate invisible environment. Over the course of the 19th century, scientists came to the conclusion that the basic stuff of the universe is not static matter, but dynamic energy, a reconceptualization topped off by Einstein's famous formula, $E=MC^2$, which provides the basis for measuring the amount of energy stored in any given quantity of matter, and in doing so making the time it takes light to travel across distance the only universal constant. In regard to sense perception, Marshall McLuhan and Edmund Carpenter characterized this paradigm shift as a return to a sense of acoustic space, as opposed to the visual space that came to dominate Western culture, especially following the printing revolution associated with Gutenberg's invention of the letterpress (Carpenter & McLuhan, 1960; McLuhan, 1964). Einstein sought to emphasize the significance of time by making the more familiar concept of space inseparable from it, hence his use of the term spacetime. But it would be more appropriate to say that we live in a timespace, that space is a function of time, traced back to the moment of origin of the Big Bang, a moment in time in which space did not exist.

Time is our most essential environment, invisible as a pure concept, but observable in the patterns of change that surround us, especially the highly stable and predictable patterns of the heavens above us. And even if the microcosm of the subatomic may possess a regularity that surpasses the macrocosm of the universe, we cannot actually see anything as small as an atom, while the planets and stars are visible to the naked eye. Of course, all perception is also a form of time travel, as what registers on our senses are reflections of events that have already passed, even if the delay is only momentary. The visual sense being our most distant of receptors, the further away the object of our gaze, the further back in time we are looking, and it is well known that as we extend our eyes through the agency of the telescope and look further and further out into space, we are in fact observing an increasingly more distant past. Whether we will one day be able to view the birth of the universe remains to be seen, but within the boundaries of the relativity of time, our relation to the cosmos is absolute. We live in cosmic time.

###

We tend to think of our environment in terrestrial terms, but the sky surrounds us and contains us. More than food and water, the air we breathe is the most pressing of the necessities for life. The atmosphere, we have come to understand, is our interface to the celestial sphere. As an interface, the sky is by nature Janus-faced, its two sides as different from one another, as antonymic as night and day. When we look at the nighttime sky, we look up into mystery, into the deepest of mysteries, while the daytime sky is comfortingly familiar, a wild blue yonder that, like the wine dark sea, is contiguous with our terrestrial comfort zone, seemingly within reach if not entirely navigable. Blue-sky may be impractical, but it is a product of unbridled optimism. Blue skies are a sign of happiness, as Irving Berlin observed, and while the opposite may be said of storm clouds, we still look for that silver lining. Yes, there is something at least a little bit friendly about the daytime skies, something somehow inviting when the sun is shining bright.

Indeed, the only thing that makes the daytime sky seem at all threatening, apart from the obvious acrophobic issues we may experience, is, ironically enough, the very source of the daytime itself. The Sun, the bane of Icarus, is the one object in the sky that overpowers the human eye, dazzles and blinds, temporarily or sometimes permanently. And yet, the intuition that we are wholly dependent on the nourishment it provides is basic to our species, and perhaps all living things understand, deep down in the molecules of our genetic material, that the fires of our Sun form the true primordial ocean from which we sprang. Moreover, the Sun may overpower, but it occupies only a small portion of the daytime sky, except during the liminal periods of dawn and dusk, during which time it expands in both size and accessibility, as sunrise and sunsets represent a shift from overpowering white heat to cooler shades of red and yellow.

The Sun lights up our atmosphere, making it opaque and visible, and when it disappears under the horizon, the air becomes transparent and invisible, a window onto outer space. This turns the nighttime sky into something altogether different, alien and foreboding. The welcoming openness of the blue disappears into an oppressive and ominous blackness, an unknowable and inhospitable dark punctured innumerably by the pale and distant light of the stars and Moon. "For the night is dark and full of terrors," goes the refrain recited by George R. R. Martin's *Game of Thrones* character, Melisandre. "Criminals are a superstitious cowardly lot, so my disguise must be able to strike terror into their hearts. I must be a creature of the night, black, terrible...," says Bruce Wayne, just before a bat flies by, inspiring him to create the identity of Batman. Far from a warm and fuzzy creature, the nocturnal flyer is the object of irrational fear, associated as it is with the monstrous image of the vampire, a creature that stalks in the shadows and cannot survive the sunlight. The other commonly invoked nighttime flyer is the owl, which, while associated with wisdom, has an air of the uncanny and intimidating about it, as a predator and a haunting presence, often heard but unseen. And then there is Edgar Allen Poe's raven, of which I will say no more.

Still, the mystery of the nighttime sky is an object of fascination as well, the ebbing and flowing of the Moon, the complexity of the constellations, the entire array of stars, planets, and other celestial bodies entices us as the source of endless wonder. The daytime sky is finite, bounded, but the nighttime sky gives us a glimpse of what is, for all intents and purposes, infinity, and eternity. It is the subject of the most intense form of awe. Psalm 8 refers specifically to the sky at night in questioning the place of humanity in the face of the vastness of the cosmos: "When I consider Thy heavens, the work of Thy fingers, the moon and the stars, which Thou hast ordained; what is man, that Thou art mindful of him?" The contrasts between day and night can be summed up in a few simple statements:

> The daytime sky is near; the nighttime sky is far.
>
> The daytime sky is immediate; the nighttime sky is distant.
>
> The daytime sky is immanent; the nighttime sky is transcendent.

We are moved to touch the sky, to go so far as to kiss the sky, as a spiritual pathway, a way to rise up through immanence towards transcendence.

But I want to note a different sense in which we might think about the Janus-faced sky, one that acknowledges the irony that our search for transcendence has only succeeded in making the transcendent recede ever further into the distance, or more aptly, placed the eternal return (Eliade, 1954), a connection to the moment of creation even further out of reach, telescopically, in space and in time. I want, in other words, to acknowledge my own ambivalence about all this, the conflict between my heart that takes inspiration from our efforts to touch the face of the cosmos, and my head that questions whether we can ever break on through to the other side of the firmament that lies above us, whether we are, in fact, searching for something that does not exist, or that cannot be found out there within the darkest of skies.

> The daytime sky is familiar; the nighttime sky is alien.
>
> The daytime sky is what is known and knowable; the nighttime sky is what is unknown and unknowable.
>
> The daytime sky represents illumination and enlightenment; the nighttime sky represents the mysterious and uncanny.
>
> The daytime sky is visible and opaque; the nighttime sky is invisible and transparent.
>
> The daytime sky reveals all that is Earthly and conceals what lies beyond; the nighttime sky conceals all that is Earthly and reveals what lies beyond.
>
> The daytime sky reflects the air that we breathe, the most basic requirement for life; the nighttime sky unveils the vacuum of outer space, an environment utterly hostile to our survival.

The sky, then, is the interface that both separates and connects us to something wholly other than us. The atmosphere is the boundary that separates our planet from what lies beyond. We become caught up in the act of touching the interface in an effort to move through it to whatever lies on the other side. But what is it that waits for us out in the void? Could it be nothing at all?

The daytime sky is being; the nighttime sky is nothingness.

###

Seventeen days after I was born, the Soviet Union launched Sputnik into orbit, the first humanly constructed satellite, or artificial moon as they were once called. It was the beginning of the Space Age, so for all intents and purposes, I am a native of that new era. It also meant a massive intensification of the Cold War, and as a consequence, I also grew up as a spectator of the Space Race, cheering Team USA on as we came from behind over the course of the sixties, and wound up the only ones to reach the finish line on the (natural) Moon. Not surprisingly, like many of my peers, I grew up wanting to be an astronaut. Sort of.

Like the older baby boomers born in the aftermath of the Second World War, I was also a science fiction native, thrust into a world that contained nuclear weapons, missiles and rockets, computers, and of course television. The Space Race was very much a part of the science fiction world that we inhabited, although, as much as we admired the pioneers of this new frontier orbiting the Earth in their space capsules, taking their space walks, and leaping about on the Moon, the images were rather low in resolution, intermittent and indistinct, and above all, slow-moving, lacking in drama and stimulation. We were ready for what lies ahead, but impatient with the slow progress being made. After all, in a sense we were already off, gallivanting about the galaxy via television programs like *Lost in Space* and *Star Trek*, old movie serials like *Flash Gordon* and *Buck Rogers*, and feature films like *Forbidden Planet* and Stanley Kubrick's *2001: A Space Odyssey*, which promised us a nearly complete space station orbiting the planet by the beginning of the 21st century, with routine airline service back and forth, and permanent colonies on the Moon. Indeed, just a few months after *2001* premiered in 1968, Apollo 8 circled the Moon, as a prelude to Apollo 11's Moon landing the following year, and while they were still in lunar orbit, one major American airline announced that they were taking reservations for the first commercial flight to the Moon, and another quickly followed suit. Not only have they failed to make good on their implied promise, but both airlines, Pan Am (the airline depicted in *2001*) and TWA, have long since gone out of business.

Peter Thiel, co-founder of PayPal, summed up the disappointment we share through the motto he created for the Founders Fund venture capital firm that he also co-founded: "We wanted flying cars, instead we got 140 characters.“ Substitute trips to the Moon and Mars for flying cars, and that sums it up perfectly. What we got, instead, was the Internet, email, websites, Google, social media, cell phones and mobile devices. And while these things are nothing to sneeze at, is it wrong to be disappointed? Were we suffering from what Daniel Boorstin (1978) referred to as extravagant expectations? Could it be that we let our imaginations get the better of us? That would certainly be nothing new for our species. Moreover, in our science fiction scenarios, we project our familiar reality onto the new setting, so that nations become planets, naval vessels and aircraft become spaceships, firearms become lasers, etc. We draw on our past, terrestrial experiences of exploration, discovery, and settlement, and transfer them onto the imagined country of distant planets and solar systems. We imagine a galaxy teeming with Earth-like planets on which we can easily survive, even thrive, setting up colonies near and far, aided by the discovery of forms of transportation moving faster than the speed of light, an impossibility according to Einsteinian physics. *Star Trek* and *Star Wars* showed us a galaxy full of intelligent, alien beings, many of whom become our friends, even though some may also become our foes, or view us as threats. The fact that these narratives are reflections of what is now, and what has been in the past, rather than on what might be, reflections of the known rather than true speculations about the unknown, suggests that they should be taken with one or more grains of salt.

I certainly do not want to argue that all of our science fiction scenarios are impossible. The champions of progress love to mock the skeptics who declared that one advance or another was not feasible, above all pointing to the invention of the airplane. I grew up hearing the declaration, if man was meant to fly, he'd have wings (or, God would have given him wings), as an example of blind, pigheaded ignorance. Given our track record of scientific and technological progress, I think it only right to never say never when it comes to extrapolations and speculations regarding the future.

Could it be that the dream we collectively dreamed is not dead, but simply deferred? That it was a mistake to expect steady progress, when history shows that innovation and change happens in fits and starts, plateauing out for a while before continuing on, that evolution is characterized by punctuated equilibria that divide periods of significant change? Perhaps.

But the future we grew up with, the future we grew up expecting to step into, remains almost entirely as distant as it did at the start of the Space Age.

At the same time that we were celebrating our repeated trips to the Moon, the great American intellectual, Lewis Mumford (1970), injected a note of skepticism into what he referred to as our space travail, writing

> I would suggest that the manned space, as now conceived, corresponds exactly to the innermost chamber of the great pyramids, where the mummified body of the Pharaoh, surrounded by the miniaturized equipment necessary for magical travel to Heaven, was placed. (p. 306)

Mumford makes clear the parallel that exists between our own efforts to send our astronauts to what constitutes our contemporary understanding of the heavens and the ancient Egyptians sending their Pharaoh and his companions to their version of heaven. In both cases, an inordinate amount of wealth, labor, and resources have been devoted to sending a select few on their journeys, with little or no benefit to balance out the enormous sacrifice required. Mumford goes on to make the following observation:

> What space technics has already achieved, within the insulated capsule, may be described as temporary mummification: a state that provides the minimal conditions for keeping the human agent alive, or rather, from decomposing in the course of his flight. If the Egyptian tomb may be properly described as a static rocket, the cosmic space rocket is in fact a mobile tomb. In each case, the most exquisite confections of technology have been provided to keep a human manikin in a state of suspended animation. (p. 306)

Mumford acknowledges the difference between the dead body placed inside the pyramid and the live one loaded onto a rocket, but notes that to be able to voyage through space, the astronaut "is forced under strict training to divest himself of every hampering attribute of life, so that what is left of human existence are just those minimal bodily and mental functions that will enable him to survive under hardships and deprivations“ (p. 307). This very much corresponds to what Tom Wolfe (1979), in a more celebratory fashion, referred to as the right stuff; still, Wolfe also makes clear the drastic difference between test pilots like Chuck Yeager, who remain in complete control of their jets, and the astronauts who were reduced to cargo during the Mercury program. If over the course of the years astronauts have progressed from passengers to more active participants in space missions, Daniel Boorstin (1978) rightly notes the difficulty in recognizing them as heroes in the traditional sense, insofar as their individual achievements are impossible to isolate from the team of scientists and technicians that support and for the most part guide them (e.g., mission control). They are cogs in a complex human organization, a true machine from Mumford's perspective, a device composed of human parts that are easily disposed of and replaced. And ultimately, Mumford (1970) draws the following conclusion concerning space exploration:

> By now this exploration has reached a natural terminus: the last frontier is closed. The landing of the first two astronauts on the moon was not the beginning of a new age of cosmic exploration but the end. The scientific technological revolution that began in the sixteenth century therewith reached its appropriately sterile terminus: a satellite as uninhabitable as the earth itself will all too soon become—unless by a massive expenditure of imagination and courageous political effort the peoples of the world challenge the age-old power complex. Without a counter-movement to slow down or reverse these automatic processes mankind comes closer, year by year, to what is in more than one sense a dead end. [p. 379)]

A dead end? Perhaps. I cite Mumford not because I am in total agreement with him, but to credit him with making me question my own assumptions about space travel, and with turning me from a complete enthusiast, a fan-boy if you will, into a divided self, ambivalent and agnostic. I am willing to ask the simple question, what for? Or as Neil Postman (1992, 1995, 1999) liked to put it, to what problem is this a solution? Mumford's more specific question would be, given limited resources and such great need here on Earth, why put all of this time, effort, and money into such projects?

###

One obvious, often unspoken answer is for military reasons. When President Reagan announced the Strategic Defense Initiative, more popularly referred to as Star Wars, science fiction fans on the liberal side of the political spectrum were dismayed to find many of their fellow enthusiasts welcoming the program, arguing that it would serve as an impetus for space travel and exploration, and the development of related technologies. And it is quite true that war, and preparation for warfare, has historically been a spur to technological development, and that all technologies of transportation, and communication, are inherently military technologies. But from a progressive stand point, or even, I would think, a neutral one, the militarization of space is hardly something to cheer about, but rather, at best a necessary evil.

Orbital weaponry is certainly not what we are looking for when we look up at the stars, and space-based warfare is not the reason why we reach for the sky, except in the case of hands raised in surrender. Nor are we especially moved by the prospect of the commercial exploitation of space, pecuniary motivations generally not being of the sort that inspires awe or satisfies a desire for transcendence, holding aside the question of whether any such efforts might be at all profitable. What then are we looking for?

One answer is that some of us are thrill-seekers. Indeed, it is evolutionarily advantageous to have some members of the species willing and wanting to take risks, which may result in great gains or in disaster, while other members of the human race play it safe. Mother Nature is a gambler who knows how to hedge her bets. So some of us are moved to wanderlust by the need for stimulation, for novelty. If successful, the result is personal satisfaction, gratification, perhaps shared vicariously by others. And while I do not count myself among them, I see no reason to begrudge our adventurers their excitement. But what is the significance of adventure alone? And what is worth sacrificing simply to ward off the possibility of boredom?

Another answer is the desire for exploration and discovery. The comparison is often made to the Age of Discovery associated with the European colonization of the New World (often taken to be the beginning of the modern era, although a much more significant event, one that made much more of a difference in people's lives, was the introduction of the printing press with moveable type about a half century before the "discovery" of the Americas). But the response, because it's there, does not answer the question of, what are we looking for? And the analogy with sailing ships crossing the Atlantic may not be an apt one, given the relative distances involved and the time it takes to make such voyages. Additionally, while the ocean may be intimidating, it is also the womb from which all life on Earth emerged, and in a more immediate sense, it is possible to survive a shipwreck, and even to traverse the ocean by raft. The vacuum of space, on the other hand, is an utterly sterile and inhospitable environment, with extremes of temperature, heavy doses of radiation, and no hope of finding safe haven if anything goes wrong. In the wake of the Space Shuttle Challenger disaster in 1986, resulting in the complete loss of its crew, exhortations regarding the need to carry on with the space program often included references to the voyages of Christopher Columbus. The Reagan years were a more innocent time, and those references were conspicuously absent in 2003, following the loss of the Space Shuttle Columbia and its crew. And the image of Columbus has been tarnished beyond repair, as the reality of the early subjugation and settlement of the Western Hemisphere has become more widely known. The advent of postcolonialism in intellectual discourse has rendered exploration and discovery a contested terrain, at best, and directed a critical eye at science fiction narratives that emphasize the conquest and colonization of space.

If the idea of space as a frontier for pioneers to settle in has become somewhat problematic, the act of exploration can still stand up as an end unto itself. It follows that another answer to the question of what it is that we are looking for is to see what is out there; simply put, the motive is curiosity, and the desire to advance human knowledge. Here too, some streams of intellectual discourse have discounted science altogether, arguing that it is ideologically driven, and while the sciences should not be shielded from critical scrutiny, I believe that the success of modern science speaks for itself. Nor would I doubt that there is much to be learned about the universe through space exploration. It is also easy enough to grant that the potential for learning is greater when there are human beings present, as opposed to automated transport and robotic or remotely-controlled mechanisms. But will we learn anything out there that we would not have learned eventually here on Earth? And if we do, how significant will that knowledge be? We place great store in our technological achievements, and space travel is a natural extension of such efforts, but after all, the Ionian physicists of the 6th and 5th century BCE arrived at the theory of the atom purely by philosophical investigation, Copernicus in the 15th century proved that the Earth circles the Sun without the aid of a telescope, and the scientists involved in the Manhattan Project first split the atom without the use of computers.

Unquestionably, the discovery of microbial life on Mars or elsewhere in space would be a truly momentous occasion in human history, and might tell us something of our own origins. And yet, what real difference would it make in our lives? Once the initial excitement wore off, would the long term response be anything more than, ho hum? I am all for the pursuit of knowledge for its own sake, but at the same time, given that there are no free rides, on Earth and into orbit and beyond, I have to ask if the result will be a difference that really and truly makes a difference?

If there is anything that would make our efforts at leaving our terrestrial home worthwhile, it would be the discovery of other intelligent life out there in outer space. But contrary to so many of our science fiction stories, and to more than a few conspiracy theories, there has been no evidence that anyone else is out there. The search for extraterrestrial intelligence is said to have begun in 1960 through the agency of the radio telescope, and the SETI Institute was founded in 1984. Nothing has come of their efforts. Perhaps this is because space is so vast and not enough time has been devoted to the search. Perhaps it is because any intelligent life that might exist out there would be too far away for their activities to register here on Earth. Perhaps it is because they do not want to be discovered. There is no way of knowing, but the fact remains that the results, so far, have not been encouraging. Moreover, the proposal to send signals out into the void, in hopes of getting the attention of some alien race, has been subjected to a great deal of criticism, insofar as our terrestrial history indicates that intercultural contact rarely ends well for the less advanced society, which in this instance would be us.

The strange truth is that we human beings, as a species, are terribly lonely. Maybe we just want someone to talk to other than ourselves, maybe we just get bored with ourselves, but from our prehistory we have sought out other beings and attempted to communicate with them, whether it was anthropomorphized natural phenomena, or supernatural entities, or animal companions, or most recently, intelligent machines. And we have enjoyed considerable success in regard to the domestication of other species, and the construction of increasingly more lifelike mechanisms. Clearly, artificial intelligence holds a much greater chance of satisfying our yearning for someone to talk to than searching the skies for evidence of extraterrestrial signals.

UFO sightings suddenly began to be reported in the aftermath of the Second World War, in the wake of the start of the Cold War, and the fear engendered by the atom bomb (Jung, 1978). While some of the rumors regarding flying saucers viewed them as hostile, there has been a persistent fantasy theme regarding UFOs that could be considered a new kind of religious belief, the idea that aliens who are more technologically advanced than us would also have to be more advanced ethically, morally, and spiritually; it follows that they are avoiding contact because they see humans as immature, and the prospect of first contact as too disruptive to our societies, but that they are studying us, and ready and willing to step in and save us should our penchant for self-destruction ever take us to the brink of nuclear war. This modern day myth forms the basis of science fiction films such as *The Day the Earth Stood Still*, *Close Encounters of the Third Kind*, *E.T.*, *Starman*, and *Cocoon*, and even, to a degree, Carl Sagan's *Contact* (it was also incorporated into a monologue delivered by Jack Nicholson in *Easy Rider*). But is there any evidence of an alien presence here on Earth, either now or in the past, along the lines of *Chariots of the Gods*? A few may say there is, but not many, and nothing generally convincing has ever come to light.

###

So what are we looking for? If it is transcendence, the problem is that we have yet to achieve the kind of epiphany depicted in *2001*, and there is no indication that we ever will.

What are we looking for? Some say it is simply a backup plan, should our planet become uninhabitable, whether due to our own stupidity, e.g., global warming or nuclear winter, or due to some other catastrophe, e.g., an asteroid colliding with our planet, or the Sun going nova sometime in the future. Rather than laughing at those who thought human flight was impossible, the theme shifts to Noah's Ark, and the ridicule that he endured because no one else believed the prophecy of imminent doom (a motif repeated in the origin story of Superman, whose father, Jor-El, was the only one to recognize that the planet Krypton was about to explode, and was only able to send his infant son to safety, Moses-like, via a small rocket). There is an ecological edge to this theme, in its emphasis on the need to preserve our species, and as much of our world's flora and fauna as possible. There is no denying the good will behind such motivations; nor can we deny the certainty that life on Earth will eventually come to an end. Whether it is at all possible to transport our entire biosphere, or even just some sort of ecosystem that would enable us to survive indefinitely, onto some sort of space ark, and ultimately transplant it onto another planet, is not at all clear. Whether it is possible to terraform other worlds is equally uncertain. It may well be that our lives and our species are inescapably bound to our Spaceship Earth, and that there is no escaping our interdependence, and the intertwining of our fates. Indeed, an environmentalist slogan turned Internet meme plays on the phrase plan B, in insisting there is no Planet B. Granted, all things being equal, there is every reason to pursue the possibility of pioneering our way out into the cosmos. But when we come back to the fact of limited resources, the question remains of whether adventures in outer space would produce the greatest good for the greatest number, or whether our time, money, and energy are better directed at the many needs that exist on the ground today, and whether any escape from disaster would serve anyone other than the elite who can afford the trip.

Moreover, the space ark's appeal to our survival instinct is not in actuality a primal one. It is not derived from the drive to survive of the individual organism, not from our instinctive motivation for self-preservation, but rather involves the abstract idea of the survival of our species. And therefore, while it seems a very base and basic reason for travelling beyond the confines of our planet, it is in fact another form of wished-for transcendence, a kind of denial of death in a collective sense, reaching for immortality, for heaven, for the infinite. But even if we leave our home behind, even if we spread out among the stars, will the universe exist forever? Science suggests that it is not eternal, so one way or another, there will be an ending, and all that we have created will vanish without a trace.

I want to make it clear that the questions I pose here, the expressions of skepticism that I introduce, go against the grain of my fondest hopes and dreams. They come from my head, contradicting my heart. I want to live in the future that I believe I was promised as a child, the future of starships flying faster than the speed of light, and travel to other planets, and encounters with intelligent, and friendly, alien beings. But I must admit that I have only seen a small portion of my own world, and only interacted with a tiny portion of the over seven billion human beings that inhabit this planet.

When we refer to the cosmos, there is a double meaning, almost contradictory in its connotations. In one sense, it refers to the cosmological research and theories of modern science. On the other, it refers to the cosmologies of religious belief systems. Religion, in its best sense, is about the spiritual quest for transcendence. Science, on the other hand, is concerned with knowledge of the immanent, and tentative rather than eternal truths. And so, we may look up into the sky with wonder, and we may travel to the stars and find inspiration in the deepest recesses of the universe, but in the end, which cosmos are we really looking for? And can either one serve as the pathway to transcendence? Or is the interface all that we can experience, a window through which we can look but not touch what lies beyond our reach in the distance. And a window through which we can look at a time that has receded into the past, and can never be retrieved, that we can never reach no matter how far and fast we travel, that we can never return to? Is the interface even actually a window, a transparent membrane through which we can at least gain enlightenment about the universe beyond ourselves? Or is it nothing more than a mirror that only shows us an image of ourselves that we may have forgotten, an extension of ourselves that also serves as an insurmountable barrier to anything beyond ourselves? Is the longing for transcendence an uplifting desire to reach beyond ourselves, or a desperate need to escape ourselves, or is it a quest simply to find ourselves?

Whatever it is that we may be looking for in the cosmos, is there anything that we can find, that we can see, and know, and touch, that is anything other than an interface?

Bibliography

Boorstin, Daniel J. (1978) textitThe Image: A Guide to Pseudo-Events in America. New York: Atheneum.

Carpenter, Edmund & McLuhan, Marshall (eds.) (1960) *Explorations in Communication.* Boston: Beacon Press.

Eliade, Mircea (1954) *The Myth of the Eternal Return or, Cosmos and History,* trans. W. R. Trask. New York: Pantheon.

_____ (1959) *The Sacred and the Profane* , trans. W. R. Trask. New York: Harvest/HBJ Books.

Innis, Harold A. (1951) *The Bias of Communication.* Toronto: University of Toronto Press.

Jung, Carl (1978) *Flying Saucers: A Modern Myth of Things Seen in the Skies*, trans. R. F. C. Hull. Princeton, NJ: Princeton University Press.

Korzybski, Alfred (1921/1950) *Manhood of Humanity, 2nd ed.* Lakeville, CT: The International Non-Aristotelian Library/Institute of General Semantics.

_____ (1933/1993) *Science and Sanity: An Introduction to Non-Aristotelian Systems and General Semantics, 5th ed.* Englewood, NJ: The International Non-Aristotelian Library/Institute of General Semantics.

McLuhan, Marshall (1964) *Understanding Media: The Extensions of Man.* New York: McGraw Hill.

Mumford, Lewis (1967) *The Myth of the Machine: I. Technics and Human Development.* New York: Harcourt Brace and World.

_____ (1970) *The Myth of the Machine: II. The Pentagon of Power.* New York: Harcourt Brace Jovanovich.

Postman, Neil (1992) *Technopoly: The Surrender of Culture to Technology.* New York: Alfred A. Knopf.

_____ (1995) *The End of Education: Redefining the Value of School.* New York: Alfred A. Knopf.

_____ (1999) *Building a Bridge to the Eighteenth Century: How the Past Can Improve our Future.* New York: Alfred A. Knopf.

Strate, Lance (2006) *Echoes and Reflections: On Media Ecology as a Field of Study.* Cresskill, NJ: Hampton Press.

_____ (2011) *On the Binding Biases of Time and Other Essays on General Semantics and Media Ecology.* Fort Worth, TX: Institute of General Semantics.

_____ (2014) *Amazing Ourselves to Death: Neil Postman's Brave New World Revisited.* New York: Peter Lang.

Werner, Jane (1955) *Smokey the Bear.* New York: Golden Press.

Wolfe, Tom (1979) *The Right Stuff.* New York: Farrar, Straus, and Giroux.

-=-

Lance Strate, Ph.D., is Professor of Communication and Media Studies at Fordham University and the 2015- 2016 Harron Family Endowed Chair in Communication at Villanova University. A Trustee and former Executive Director of the Institute of General Semantics, he is a founder and Past President of the Media Ecology Association, and a Past President of the New York State Communication Association. He is the author of *Echoes and Reflections: On Media Ecology as a Field of Study* (2006), *On the Binding Biases of Time and Other Essays on General Semantics and Media Ecology* (2011), *Amazing Ourselves to Death: Neil Postman's Brave New World Revisited* (2014), and *Thunder at Darwin Station* (2015), and co-editor of several anthologies, including *The Legacy of McLuhan* (2005), *Korzybski and...* (2012), and *The Medium is the Muse: Channeling Marshall McLuhan* (2015). He is president of Congregation Adas Emuno of Leonia, New Jersey, has been an advisor for several autism advocacy groups, and is the recipient of the Media Ecology Association's 2013 Walter J. Ong Award for Career Achievement in Scholarship.

Faith in Space: A Christian Perspective

Michael O'Neal

Many of us cherish nurturing our spiritual sides and take part in a number of activities that we deem important to the health of our faith-lives. Can you imagine giving up these practices for a significant period of time? Not only do they help us spiritually grow, but they keep us connected with who we are and aid us to make meaning of what we encounter in our daily walks. Removing someone from their normal spiritual support structures could lead to unexpected behaviors and consequences. So as you might expect, many astronauts desire to engage in activities that enrich their faith. Of course this brings many unique challenges because of their isolation and close quarters with others of differing beliefs.

Astronaut Jeff Williams attested to the importance of nurturing his faith while on the International Space Station (ISS). Back in May of 2006, Jeff joined a few hundred Kennedy Space Center employees via a live video feed from the ISS during their annual National Day of Prayer Ceremony. The moderator asked Williams to comment on the importance of maintaining his faith-life while up on the ISS. This was his response.

> I don't think I could sustain the 6 months day-to-day up here, doing what we do, without my faith-life, without my faith in Jesus Christ, without spending time with prayer and devotion, and reminding myself who He is as He is revealed through His word. Especially as I look out the window and view the grandeur of creation, which of course reflects His glory, so that is a big part of my life on-board....

I don't think I could sustain the 6 months day-to-day up here, doing what we do, without my faith-life, without my faith in Jesus Christ, without spending time with prayer and devotion, and reminding myself who He is as He is revealed through His word. Especially as I look out the window and view the grandeur of creation, which of course reflects His glory, so that is a big part of my life on-board....

The following stories and observations will provide you with a glimpse of how some of the astronauts chose to engage and cultivate their faith during their missions.

Message to the Earth

As clocks approached 9:30 p.m. EST on Christmas Eve in 1968, almost everyone in the U.S. parked themselves in front of a television. Earlier that day, three NASA astronauts had entered lunar orbit for the first time, and a captivated world eagerly awaited their live broadcast to begin from our nearest celestial neighbor.

Streaming in from about three quarters of a million miles away, Frank Borman's (Apollo 8 Commander) voice invaded millions of living rooms. The otherworldly tone of the transmission seemed remarkably appropriate as Borman welcomed the largest TV audience in history up to this point in time. From sixty miles above the lunar surface, Jim Lovell and Bill Anders joined Borman in providing a guided tour of the Moon's features as the spacecraft's orbit traversed this eerie, unfamiliar world. When the grainy images from Anders' handheld camera appeared on TV screens for the first time, Borman's impression of this barren landscape hit the nail on the head, describing the Moon's surface as a "... vast, lonely, forbidding-type existence, or expanse of nothing, that looks rather like clouds and clouds of pumice stone" (Woods & O'Brien, 2001).

After introducing the Earth to some of this alien world's breathtaking geography, the spacecraft approached lunar sunrise. With only a couple minutes left in the broadcast, the astronauts shifted to a more reflective tone. Prior to launch, they discussed their desire to leave the Earth with a special Christmas Eve message, so they agreed in advance to the following as they each took turns reading from a scripted set of words attached to the back of their Flight Operations Manual (Lovell, & Kluger, 1994, p. 53). While Anders continued to provide his captivated audience with images of the Moon, he started off the discourse:

> We are now approaching lunar sunrise, and for all the people back on Earth, the crew of Apollo 8 has a message that we would like to send to you.
>
> In the beginning, God created the Heaven and the Earth. And the Earth was without form and void, and darkness was upon the face of the deep. And the spirit of God moved upon the face of the waters, and God said, "Let there be light." And there was light. And God saw the light, that it was good, and God divided the light from the darkness.

Followed by a short pause, Lovell took the microphone and continued with their Christmas Eve blessing.

> And God called the light Day, and the darkness he called Night. And the evening and the morning were the first day. And God said, "Let there be a firmament in the midst of the waters. And let it divide the waters from the waters." And God made the firmament and divided the waters which were under the firmament from the waters which were above the firmament. And it was so. And God

> called the firmament Heaven. And the evening and the morning were the second day.

With the Sun now approaching the Moon's horizon, its glare started to taper off which resulted in much clearer images of the Moon's foreboding craters, mountains, and rilles for the Earth's viewers. With a click of the microphone, Borman's voice started reverently closing out the soliloquy.

> And God said, "Let the waters under the Heavens be gathered together into one place. And let the dry land appear." And it was so. And God called the dry land Earth. And the gathering together of the waters called He seas. And God saw that it was good. And from the crew of Apollo 8, we close with good night, good luck, a Merry Christmas and God bless all of you - all of you on the good Earth. [Woods & O'Brien, 2001]

Silence abruptly replaced the Commander's voice, and static filled the TV screens before the networks resumed control. Struck by a sense of awe, I am sure many from around the world joined Susan Borman in tears and shared her sentiments as she pondered, "What a thing to do . . . . How perfect a choice" (Zimmerman, 1998, p. 211).

Only hours before the broadcast, these astronauts experienced a profound event. As their spacecraft entered lunar orbit and proceeded to go behind the Moon for the first time, these explorers suddenly became totally cut off from their home-world, unable to see it or communicate with anyone on it. But as the horizon continued to advance, these privileged few beheld a sight reserved only for God's eyes through the eons – an *Earthrise*. After experiencing the color-filled splendor of the Earth rising on the horizon of this monochrome world with space's dark void as its backdrop, could you imagine any other reading so full of meaning as the creation account in Genesis?

In his book *Genesis, The Story of Apollo 8*, Robert Zimmerman made the following comment concerning the Flight Crew's beliefs behind the decision to read Genesis 1:1-10.

> Those words, however, expressed for these three men a heartfelt belief that the universe was more than mere energy and matter. Not only did a spirit lurk behind the veil of the terrifying black dark that surrounded them, it impelled them to live their lives a certain way, in a certain manner. [p. 212]

Prayer

Sam Durrance shared that he often prayed silently during his Shuttle missions (2005). This private feature of prayer perhaps makes it the most practiced aspect of faith in space. Many astronauts have commented on how they maintained their prayer habits while in space, along with the role it played during their missions. Concern for their families, mission success, and safety draw them to prayer, but the emotional impact of experiencing the wonders of space naturally evoke prayer as well. Thomas Jones stated, "... prayer came easily, whether I was floating weightless in my sleeping bag or gazing quietly at the Earth" (2004).

For Clayton Anderson, his prayer-life became an important resource for him when an Earthbound family crisis arose during one of his missions. While on the ISS and physically isolated from his loved ones, Anderson learned that his mother had been diagnosed with lung cancer. Though feelings of helplessness surely plagued him, he was not powerless. Anderson reached out to God in prayer for his mother as she fought this horrible disease, as well as for his family who were trying to cope under these dreadful circumstances without him (2008).

Alone and orbiting the Earth in Faith 7, Mercury astronaut Gordon Cooper peered out his capsule's window and verbally noted the nocturnal beauty of the lit-up eastern coastline of Australia. Nine to ten minutes of voiceless silence then passed before his own words again pierced the peace of his orbiting abode's tight quarters. As his eyes shifted toward the Earth's horizon to the east, he reported a hazy band through which he could only faintly see the stars.

While his spacecraft continued to effortlessly streak along its orbital trajectory at about 17,500 miles per hour, Cooper's thoughts turned to his good fortune and to the many involved in this noble endeavor. Not only had a feeling of thankfulness permeated his soul, his orbital vantage point had profoundly affected his worldview. So on this fourteenth orbit of his twenty-two orbit mission, he paused for a moment and expressed his gratitude, desires, and concerns to God.

Configuring the communication system to only record his prayer, those on the Earth would not hear his reflective petition until the capsule's return, and the voice recorders were retrieved and played back. After prefacing what he was about to do, Cooper then went to God in prayer, while the on-board recorders captured the first event of its kind in space (2000, p. 68).

> I would like to take this time to say a little prayer for all the people, including myself, involved in this launch and this operation.
>
> Father, thank You, for the success we have had in flying this flight. Thank You for the privilege of being able to be in this position, to be up in this wondrous place, seeing all these many startling, wondrous things that You've created. Help guide and direct all of us, that we may shape our lives to be good, that we may be much better Christians, learn to help one another, [and] to work with one another, rather than to fight. Help us to complete this mission successfully. Help us in our future space endeavors, that we may show the world that a democracy really can compete, and still are able to do things in a big way, [and] are able to do research, development, and can conduct various scientific, very technical programs in a completely

> peaceful environment. Be with all our families. Give them guidance and encouragement, and let them know that everything will be OK. We ask in Thy name. Amen. [*Mercury-Atlas Transcription*, 1963]

On July 30th of 1971, James Irwin worked diligently on deploying the Central Station at the foot of the Moon's Apennine mountain range. Keenly aware that this hardware served as the central hub for several other scientific instruments, this Apollo 15 astronaut knew that many scientists back on the Earth depended on him to successfully bring it on-line. Keeping to the procedure which was integrated into the cuff of his spacesuit, Irwin was making good progress until an unexpected malfunction occurred. Erecting hardware in a bulky spacesuit on the lunar surface was challenging enough, but when combined with an unforeseen anomaly and not much time to spare, much of the Apollo 15's scientific mission now faced failure.

Because of the time constraints, Irwin did not feel that consulting Houston was a workable option, so he sought heavenly advice. The following two excerpts from Irwin's book, *To Rule the Night*, documents the result of his prayer for help, and his thoughts on the step of faith he took.

> ...I prayed. Immediately I had the answer. It was almost like a revelation. God was telling me what to do. ...I am not talking about some vague sense of direction. There was this supernatural sensation of His presence. If I needed Him I could call on Him, call on His power. [1973, p. 19]
>
> There I was, a test pilot, a nuts-and-bolts type who had gotten rather skeptical about God, and suddenly I was asking God to solve my problems on the moon. I was relying on God rather than on Houston. [1973, p. 123]

Irwin successfully deployed the Central Station and directly credits God's guidance. God's presence and involvement during the lunar surface phase of the mission thrust this unsuspecting astronaut into deep reflection. This served to remake his faith and forever change his life (some of the text in this story repeated, with publisher's permission, from O'Neal, 2010, p. 125).

Times of Devotion & Worship

Music possesses phenomenal power. Depending on what you choose to listen to, music can soothe, energize, or inspire and possibly even shift your mood. Certain songs transport you through time to an event in your past or take you to another place, perhaps with that "special someone." Some songs also possess the uncanny ability to keep repeating themselves over and over in your head.

Since many tasks easily allow for listening to music and being a favorite free-time activity for many, it should be no surprise that music finds its way into many of the astronauts' activities in space. Through the private means of compact electronic devices with headphones, many astronauts have used music as a means to stay in touch with their faith and facilitate reflection.

Guy Gardner was blessed by two separate groups who recorded for him a collection of songs on tape that he listened to on his STS-27 Shuttle mission. The Minister of Music at his Baptist church put together an arrangement of hymns sung by the choir. And KSBJ, a contemporary Christian radio station in Houston, also prepared for Gardner a tape that contained a series of messages from the radio personalities with corresponding Bible verses and songs. Not only did these acts of kindness serve to spiritually nurture him, but it was a wonderful way to keep him connected with his faith community.

Joe Tanner listened to several Contemporary Christian CDs during one of his missions, including *Saviour: The Story of God's Passion for His People* that included performances from several Christian song artists (2006). Clayton Anderson took along on his ISS mission a concert recorded at his church that included his own performance of a song by Steve Green titled "I Will Go." He also noted that he often sung to himself as he went about the Station (2008).

Sundays were Carl Walz's day off during his six-and-a-half-month stay on the ISS, unless mission requirements dictated otherwise, so he utilized a portion of this precious time to nurture his faith-life. Each week his wife emailed him the Bible readings from their church's worship service, which typically contained a collection of passages – one each from the Old Testament, the Gospels, and the Epistles. While sitting in his quarters in the Russian segment of the ISS, Walz utilized Bible study software on his laptop to look up and read these passages. Since the software provided access to Bible commentaries, he also dove into a more detailed study of each of these verses.

Isolated from his home congregation, this virtuous routine held deep meaning for this space-tenant. His time of study and reflection created an important connection for him with his Earth-bound faith community. He was studying the "same Bible passages as the folks back home were." On Christmas Eve, Walz did a little real-time bonding by calling his Parish Priest from the ISS. Not only was this encouraging for Walz, but their conversation inspired part of the Priest's evening homily, as he thought about Walz's current residence amongst the heavenly hosts.

When times got tough or an important event was taking place, Walz "leaned on" and garnered strength from one of the Bible's most encouraging verses.

> What then shall we say to these things?
>
> If God is for us, who is against us (Rom. 8:31)? [All biblical references in this essay, unless imbedded in other quotes, are taken from *The Hebrew-Greek Key Study Bible,* 1990]

Many astronauts have such "go to" verses for stressful times.

Music holds a special place in Walz's heart. He has participated in his church's music ministry since the age of seventeen, and at the time of his Expedition 4 mission to the ISS, he was the lead singer for the astronaut rock band

Max-Q (Max-Q is the point where maximum dynamic pressure is encountered on a vehicle in atmospheric flight). So there is no way he could leave planet Earth without addressing such a love, consequently a piano keyboard was kitted with his personal belongings. And once he arrived at his new orbiting home, a previous astronaut's guitar beckoned him to learn to play it during his stay.

Walz's Sunday routine typically included playing hymns and other Christian songs from sheet music. One songbook he enjoyed playing from was *In the Breaking of Bread* by Christian song composer Bob Hurd. Singing these lyrics held deep meaning and had life-shaping power for him. One of the hymns he played was "Be Thou My Vision," and he said the following about how this song touches him.

> ... especially the lines, 'Riches I need not, nor man's empty praise, Thou mine inheritance, now and always.' That always runs through my mind...and whenever I get discouraged I think of that, and it's like, well, who cares what people think? It's what God thinks that's important. [Tracy, 2002]

So with Bible study software, the Sunday readings from his church, two musical instruments, and sheet music, Walz was equipped to hold his own zero-g time of worship. He said, "I would go and play hymns on the guitar or keyboard, and so I almost had my own little church service." [Tracy, 2002]

Walz also utilized music's spiritually rich influence to affect his life in other ways while on-board the ISS. You probably have seen videos and images of astronauts vigorously exercising on various devices in space. Without gravity's influence on one's muscular-skeletal system, lengthy workout requirements serve as a countermeasure against muscle and bone loss for those on long-duration missions. Walz constructively utilized this protracted exercise period (up to two and a half hours a day) to address his spiritual health as well by listening to Christian music. His repertoire included a series of CDs of beautiful songs by contemporary Christian song-artist Twila Paris (Walz, 2014).

Sometimes recorded music is just not satisfactory. Doug Wheelock loved using the Station's Cupola module as his "personal cave." It contains seven windows and points directly down toward the Earth. For Wheelock, the Cupola provided him a wonderful place to view the Earth and other celestial objects. From this perspective, the Moon could be seen as an orb not just a flat plate as when viewed from the Earth. And when viewing his home-world at night, it became a "raging place" with lightning flashing to and fro, the auroras dancing at the poles, and shooting stars burning up in the atmosphere.

On one occasion, Wheelock was so *overwhelmed* by the beauty and majesty of what he beheld -- he just broke out in song. With a fresh and intensified meaning, the worshipful words of "How Great Thou Art" naturally flowed from this spellbound space-dweller (2013).

> *O Lord my God! When I in awesome wonder*
> *Consider all the worlds Thy hands have made,*

> *I see the stars, I hear the rolling thunder,*
> *Thy power throughout the universe displayed...* [Boberg/Hine, 1885]

Bringing Bibles, Christian literature, and devotional material is a common practice among some of the astronauts. Typically, the medium of choice is electronic because of weight and volume constraints, but at times some of these items are brought in book form as well.

As the STS-101 Shuttle mission wound down, Jeff Williams and another astronaut had some free time to observe the Earth through the windows of the Atlantis. With Bible study software loaded on Williams' laptop, they searched on words such as "creation" and "Earth" while viewing the beauty of sunrises, sunsets, and other design features of God's creation. As the software yielded up its biblical treasures, they then read these sacred gems while surveying God's handiwork. Surely this brought life and intensified meaning to these ancient words (2000).

Jerry Ross also allowed God's Word to take hold of his heart while viewing the Earth on his seventh and last Shuttle mission. With major elements of the ISS in its cargo bay, the Atlantis was docked to this international construction project. Ross's tasks during the upcoming days included two spacewalks to help out with the Station's assembly. Prior to going to sleep one night, Ross opened his Bible to Genesis and read the creation account while surveying the Earth. He made the following statement about this event in his book, *Spacewalker*, "... reading the creation story in Genesis while looking down on the beauty of the Earth from space was a very powerful moment for me." (2013, pp. 213-214).

Ross also read one of his favorite verses, Philippians 4:13, one night on that last mission. The thought that Christ had given him the strength to perform what God had laid before him caused him to reflect on his phenomenal life's journey. A journey where he chose to follow God's guiding hand (pp. 78, 213).

Skylab astronaut Jack Lousma gained a "greater appreciation" for God's creation from his orbiting vantage point but likened his religious experiences to what he had encountered on the Earth. Reading God's Word was a daily priority for him, even when life took him 270 miles above the Earth's surface.

> Reading my Bible in Skylab was no different than reading it on Earth, as I had been doing daily for years. Well, there was one small difference. The pages were a little easier to turn in that weightless environment. That book tells us a lot about the world in which we're living and how it got to be the way it is. I think it's important to keep in touch with the One who made the total universe. I read that book on a daily basis here on earth and I talk to the One who wrote it. So why should I do any differently in space? [1983, pp. 10-11]

Jeff Williams's involvement and relationships at the Gloria Dei Lutheran Church in Houston was an important part of his life. Not only would his Expedition 13 mission to the ISS remove him from his cherished church-family for 6 months, but his last few months of training before liftoff was in Russia. Leaving his faith community for such a lengthy period of time was destined to create a void in his life, but Williams did an amazing job of preparing for the spiritual journey that he would experience during his time away.

While on board the ISS, Williams tried to make time for daily devotionals. He listened to sermons from his church and *Grace to You* ministries. One of his Pastors stated that Williams was a voracious reader and enjoyed constant intellectual stimulation, so he brought devotional material and Christian literature to ponder over, such as *Valley of Vision* which is a collection of Puritan prayers and devotions. Outside the crew quarters, Williams would read his Bible and annotate his observations in the margins. While viewing the wonders of the universe from one of the ISS's windows, he would enrich the experience by listening to traditional hymns and contemporary Christian music that included songs by Michael Card and Rich Mullins.

Prior to the start of Gloria Dei's church activities on Sunday mornings, Williams routinely called one of the Pastors from the ISS. These calls served as a source of encouragement for Jeff. They took time to pray together, but much of the call consisted of just a friendly chat between two Christian brothers. Williams was especially uplifted on one occasion, when he called during a choir rehearsal for Easter Sunday. After spending a few moments sharing with the choir, they in turn gave him a loud vocal response (2013).

All the above went a long way in aiding him to stay connected to his faith community and continue to develop his faith; nevertheless, he sorely missed participating in his church's Sunday worship service. Anticipating this great need before his flight, he requested that NASA connect him to one of Gloria Dei's worship services during his mission. So on July 2, 2006, Gloria Dei welcomed Williams to their worship service as they received a live video from the ISS while he received only the audio. Overcome with emotions, this space flight veteran appeared to be in tear suppression mode as he joined his congregation. Gloria Dei's Pastor asked Williams to share a word with them, and this was his earnest response.

> Great to talk to you Pastor K, great to talk to the people at Gloria Dei. I've been listening for the last 30 seconds or so, and frankly, I am overwhelmed. It's such a great privilege to be joining you in worship today. As you know, I have not had a chance to worship since January, and it is an important part of my life. So it's great to be with you today.

Asked next to lead the congregation in prayer, Williams closed his eyes while bobbing about in the zero-gravity and directed the following words heavenward.

> Dear heavenly Father, we thank You for the opportunity to gather together even in such unusual circumstances as this Lord. We thank You for the provision of the technology that enables us to do this. Lord, we are in awe in wonder of You. You are the Creator, as I

> can testify that to see Your creation from here is just absolutely magnificent. And we know from Your word, from the book of Job, that it is only a glimpse of Your wonder and majesty Lord. And we are overwhelmed by the glimpse that we have of You. And Lord, we thank You also that You are our redeemer; that You redeemed us through the provision found in Christ. Lord, we thank You for sustaining us each day. Lord, I ask for a special blessing over the people of Gloria Dei today as they worship You, our Risen Lord and Savior. In Christ's name, Amen.

His pastor in turn led a prayer for Williams and his crewmates, and then graciously said, "God bless you Jeff, God keep you." Remote and yearning for the fellowship of his church, the gift of worship gave this appreciative astronaut sustenance to carry on (2006).

Drawing on God's Word and His Presence

One of the last sounds anyone wants to hear when preparing for bed is the shrill noise of an alarm going off. But such was Doug Wheelock's late night experience back on July 31st of 2010 aboard the ISS as his sleepy state was quickly snatched away from him.

Earlier that night Wheelock decided to go for a run on the Station's treadmill. Prior to starting, he disabled the smoke detector under the treadmill per their standard procedures to avoid setting off any false alarms. By the time he finished his run, Wheelock noted that his crewmates were off in their sleep chambers. He then re-enabled the smoke detector and started to go through his normal routine to prepare himself for a night of peaceful slumber. However, this space-farers' home had other plans for him this night.

At 11:32 p.m., the Station's Caution and Warning System's pulsating alarm started to scream. Promptly Wheelock made his way to the monitoring console and noted several fault annunciation lights on and numerous failure messages scrolling on the screen. The other crew members sleepily joined him wondering what he had done. Of course, he assured them that he had only re-enabled the smoke alarm via the Station's computer system and started his bedtime routine when the alarm went off.

Months later, Wheelock explained to an attentive group of faculty and students at a chapel service on the campus of Oklahoma Christian University (OCU) that we all eventually face those significant emotional events in life that challenge us and have the ability to re-shape our faith. Such was Wheelock's experience on the ISS that night, along with the trouble-filled days that followed. He intensely explained that

> ... the Space Station started to die - ... alarms [went] off, ... warning lights were flashing, all kinds of sirens going off, lights started to turn off, fans shutting down, [and] the spaceship now starting to go into a stability tumble....

He said the failure messages scrolled so fast across the screen, he could not even read them let alone interpret them. Confronted with one of his life's greatest difficulties, what defined him as a person would be severely tested. For Wheelock, his faith would have to play a pivotal role if he was to successfully navigate this turbulent night and the demanding days that ensued.

Not much time passed that night before it was determined that one of the Station's external ammonia coolant pumps had failed. Basically, this left the Station without the ability to cool about half of its electronics and power systems. So a number of the Station's systems would need to be reconfigured or taken off-line until the pump could be replaced, leaving the crew one failure away from potentially abandoning the Station. A spare pump package was externally available on one of the trusses, but the crew's home would remain crippled for three weeks as problems arose with the removal and replacement of the failed pump.

Three tiring and frustrating emergency spacewalks faced Wheelock and one of his companions as they encountered multiple unexpected problems, necessitating considerable re-planning, patience, and ingenuity. Initially one of the Quick Disconnects (QD) on the pump package malfunctioned, later requiring Wheelock to use a hammer on it. With a little friendly persuasion, the QD freed-up, allowing him to disconnect it; unfortunately it started to leak ammonia, requiring it to be immediately reconnected. Ammonia at this strength can be toxic, so much care was necessary to keep this hazardous commodity off their spacesuits.

On the third attempt to remove this QD, Wheelock encountered a seriously frozen connection that did not want to budge, which eventually required him to violently shake it to free it up. And if these problems were not enough, Wheelock's CO2 sensor in his spacesuit started to malfunction. Of course performing carefully planned out tasks in zero-gravity is inherently tricky, but when the "unknown" arises, a whole new level of difficulty and risk must be dealt with.

Wheelock's faith served him well throughout this anxiety-filled period. Years ago, he had started memorizing Bible verses in his youth as a participant in AWANA (Approved Workmen Are Not Ashamed; from 2 Timothy 2:15). Some of these passages and a number of others served to remind him of the promise of God's presence, guidance, and strength that was at his disposal. Prior to his flight to the ISS, Wheelock made the following comment in an interview with the *Christian Chronicle*:

> God's word has such power, and for me, my favorite passages of Scripture are those that focus on God's promise of strength in times of weakness, restoration in times of brokenness and peace in times of turmoil and despair. [McMillion, 2010]

Drawing on selected passages (such as Prov. 3:5-6, Isaiah 40:31; 55:12 and Phil. 4:13), Wheelock was reminded that he "was not alone." He also had the practice of trying to include God in all things that he undertook because then he knew that "God was there." When facing difficulties and the unknown, he wanted a divine partner at his side. Even if his human frailties assailed him, Wheelock took comfort in knowing that "when we are weakest we can feel His strength." By letting his spiritual faith permeate the confidence he had in his technical and problem-solving skills, he calmly tackled the difficult issues at hand with his crewmates and the Mission Control team.

After the third space walk, the cooling system along with the rest of the Station was fully operational. With everyone safe and the concern of abandoning their celestial home overcome, "normal" again became the rule of life on the ISS. With the difficulty defeated, Wheelock told his OCU audience that the verse rang true, "I can do all things through Him who strengthens me" (Phil. 4:13). [2013 & 2015]

Faith in space - a natural and integral part of the human experience as we continue to venture out from our home world.

Bibliography

Anderson, Clayton (2008) interview by author, 28 August.

Boberg, Carl Gustav (1885) "How Great Thou, Art," trans. Stuart K. Hine.

Cooper, Gordon (2000) *Leap of Faith: An Astronaut's Journey into the Unknown* (New York: HarperCollins, 2000), p. 68.

Durrance, Sam (2005) interview by author, 18 August.

Hebrew-Greek Key Study Bible, The: New American Standard Bible (1990) Chattanooga: AMG Publishers.

Irwin, James (1973), *To Rule the Night: The Discovery Voyage of Astronaut James Irwin.* Philadelphia: A. J. Holman.

Jones, Thomas (2004) "Reaching the Heavens: An Astronaut's Journey," *St. Anthony Messenger,* June. http://www.americancatholic.org; accessed 19 August 2005.

Lousma, Jack (1983) "Astronaut on Creation," *Creation* 1 April, pp. 10-11.

Lovell, Jim & Kluger, Jeffrey (1994) *Lost Moon: The Perilous Voyage of Apollo 13.* Boston: Houghton Mifflin.

McMillon, Lynn (2010) "A Conversation with Doug Wheelock," *The Christian Chronicle,* 23 June. http://www.christianchronicle.org/article/a-conversation-with-doug-Wheelock?A=SearchResult&SearchID=2542201&ObjectID=436489-8&ObjectType=35; accessed 15 August 2010.

Mercury-Atlas 9 Composite Air-to-Ground and Onboard Voice Tape Transcription (1963) 24 June. http://www.jsc.nasa.gov/history/mission_trans/all_transcripts.htm; accessed 17 Aug 2013.

O'Neal, Michael (2010) *An Angel's View: Encountering God Through the Stories of the Heavenly Hosts.* Nashville: 21st Century Christian.

Ross, Jerry L. (2013) *Spacewalker: My Journey in Space and Faith as NASA's Record-setting Frequent Flyer.* West Lafayette, IN: Purdue University Press.

Tanner, Joe (2006), interview by author, 8 February.

Tracy, Shirley (2002) "Cleveland Native, Returns from Record Setting Space Mission," *Connection Magazine*, October. http://connectionmagazine.org/2002_10_/ts_space_mission.htm; accessed 5 August 2005.

Walz, Carl (2014), interview by author, 10 January.

Wheelock, Doug H. (2013), interview by author, 20 June.

_____ (2015) *Doug Wheelock - Space Chapel*, on-line video. http://vimeo.com/29686864; accessed 27 May 2015.

Williams, Jeff (2000) "Grace in Space: An Interview with Astronaut Jeff Williams," interview by John MacArthur, *Grace to You*, 15 March http://www.gty.org/resources/sermons/GTY75/grace-in-space-an-interview-with-astronaut-jeff-williams; accessed 1 January 2010.

_____ (2006) *Jeff Williams Call from the ISS*, Gloria Dei Lutheran Church 9:30am Worship Service, 2 July, DVD.

_____ (2013) interview by author, 6 June.

Woods, David W. & O'Brien, Frank (2001) "Day 4: Lunar Orbits 7, 8, and 9," *Apollo Flight Journal.* http://history.nasa.gov/ap08fj/15day4_orbits789.htm; accessed August 7, 2013.

Zimmerman, Robert (1998) *Genesis, The Story of Apollo 8: The First Manned Flight to Another World.* New York: Four Walls Eight Windows.

-=-

Michael O'Neal worked for NASA at the Kennedy Space Center for over 31 years. Awarded NASA's Outstanding Leadership Medal and two Exceptional

Service Medals, he served as Deputy Director in the Space Station and Space Shuttle Engineering organizations, and investigated mechanisms to provide spiritual support for astronauts. Along with his degrees in Electrical Engineering and Engineering Management, he has an M.A. in Christian Ministry from the Harding School of Theology. Mike has authored two books including, *An Angel's View: Encountering God through the Stories of the Heavenly Hosts.* Mike preaches part-time and speaks on his books and on spirituality and spaceflight (see www.angelquakeministries.com).

Faith to Face

Jeremy Saget

Destiny Mars

Humans have always been fascinated with the planet Mars. The Red Planet, as it was before its name adopted the Roman god of war, evokes the color of blood and rusty iron, and has intrigued Earthlings since ancient times. From the Egyptians more than three thousand years ago, followed by the Babylonians, Chinese, and Greeks providing the first observations, its early history was associated with the color of conquest, passion, and antique divinity through beliefs and religions. Through the ages, interpretations have abounded. We owe a debt to the Arabs and Indians for calculation of its size and its relative distance, and to Galileo for its first telescopic viewing. More recently, the nineteenth century brought us the birth of the imaginary "Martian," fed by the fantasies of an extraterrestrial civilization, the origins of the "canali" that Schiaparelli observed and then Lowell interpreted, through to Wells' *War of the Worlds*. The twentieth century saw a growing number of authors cultivate the Martian myth to an extent that is out of this world. Science fiction has long since anticipated the history of our neighboring and next home planet.

Since entering the space age less than sixty years ago, for the first time in two hundred thousand years, humankind today has the technological ability to physically reach Mars in the coming decades. We are now seeing renewed interest in this space epic, revisiting the big questions regarding the nature of humanity, the birth of life in the universe, between science and conscience. The exploration of Mars has been the sure priority for all the experts, right from the days of the astronautical pioneers. The robotic exploration of the planet, dominated by the Russians and Americans, a little more successfully in the case of the latter, stimulates international cooperation and draws us an ever more detailed portrait of Mars, while we are still learning more about our own planet. But despite advances in robotics and artificial intelligence, nothing beats placing a human being on the site. First, we are more capable and adaptable in that we can move around more flexibly and more objectively select relevant samples (Apollo 17, 1972, to compare with Lunokhod 2, 1973 & Opportunity, 2004-15: Apollo 17, 35.9 km traveled in 4:26 hours by Cernan and Schmitt to collect 110 kg of lunar rocks by a geologist versus 37 to 42 km in 4 months by Lunokhod 2; Opportunity to cover more than the distance of an out-of-this-world marathon, although it took eleven years all the same). Then, as we do not always find what we seek, we are endowed with the gift of creativity, the serendipity that is not coded into the software. Finally, and above all, because the marstronauts can transport the whole of humanity with them to share in their curiosity and their feelings.

We will see how the re-enchantment of the world allows the reanimation of our curiosity for exploration during the development of the mind, but first it is necessary to ask the right questions.

Why Mars? “Because it’s there!” (Mallory, 1924: famous answer about the reason to persevere in his Mount Everest ascent; he would be the first ever to reach the very top, with Irvine – 8 June 1924 – but unfortunately didn’t survive unlike later first successful expedition by Hillary & Norgay, 29 May 1953). “It’s all there. . . . ” (Kabat-Zinn, 1994).

Where do we come from? Where are we going? Who are we? These three huge questions emerge from our reflective consciousness and remain paramount in our lives. But to find one’s place, a person must also ask: What can I do? What would I do? What will I do? Each of these great metaphysical questions is exactly what we envisage in the exploration of the cosmos. And indeed on Mars can be found the basic building blocks for solving the equation of life in the universe. Indeed, all the elements necessary for life as we know it, depending on liquid water and carbon, are there on Mars. If we find evidence of a past or present life on Mars, it will mean that life is common in the universe and intensifies the question of intelligent life and the Fermi paradox (Fermi, 1950 cited by Sagan, 1975). If we do not find it, this could suggest that life is very rare, or that some determining factor still eludes us.

In other words, the human philosophical quest transits the world of ideas and is taken on an interplanetary voyage. Poets and space engineers agree, "Earth is the cradle of humanity, but one cannot live in the cradle forever“ (Tsiolkovsky, 1911: “A planet is the cradle of mind, but one cannot live in a cradle forever”, from a letter, usually cited as above) succeeding "It is the destiny of man in the end escaped“ (Victor Hugo, 1859: “*La Légende des siècles*”, XIV. Vingtième siècle: II. Plein Ciel; first series : a prophetic poem expressing an epic eloquence). Could the real world, as an emulating phenomenon, follow simulating noema according to a holographic formula adapted to the structuralist world of ideas? "Anything one man can imagine, other men can make real“, according to the famous apocryphal aphorism of Jules Verne. The future is standing there among our dreams.

In line with the doomsday scenarios predicting the inevitable extinction of humanity if it fails to expand onto other planets, this determination to explore the cosmos seems to be intrinsic to our nature. Our essence is the fuel that drives us on, the propellant of our space adventure that will continue to oppose the Earth’s attraction. Gravity and freedom. Our world can sometimes appear to be retracted, closing us in. The resources of such a world tend to be exhausted and the resulting adverse global events are constantly repeated, what’s more, magnified by our media. It is time to stand back, re-invigorate the world, open up to infinity. The prospect of an open world, the extraterrestrial imperative in a philosophical sense (Ehricke, 1978), changes the angles of view, offering sustainable solutions and new resources, launching our civilization into a new dimension on the Kardashev scale (Kardashev, 1980; see also Annis, 1999). This valuable momentum supports positive global dynamics and events inside their virtuous circle.

We are well underway in our preparation for the experience that will come with the next giant leap for humanity. As we head towards a pluriplanetary age, *ad astra per aspera*, ("the road to the stars is a rocky one"), from inspiration to aspiration, it may be appropriate to inhale deeply and reflect on the likes of Odyssey from where we draw the breath that guides us. This trend explores the link between our inner world and the discovery of the outside world.

With respect to this link, it must be remembered that faith concerns the relationship between the subject and the object of the faith while belief implies a judgment, which is very different. Traditions, rituals, and religions structure these beliefs in our societal cultures. We will try here to present rather the awakening and development of a faith placed in exploring the cosmos, in a shared philosophical and spiritual quest in its intelligible and explicit form. This is a reflection based on this experience that questions the very meaning of existence. This extravertive introspection naturally leads us to the planet Mars, guided by space exploration as a specific metaphor reflecting what we learn about ourselves. Beyond the logic of this spatial quest as far as the search for the truth of humanity, we will see that faith reestablished here could be the real key to change, opening up the world and the infinity that it offers us. A faith such as this would seem to be the main source of intrinsic energy that propels men and women who are ready to meet the challenges of our great adventures, moved by the desire to explore, constantly pushing our frontiers and embracing the wide sky.

Calling to Mars

I remember the second time I was born with clarity. I was twenty.

My childhood was relatively free from religious influence apart from cultural exposure. The father of our large family, eminently rationalist and probably agnostic, personifying the intelligentleness, wanted his children to make their own spiritual choices at the time of the awakening of their conscience. Innocent, we therefore received no particular religious education but rather a culture of active listening and openness. Our family motto emphasized the three words: be constructive, open, and independent. After an initial childlike period marked by a primary, magical, intuitive, and intense faith, at the age when I actually wanted to become a "sage", at the age of two, then an astronaut exploring space, at the age of five, I then felt the age of reason growing. This brought about a personal theorization that was somewhat atheist, rationalist, scientist though reductionist, and always with a dash of optimistic idealism. This model of the world worked relatively well, satisfied the desire to understand and had the elegance of consistency, respecting the ready-to-think aversion, but somewhere I still perceived incompleteness. I thought that enriching our scientific knowledge would gradually complete an understanding of the entire worldly phenomena, where each unique property, even human consciousness, would emerge from its increasing complexity. This was a scientific design from knowledge based primarily on sound deterministic deduction, perched on the shoulders of giants and their operative paradigms.

Then I had two very strong intuitive experiences.

The first, when I was sixteen, came while I was under a tree sharing a poetic moment with the woman who would become my wife, and concerned the acute sense that chance does not exist. I had the sudden implicit certainty that so-called "happenchance" emanated from an unintelligible information source, a field surrealistically baptized the "bachido effect" after some amusing discussion. Twenty years later, I was equally amused when I came across some very recent readings revisiting Gödel's incompleteness theorem (Kurt Gödel, 1933, his second incompleteness theorem and concept of undecidability: a complete and consistent finite list of axioms can never be created within any system, some true statements remaining unprovable without out-of-field information), the fundamental indeterminacy of quantum physics and the need for an informational field outside of space-time (Laszlo, 2004). For me, this anecdote underlined the conative potential of our intuition and strengthens the justifications that follow.

The second would bring lucidity to my entire life, originally a sort of vibration in a partially configured (Klein, 2014) "past-present-future" wave through which I regularly felt the effects.

So I was twenty years old, immersed in a prospective article alluding to the possible first manned mission to Mars, then projected for 2020. It was a real intuitive shock, a real "cognitive shift" experience, probably what could be called a revelation. Without doubt, that moment brought about the exciting awareness that our generation, the first in the history of humankind, was capable of reaching another planet. This would be the start of our universal history, leaving the cradle, being pluriplanetary, the direct testimony of the space age, the transition from a retracted finite world into the infinite, the opening of the "world" of possibilities, the next giant leap for humanity, where the infinity returns to the infinite regress. What exciting times we live in! The intentionality of the moment could actualize a future potential that we could realize together. But at the same time, there was another dimension present in that indescribable revelation. Astronauts frequently, while observing our blue planet offered up in its entirety right before them from a space station or even the Moon, describe an "overview effect" (White, 1987). This is an experience which, at the same time, offers a spectacular awareness of the beauty of our planetary-spacecraft and fragility of its thin living surface layer, and the interdependence between humankind and the environment. This is the very moment when I was transported to Mars, a short journey for the imagination, and I somehow saw this "pale blue dot", which I imagine could induce a similar psychological effect. What interests me here is the power of the intention, the light carried along the trajectory of life. I have no idea of the how or when, but from this I glimpsed some transcendent causality in the very depths of my being that would lead me to dedicate my efforts and patience to this common goal which would see Humans on Mars in our lifetime, overcoming all. Since this moment of enlightenment, a serene power that we call faith has once again echoed within, in the sense of irrefutable confidence in that which escapes judgment and the exercise of conditionally formatted reason, the irresistible purpose and dedication that we set in motion. It is a universal human concept *par excellence* that structures an image of life as a whole. Our spiritual nature harmonizes perfectly with the predilection that drives us to explore the cosmos in all its dimensions and refocuses our date with Mars as the next destination awaited by all.

A certain synchronous reconfiguration of the mental software that perhaps consisted of decentration, a new mode of understanding (Immanuel Kant, 1787: *The Critique of Pure Reason*: according to the philosopher, the "Understanding" allows the synthesis of the miscellaneous, that consists of the unification of sensitive intuition's data by ordering them through categories, transcendental foundations of knowledge, and creating mind-operable concepts), a metacognitive way of reading the world. Accordingly there was a reinvestment of the potential for intuitive awareness. There is in fact another type of neural processing, quite neglected in our academic activities or our conscious workspace because it is not structured like logic. Language is very closely coupled with the discursive epistemological tradition and the dialectic of the refutability criterion (Popper, 1978) defining knowledge through science, the most reliable method there is. This second type of fluency is proven to be much faster than explicit sequential processing, based on a tree network architecture. It is swift, global, multi-modal, differential, integrative, inductive, with efficient extraction of relevant data by significant correlations or inferences. It is this way of thinking that gives us the solutions to difficult problems in the early morning, that permits serendipity (Cannon 1945; see also Kingdon, 2013) and flashes of paradigmatic revolutions, which is again working toward our famous "eureka" moment. It allows us to recognize a good idea, but does not allow us to explain it, which may seem confusing. It is, however, just the best way of pointing us in the right direction, but we have to choose to follow it. We often turn away from it through very reassuring but blinkered rationalist molding, and we should remember that he who recognizes the truth is ahead of he who models the approximation. Intuition lets you know immediately that a venture is good and allows complete confidence in a subsequent incremental approach, even before knowing all the specifications. This is also probably why science and literature each speak of the truth, one demonstratively, the other through the suggestion of a profound hidden truth. Pure reason never produced anything reasonable (Friedrich Hölderlin, 1799: "Pure intellect has never produced anything intelligent, nor pure reason anything reasonable"). The exploration of the cosmos is open equally to poets and scientists.

Aspects of Social Psychology

The main selection challenge concerns the psychology of the crews to find the chosen few. It begins with the "select out" according to individual criteria arising from social psychology studies into containment and isolation in extreme environments (Kraft et al., 2003). The oddity is that it has more to do with multi-criteria compatibility than to the level of performance in a specific area. This especially continues during the "select in" of the "what it takes" during a continuous process of intensive training -- immersive multipurpose workouts, extended simulations in Mars analog outposts, group challenges. This is not about selecting individuals but multicultural mixed groups of two men and two women. The makeup of these groups must be sufficiently different to extend the viewing angles, the usable range of adaptability and the solving of unexpected problems while maintaining synergistic understanding and level of performance in trying conditions. Success must be collective, a positive team spirit is a key factor, along with a willingness that moves in the same direction, a cohesion constituting the main propulsion energy.

A recent review of the literature highlights the principal protective psychological factors in mission situations involving longterm isolation and confinement in extreme environments (Vanhove et al., 2015). The Mars One selection committee, an expert social psychology team for such missions, has pre-identified certain relevant personality criteria (Mars One, 2013), and plans to highlight the relevant strategies for coping, the adaptation and positive adjustment to adversity through simulated group dynamics. If one tries to draw a portrait of the pioneers in the exploration of outer space and of Mars, these are some of the traits that one could imagine: endurance, resilience, adaptability, curiosity, confidence, creativity, optimism, kindness, willingness, hardiness. Endurance and resilience require excellent internal and external connection, perseverance, with consistency in a stable thought process, and an ability to maintain consistent performance in extreme situations. This means being oriented and focused on the goal. A spirit of integrity, balanced and patient, strengthen a "can do" attitude. Adaptability is about situations, contexts and individuals. It is necessary to understand fields of competence, limitations and the search for how to overcome them. Active listening, openness to differences is essential. Great curiosity will be a characteristic, with a thirst for learning, a search for understanding and the passing on of skills. The future explorers of the extreme will be particularly optimistic and confident in themselves as well as in their companions and their fate. It will be necessary to have developed social skills, experience, and be equipped with wisdom, shrewdly integrating social interactions and self-informed feedback. Creativity will be very helpful, to which can be added flexibility, plasticity, versatility, context appropriate humor, playfulness, and a rich and resourceful imagination. This last point was understood by Shackleton when establishing his crew for the "Endurance" mission, a reference model in the field (Kraft & Kass, 2012). This is the vivacity of the inner world brought onboard by the crew, conscious of the uniqueness they bring and take along with them, which represents the best way of coping with the containment, the search for an absolute link to the extreme isolation and the "out of view" effect.

So, it seems there is a change in the astronaut profile, very professional versatile operators, a departure from the "space cowboys" or the stuff of heroes, the very resilient test pilots with a pronounced taste for risk and the search for an adrenaline rush, toward a scientific profile with an explorer attitude where psyche is well-balanced, flexible, open, creative, even-tempered, with a goal-oriented team spirit and accomplishment-driven. Little by little, through intensive development and prolonged training, the prerequisites for the selection of crews should expand and focus primarily on the personalities, the group dynamics and the coping strategies rather than on the background itself. With regard to the strategies, more protective factors have been identified: problem-focused coping strategies, stress avoidance coping, effective positive cognitive reappraisal, self-efficacy, perceived social support (Vanhove et al., 2015). Also, between the sense of coherence and the feeling of self-efficacy, the intrinsic characteristic of a bold nature, or hardiness, is what seems to facilitate such coping and growth, a positive adjustment to adversity (Kobasa, 1979): "hardiness" brings together the cardinal notions of commitment, sense of challenge, confidence, and perceived control, in other words, the feeling that one's own actions can change the course of events. Commitment is specifically an active attitude in relation to the environment, to give meaning to the experiences and to feel involved in what is being undertaken. The ability to meet challenges implies the attraction to innovation, motivation through difficulty, the sense of effort. We do not give ourselves because it is easy, but because it is difficult (see Kennedy, 1962). "They did not know it was impossible, so they did it" (Mark Twain aphorism). Day by day, it is always possible to push the perceived boundaries a little further to better discover the real limits. Finally, perceived control is therefore based on an attribution system of factors internal to the decision process, underpinned by trust and a second innocence. It is necessary to want to change the world a little, through actions, and according to ideals. An idealistic personality here strengthens this psychological robustness, based on introspective dominance, intuitive, with preference for feeling and perception (Briggs Myers, 1990).

The human dimensions concern above all the psychological barriers, but also the physical constraints, of course, as demonstrated by our technological aids and life support systems. Here, we should remember that the study of the ontogeny of the human species suggests the hypothesis that neoteny (Margulies & Sagan, 2002) plays a special role in the evolutionary emergence of human hypercognitive characteristics, including reflective consciousness and spirituality. This entails the conservation of juvenile-like characteristics in adulthood, much more than in other species. The human being, in this unfinished form, inherently premature, depends more than any other species on prosthetic creations and technology, on the one hand, yet on the other, has a cultural and cerebral adaptive plasticity which bestows a selective advantage which replaces our instinctive programming. This retarded autonomy, requiring a long period of socialization, learning, technological differentiation and maturation, is paradoxically the greatest asset of humanity in our hope to adapt to life on another planet. And all this goes hand in hand with a long moral and spiritual maturation that emerges from this teleonomic process. We should not forget the child that exists within us.

Aspects of Developmental Spirituality

In my experience, there appears to be an open spiritual cycle, and we can allow ourselves to be touched by a secondary faith, following a surface rational latency that is much needed for the consistent construction of our deep spirit. In the way that paradigms and civilizations overcome their limitations by heuristic spirals arising from revolution, so it is for the individual interested in spiritual development. James Fowler described six stages of spiritual maturation (Fowler, 1981; see also Kohlberg, 1981) that appropriately illuminate our analysis.

The first spiritual stage is the intuitive projective between the ages of two and six years old.

Here there is a cognitive egocentrism, the child's perspective is the only perspective considered. Stories provide the symbols that structure reality. Faith is imitative, full of imagination, not restricted or inhibited by logical thinking. The child and its fluid thought patterns constantly encounter new things for which the knowledge modes are not yet formed. The emerging strength here is the ability to capture the experience of the world, to transform it into powerful unified images that advise the intuitive understanding of the child of the conditions of existence. The transition to the next stage involves the emergence of operational thinking.

The second spiritual stage could be described as mythical-literal, between the ages of seven and twelve on average.

The subject begins to internalize the stories, beliefs, and rituals that symbolize its membership in a group, and appropriates moral rules and attitudes. One-dimensional symbols are understood literally. The emergence of concrete operations orders the composition of the previously acquired world by more coherent linear construction. The story gives value to experience. Some empathy emerges with a sense of immanent justice based on reciprocity. The cosmos appears anthropomorphic; without the perspective to allow the formulation of reflection, the meaning is both carried and enclosed by the story. The narrative capacity emerges and myths provide coherence to experience. Implicit contradictions and disappointments initiate a self-transition allowed by the acquisition of formal operations.

The third spiritual stage is the synthetic-conventional, generally between the ages of twelve and twenty. The experience of the world thus extends to society. This deals with coherently navigating through this increasing complexity. Faith forms the basis for identity and worldview by synthesizing a system of values and by structuring relationships. This conformist stage is adapted to conventional expectations and judgments and for some becomes a permanent balance without the construction of autonomous judgment or independent perspective. Beliefs and values are deeply felt, tacitly held, forming limits without any explicit systematic review, and a tendency toward categorization of individuals and consensual membership. There is a personal myth in formation, resulting in the cutting of identity and the development of faith, incorporating the features of personality. The conflicts or, often the experience of escape, emotional and physical, precipitate self-examination, the construction of fundamental values and hence lead to the next spiritual step.

For some, a fourth stage of spiritual development corresponds to an individual-reflective stage, most often between the ages of twenty and forty.

This transition is especially critical because of the contemporary assumption of responsibilities and undergoes paradoxical tensions, including the seeming opposites of subjective power versus objectivity (the latter necessary for critical thinking), self-realization versus altruism, and the dedication to a relative cause versus the search for an absolute. This stage is marked by a dual development: the development of the self, where the identity is no longer defined by the relationship to others, but supported by the awareness of its own limitations, its internal connections and the composition of a rational vision of the differentiated world. It includes a demythologizing. The capacity for critical reflection of the identity itself and perspective is a growing force as well as a second narcissism given that the perspectives of others are integrated into our own worldview. However, the resurgence of a deeper self from childhood, the paradoxes, the compromises, and even the logic that distinguishes the complexity of the dialectic between abstract concepts and levels of truth, life, and representation, provoke the overcoming of limits and illusions of this spiritual stage.

Some may well reach a fifth stage, occurring between thirty and fifty, the stage known as conjunctive.

Conjunctive faith implies integration into the self of that which individualism with its certainties could ignore by emotional adaptation of reality. A second innocence, which unifies the power of the symbols, is accepted and the new conceptual signifiers allow the history of the subject to be reconsidered. The subject opens up his "deep self" to his unconscious, which implies a critical recognition of his ideals, prejudices, value system, and moral cultural content. Unusual without irreversible commitments and before mid-life, this spiritual level is again receptive to the apparent paradoxes and contradictions. The subject accepts his vulnerability, proximity to otherness but the difference is the commitment to the conservation of each identity and of alternative worldviews. His strength is rooted in the ability to recognize his deepest values and the group who shares them, while accepting their relativity. The subject can appreciate symbols, myths, rituals without being literal, and grasps the imperative of an inclusive community of beings. However a division can result from living in an untransformed world, with the need to preserve his own welfare and maintain an ambiguous balance, with a transforming vision of the world and of loyalties. In rare cases this tension leads to a radical change, the final stage of spiritual development described.

And, indeed, there are a rare few who reach universalization, the sixth spiritual stage. This is probably, along with the preceding stage, a key operating stage for the pioneers who will show us the way to Mars.

Reaching this spiritual level involves overcoming paradoxes. It is about the subject reaching universal values, looking for an absolute, giving priority to others over his own interests and preservations, which give an outstanding quality to his actions. The depth of the devotion to the object of faith, embodied in a just cause, well-understood in all its dimensions, can disturb the common sense of pertinence. Perseverance and renunciation. Fulfillment and self-denial. Detachment and connection. Autonomy and sharing. Ecumene and isolation. Presence and absence. Action and meditation. Integrity and risk. Freedom and confinement. Acceptance and defiance. Related and absolute. Some of the many paradoxes that must be overcome to consider a trip to Mars. The way of resolving these contradictions is probably eminently spiritual. For example, the detachment (Luong, 2002) in Eastern spirituality aims for, far from indifference or callousness, unconditional love, an absolute, which frees us from the fear of losing, the characteristic of attachment. Hence the distance taken gives a new force and another depth to essential links. Self-denial is not self-extinction, but the gift of self, complete and in full conscience, the creation of a link between the surface and the new level. Sometimes in the life of a person the distance is relative. To arrive, it is necessary to be the path (Siddhartha Gautama, circa 400 BC: "You cannot travel the path until you have become the path itself").

Humanity could thus be the real vessel that explores the cosmos and paves the way. Be the captain of your soul ("I am the master of my fate: I am the captain of my soul," thereby ended the famous poem written in by William E Henley in 1888; later entitled "Invictus" by an another poet, Quiller-Couch, in 1900), and allow the curious child that we all have within take the helm, in a new cycle guided by the compass of intuition, in the harmony of full spiritual maturity. Faith is the first and last key for humans in the challenge of Mars exploration. A spiritual awakening to become part of the adventure and to overcome the ultimate challenges. A journey to the end of what we can know about ourselves.

In summary, considering all psychological elements known or thought to be critical to lead a mission to explore the planet Mars, and the installation of a first permanent human settlement, it becomes clear that the spiritual maturity described appears as the ideal success vector, resonating correctly with each of the notes of the score. A proper spiritual development seems to be the best medium to support the growth, for the individual and for the group, of trust, openness, overcoming, guidance, communication, sharing, mindfulness, to which it is possible to add stepping-back, sharing and the necessary degree of self-denial.

In conclusion, faith is probably the real cornerstone, transcending the paradoxes of such a human challenge, an unprecedented one as it involves leaving our reassuring blue planet for the first time, beautiful but fragile, until it is lost from sight. This is thus a renovation of the way to be part of the world to be invented. Could humanity be the best chance for the universe to learn about itself? Aiming for a sense of coherence, with unified science and global awareness, where a supplement of soul determines the quantum field? During the voyage, when sublimating the gravitational field, I will weigh my words: "faith to face, touching the face of the cosmos."

Bibliography

Annis, James (1999) "Placing a limit on star-fed Kardashev type III civilizations," *Journal of the British Interplanetary Society, 52*, pp. 33-36.

Briggs Myers, Isabel (1990) *Introduction to Type: A Description of the Theory and Applications of the Myers-Briggs Type Indicator.* Gainesville, FL: Center for Applications of Psychological Type.

Cannon, Walter (1945) *The Way of Investigator.* Norton, New York.

Ehricke, Krafft (1978) "The Extraterrestrial Imperative," *Air University Review*, January-February.

Fowler, James (1981) *Stages of Faith: The Psychology of Human Development and the Search for Meaning.* San Francisco: Harper & Row.

Hölderlin, Friedrich (1799) *Hyperion or the Hermit in Greece, Vol 2.*

Kabat-Zinn, John (1994) *Wherever You Go, There You Are: Mindfulness Meditation for Everyday Life.* New York: Hachette Books.

Kardashev, Nikolaï (1980) "Strategies of Searching for Extraterrestrial Intelligence: A Fundamental Approach to the Basic Problem," *Cosmic Search, 7 (2)*, pp. 36-38.

Kennedy, John F (1962) "We Choose to Go to the Moon" aka "Address at Rice University on the Nation's Space Effort," speech delivered at Rice University, Houston, Texas, 12 September.

Kingdon, Matt (2013) *The Science of Serendipity: How to Unlock the Promise of Innovation?* Hoboken, NJ: Wiley.

Klein, Etienne (2014) "Le Futur Existe-t'il Déjà dans l'avenir?" *Revue Temps, 1*, pp. 3-7.

Kobasa, Suzanne (1979) "Stressful Life Events, Personality, and Health: Inquiry into Hardiness," *Journal of Personality and Social Psychology, 37*, pp.

1-11.

Kohlberg, Lawrence (1981) *Essays on Moral Development: The Philosophy of Moral Development.* San Francisco: Harper & Row.

Kraft, Norbert; Binder, Heidi; Lyons, Terence; Kass, Raye (2003) "Types of Relationships Formed by a Mixed Gender, Multinational Crew while in Isolation," 54th International Astronautical Congress of the International Astronautical Federation, the International Academy of Astronautics, and the International of Space Law.

Kraft, Norbert; Lyons, Terence; Binder, Heidi(2003) "Intercultural Crew Issues in Long-Duration Spaceflight," *Aviation, Space, and Environmental Medicine, 5 (74)*, pp. 575-578.

Kraft, Norbert; Kass, Raye (2012) "The Uncharted Territories of Mars: Is Science Enough?" *Huffington Post, Science*, 3 July. http://www.huffingtonpost.-com/norbert-kraft/mars-travel_b_1646458.html

Laszlo, Ervin (2004) *Science and the Akashic Field: An Integral Theory of Everything*, Rochester, VT: Inner Traditions.

Luong, Can-Liem (2002) *Psychothérapie Bouddhique: Meditation, Éthique, Liberté.* Paris: L'Harmattan.

Margulies, Lynn & Sagan, Dorion (2002) *L'univers Bactériel.* Paris: Le Seuil.

Mars One (2013) "Selection and preparation of the Astronauts: Five Key characteristics of an Astronaut." http://www.mars-one.com/faq/selection-and-preparation-of-the-astronauts

Popper, Karl (1978) "Natural Selection and the Emergence of Mind," *Dialectica, 32*, pp. 339-355.

Sagan, Carl (1975) *Cosmic Connection: An Extraterrestrial Perspective.* Paris: Seuil.

Vanhove, Adam; Herian, Michel; Harms, P. D. ; Luthans, Fred (2015) "Resilience and Growth in Long-Duration Isolated, Confined and Extreme (ICE) Missions. A Literature Review and Selection, Training and Countermeasure Recommendations," NASA technical report.

White, Frank (1987). *The Overview Effect: Space Exploration and Human Evolution.* Boston: Houghton-Mifflin.

-=-

Jeremy Saget is a French aerospace physician, weightless flight surgeon, and zeroG instructor. He holds a Masters degree in cognitive science, specializing in human factors. Currently involved in spaceflight participant training, he is working on psychological aspects of "isolated confined missions in an extreme environment". Passionate about humanity, space, exploration, science, and ingenuity, he is an advocate for the "space for all" era. Being a lifelong Mars enthusiast, he has been preselected as a *Mars One Astronaut Candidate*. This project aspires to establish a permanent human settlement on Mars in the very near future.

One Earth

Rabbi Barry L Schwartz

I have a confession to make. Ever since I was a kid, I wanted to become an astronaut. But even the merry-go-round made me dizzy. So I became a rabbi. But long before I could quote a verse of Bible, I knew everything about every space flight ever launched. I had scrapbooks of every Apollo mission. I was one of those kids enthralled by our quest to have "slipped the surely bounds of Earth, and danced the skies on laughter-silvered wings". I consider it a blessing to have come of age during the space age.

On July 20, 1969 I begged my parents to stay up, all night if necessary, to watch Neil Armstrong take "one small step for a man, one giant leap for mankind". Fortunately they agreed and those grainy images on our black and white TV stirred my heart. Over the years I've met people of a certain age, mine, who smile knowingly when I try to describe my feelings. Call it the Apollo brotherhood. In our childhood naiveté we thought the Moon landing was the beginning of a new era when all things were now possible. In some ways, it was. A thousand years from now humankind may not remember much from the 20th century, but the first steps into the universe will be one of them. In other ways, it was not. The weight of the world seemed too heavy for the nascent star trekkers. Next steps into the solar system stayed firmly mired in the realm of science fiction.

Keeping up my youthful (and irrational?) exuberance has been challenging. When I wax poetic on the promise of space exploration people look at me funny. On the twentieth anniversary of Apollo 11's triumph, July 20, 1989, now grown up and living in Washington, I took my wife to a "lunar landing party" at the Smithsonian. It took some convincing. Now more than forty years have passed, and like the Israelites, much of the time has felt like wandering in the desert. The Sinai moment is a distant memory; the promised land of a base on the Moon, a manned mission to Mars, and the active pursuit of the final frontier "to go where no man has gone before" is elusive.

Yet I still envy former senator Jake Garn, the first politician in space. I would like to be the first rabbi in space. Something tells me that fantasy will not come to pass. So I harbor a much more modest fantasy: just this little sermon on the subject. The question before us: What have our first baby steps into the solar system taught us? What have we seen? As I write this, the Hubble telescope is celebrating its 25th anniversary. The myopic instrument that couldn't focus turned into a galaxy gazing marvel. The images of worlds beyond words, of spiraling constellations and storm-swept nebulae hint at a universe of breathtaking grandeur beyond imagination. There's certainly a sermon in those stunners, but for now I want to hold forth on another image. It's the one that hung outside my office door for years and I still cherish. It's an iconic photo and it's even been given a name: *The Full Earth*. The photo was taken by Apollo 17 on its way to the Moon. Of all the splendid images of Earth this one is the most famous and recognized.

What strikes you right away is color. There is our planet, a brilliant sphere of blue and white, in a sea of utter black.

Nearly a half century ago pioneering astronomer Fred Hoyle uttered these prophetic words: "Once a photograph of the Earth, taken from the outside is available ... a new idea as powerful as any in history will be let loose."

This new idea is really what I want to talk about. Permit me to introduce the idea, not through my own words, but through those of my childhood heroes; a select group of men and women who have experienced something we can only dream about. I speak of those we call "astronauts". They have seen "the full Earth". They have glimpsed our planet, from beyond. They are the ones who have left home, in a profound sense, only to return home, with a unique perspective. We often think of astronauts one dimensionally as can-do, top-gun, right-stuff pilots. But they are more. They are explorers and seekers. They are philosophers and poets; even mystics.

Sometimes, not often, these astronauts try to put into words what their experience has meant. In the din of our lives I think we have missed what they are saying. But if we take a moment to listen, a message is emerging; indeed "as powerful as any in history". Allow me to quote from their journals. Listen to their words, to their stream of consciousness, and feel the birth of an idea, and the shift of a paradigm:

> Looking outward to the blackness of space, sprinkled with the glory of a universe of lights, I saw majesty- but no welcome. Below was a welcoming planet. There, contained in the thin, moving, incredibly fragile shell of the biosphere is everything that is dear to you, all the human drama and comedy. That's where life is; that's where all the good stuff is. *-Loren Action, USA*

> I have been in love with the sky since birth. And when I could fly, I wanted to go higher, to enter space and become a "man of the heights." During the eight days I spent in space, I realized that mankind needs height primarily to better know our long-suffering Earth, to see what cannot be seen close up. Not just to love her beauty, but also to ensure that we do not bring even the slightest harm to the natural world. *-Pham Tuan, Vietnam*

> What struck me most was the silence. It was a great silence, unlike any I have encountered on Earth, so vast and deep that I began to

> hear my own body; my heart beating, my blood vessels pulsing, even the rustle of my muscles moving over each other seemed audible.
>
> But there was the Earth. The Earth was small, light blue, and touchingly alone, our home that must be defended like a holy relic. *-Aleksei Leanov, USSR*

> Once during the mission I was asked by ground control what I could see. “What do I see?” I replied. “Half a world to the left, half a world to the right, I can see it all. The Earth is so small.” *-Vitali Sevastyanov, USSR*

> Before I flew I was already aware of how small and vulnerable our planet is; but only when I saw it from space, in all its ineffable beauty and fragility, did I realize that humankind's most urgent task is to cherish and preserve it for future generations. *-Sigmund Jahn, German Democratic Republic*

> As I looked down, I saw a large river meandering slowly along for miles, passing from one country to another without stopping. I also saw huge forests, extending across several borders. And I watched the extent of one ocean touch the shores of separate continents. Two words leaped to mind as I looked down on all this: commonality and interdependence. We are one world. *-John-David Bartoe USA*

What these modern day explorers are telling us is a truth at once ancient, but radically new. Something we have always known, but never really understood:

We are one Earth. We are one planet. We are one world.

We are not so much independent, as interdependent. Amidst our astonishing diversity is an even more remarkable unity; amidst our deep disparity is an even more fundamental commonality. This is it: the home planet; our wondrous but fragile home; our shared home, and so far, our only home.

Our journey into space is really about our journey back home. Soviet cosmonaut Vladamir Lyakhov wrote: "while out there in orbit, our dreams were usually about Earth.“ American astronaut Alfred Worden realized, “Now I know why I'm here. Not for a closer look at the Moon, but to look back at our home, the Earth.” Saudi astronaut Bin Salman put it most incisively: “The first day or so we all pointed to our countries. The third or fourth day we were pointing to our continents. By the fifth day we were aware of only one Earth.”

Gifted to us by our journey into space, the power of the “one Earth” idea is only slowly beginning to take root in our emerging global consciousness. When I was a kid I also read a lot of science fiction. Arthur C. Clarke, perhaps our greatest cosmic clairvoyant, has a story that begins, "Down there at the end of the 20th century the Earth is dying“. Those words have always haunted me. You and I will continue to enjoy the blessings of this good Earth. We dance as the clock ticks, we celebrate as the clouds thicken and the planet warms. But what of our children? And our children's children? It is difficult enough to grasp the global dimension of our ecological problems. The generational dimension: even harder. The real effects of what we do now will be felt long after our own brief sojourn on this planet. The true consequences of our behavior belong not to us, but to the ones who will bear our names.

What will it take for us to realize that we act today for sake of tomorrow? What will it take for us to comprehend the wisdom of the Native American teaching that every generation must act for the welfare of seven generations that succeed it? What will it take for us to comprehend the wisdom of the African proverb: "Let us consider our world not so much as inherited from our ancestors, but as borrowed from our children"? What will it take for us to comprehend the wisdom of the rabbinic adage that "Just as my ancestors planted for me, so I will plant for my children"?

An idea as powerful as any in history has been let loose. It is a life affirming idea. It is an idea worthy of guiding us and our children. We have journeyed beyond the Earth to see the Earth. We have taken a new look at our planet. From outer space we have gained an inner understanding; a fresh perspective. We are one community on one Earth; a dazzling bundle of interdependent life, hurtling through the void. We are one human race; and must we not join hand in hand across the globe, to care for this our home?

And perhaps this global perspective, if we take it to heart, will mitigate our Earthly problems in a way that rekindles our cosmic quest. "Behold the time is coming," proclaimed the prophet Amos, "when [our] hunger shall not be for bread nor our thirst for water, but for hearing the words of the Lord." And I might add, for discovering the wonders of the Lord, strung like jewels across the universe. The Psalmist gazed upward and declared, "When I behold Your heavens, the work of Your fingers, the moon and the stars that You set in place, what is man that You have been mindful of him, mortal man that You have taken note of him." In awe and in humility do we dare to touch the face of the cosmos?

We have looked up to the heavens, and now we have looked down to the Earth. "The first day or so we all pointed to our countries. The third or fourth day we were pointing to our continents. By the fifth day we were aware of only one Earth." Behold the home planet, and behold its place in the endless expanse of the universe.

-=-

Barry Schwartz is Rabbi of the Congregation Adas Emuno in Leonia, New Jersey. He is author of four books, a prize winning short story, and his articles that have appeared in the *Journal of Reform Judaism*, *American Jewish History*, and the *Hebrew Union College Annua*l. His latest textbook, *Jewish Heroes, Jewish Values*, (1996) is currently used in over 300 religious schools nationwide. A previous text, *Jewish Theology: A Comparative Study* (1991), explores Jewish denominational thinking. *Honi The Circlemaker – Eco-Fables*

From Ancient Israel (1993) is a series of folktales for children. He recently authored *Judaism's Great Debates*, which was published in both adult and youth editions.

Shall the Sacred Heavens Be Cast Down?

Kathleen D. Toerpe

As a child, I never understood my friends' fascination with looking up at the stars. Why did they gaze with painfully craned necks towards a black sky that, to me, looked like it was merely a swath of ordinary velvet cloth scattered with faded lint? Even with the Coke-bottle glasses that aimed to correct my extreme myopia, I could only make out a few scattered twinklings of light. On a clear night, at most a dozen or so stars revealed themselves to me - hardly enough to tempt me from my real love affair with space. As a child, the reality of the night sky - stars, planets, meteor showers, even the aurora borealis, were simply not all that impressive to me, because I had not the physical sight to appreciate them. Instead, like many other tail-end Baby Boomers, the wonders of space came vicariously to me through the exploits of Captain Kirk, Will and Penny Robinson, Luke Skywalker, and, later, the multifaceted and multi-faced Doctor from Gallifrey. For me, the mystery of space wasn't so much the vastness of the cosmos - though I distinctly remember being puzzled as to how a "light year" could be a unit of distance, rather than of time - as it was the portability of our fears, weaknesses, and aspirations. What seized my imagination was the perplexing ability of the fictional extraterrestrial species that I encountered each week - Vulcans, Klingons, Time Lords, and, especially, the rather ludicrous aliens of Lost in Space - to act so frustratingly and disappointingly ordinary and human. Were extraterrestrials nothing more than the comic or savage or logical reflections of us? Is this what awaited humanity in my hallowed imaginings of First Contact? Were humans really the reference point by which all species of the universe were measured? This rather ontological and sociological dimension of outer space fascinated me much more than the stars themselves, and, thus, for better or worse, I became a social and cultural historian, rather than an astronomer or cosmologist.

I had it wrong, of course, when I short shrifted the immense majesty and mystery of our cosmos. One hundred billion galaxies, each one hosting another hundred billion or so stars; each star likely anchoring multiple planets, with perhaps a tenth of all planets - a paltry ten billion or so in our Milky Way alone – capable of mimicking Earth's ability to maintain liquid water and, thus, the possibility of biological genesis. The possibilities strain our creative ability to imagine! What once my poor eyesight couldn't envision, however, my trained intellect can now conceive and, as an adult, I find myself lost in the sacred awe of a universe whose grip on the human imagination began, I suspect, the first time human eyes opened skyward on a clear evening many millennia ago.

No one knows, exactly, what the earliest humans thought when they looked up at the night sky. Confusion, perhaps, or fear or profound wonder? Prehistoric societies, of course, by definition left no written record. We have no official documents, no corroborated eyewitness accounts or oral histories, no valid or reliable quantitative data – nothing that historians commonly use to understand the historic past. At best, we have cave drawings, such as those of Lascaux in southwestern France, representing late Upper Paleolithic culture c. 15-18,000 BCE. Though detailed and sophisticated – revealing the ancient mental pairing of terrestrial animals and heavenly constellations – these paintings give only a tantalizingly cryptic and incomplete testimony to ancient beliefs.

We can presume, however, that these ancient peoples who contemplated the universe used whatever philosophical constructs they had developed within their cultures to make sense of their observations. Or, perhaps, lacking sufficient ones, they created new constructs and paradigms passed down through oral folklore and chiseled stone. In *The Inner Reaches of Outer Space*, comparative mythologist Joseph Campbell suggests that "the mystery of the night sky, those enigmatic passages of slowly but steadily moving lights among the fixed stars, had delivered the revelation, when charted mathematically, of a cosmic order, and in response, from the depths of the human imagination, a reciprocal recognition had been evoked. A vast concept took form of the universe as a living being . . . " (1986/2002, p. 13). But as formal recorded history emerged, this universe, this cosmos, was clearly no ordinary living being, and definitely, no ordinary human. Rather, this space that stretched above, below, behind, and beyond Earth, was clearly home to forces greater and more powerful than mere humans could ever be. Outer space took on metaphorical meanings of "good and evil, light and dark, even of life and death . . . Where formerly there had been the planetary cycles, marking days and nights, the months, years, and eons of unending time, there was now to be a straight line of progressive world history with a beginning, a middle, and a prophesied end –Gayomart, Zarathustra, and Saoshyant: Adam, Jesus, and the Second Coming" (Campbell, p. 16).

Thus, space became extraordinary – above, below, behind, and beyond human – and became, over time, a sanctified or sacred expression and reflection of human longing for meaning, purpose, and transcendence. Gods descended from the heavenly skies, bellowed out anger in claps of thunder and flashes of lightning, and even ascended in perfected glory after conquering death itself.

The foundational scriptures and tenets of many of humanity's ancient belief systems – those both enduring and those no longer practiced – often cast space itself as the creative and artistic work of divine hands, equated "the heavens" with what is "sacred," or juxtaposed the immensity of space with the meager existence of humans:

> When I consider your heavens, the work of your fingers, the moon

> and the stars, which you have set in place, what is mankind that you are mindful of them, human beings that you care for them? (Psalms 8:3-4, c. 1400 - 400 BCE, New International Version [NIV])

From the mathematician and poet, Claudius Ptolemy:

> . . . if one should seek out in its simplicity the first cause of the first movement of the universe, he would find God invisible and unchanging. (Preface, *Almagest*, c. 150 CE)

In this next passage, the Sun represents the eyes of Vishnu, the Supreme Lord, while Krishna's symbol is the Moon:

> Of the Adityas I am Visnu, of lights I am the radiant sun, I am Marici of the Maruts, and among the stars I am the moon. (*Bhagavad Gita* 10:21, c. 400 BCE - 200 CE)

In its apocalyptic prophecy, the Book of Matthew uses celestial bodies as symbolic forewarnings of "End Times":

> . . . the sun will be darkened, and the moon will not give its light; the stars will fall from the sky, and the heavenly bodies will be shaken. Then will appear the sign of the Son of Man in heaven. And then all the peoples of the earth will mourn when they see the Son of Man coming on the clouds of heaven, with power and great glory. And he will send his angels with a loud trumpet call, and they will gather his elect from the four winds, from one end of the heavens to the other. (Matthew 24:29-31, NIV, c. 50 - 70 CE)

Back and forth across the ancient world, deities were symbolized or equated with celestial bodies; the Egyptian sun god Ra, the Greek chariot-riding Helios, the Roman moon goddess Luna, and the Chinese sun goddess Xihe marked the heavens as their own, with even the Greek naming of the constellations and the Roman naming of the planets betraying a mix of emerging science and ancient mythology. Often tethered to the image of an anthropomorphized deity, the spiritual awe that one encounters when looking up at the sky has also evoked throughout history a more incorporeal, but equally ineffable, sense of wonder in what Albert Einstein has described as a "cosmic religious feeling" communicated most keenly through art and science (1954, p. 38).

Western Medieval and Renaissance societies both challenged and reinforced the sacredness and extraordinary nature of outer space. Building upon Aristarchus' s (310-230 BCE) early postulation of a heliocentric universe, Nicolaus Copernicus (1473-1543 CE) envisioned a universe of concentric circles anchored by a stationary sun. Though he challenged the widely accepted Ptolemaic geocentric model and the religiously ensconced worldview that put the Earth at the center of the universe – as did the Islamic astronomer and mathematician Ibn al-Haytham (965-c.1040 CE) nearly four hundred years earlier – Copernicus nonetheless accepted the a priori partiality of both Aristarchus and Ptolemy for the pleasing mythology, geometry, and symbolism of circular orbits. Thus, though slowly emerging, observational-based astronomy, at least in the West, was still subordinate to prevailing cultural worldviews. It would take the shattering cosmological claims of Giordano Bruno (1548-1600CE) that not only was our Earth not exceptional in the universe, but neither was our Sun, and perhaps we as well, along with the painstaking astronomical observations of Tycho Brahe (1546-1601 CE) and Galileo Galilei (1564-1642 CE), Johannes Kepler's (1571-1630) laws of planetary motion, and Isaac Newton's (1642-1727 CE) research on universal gravitation to complete the Copernican Revolution's paradigm shift. Still, by Newton's death and the end of those tumultuous two hundred years, outer space was still largely regarded in the West as the sacred handiwork of the God of the Old and New Testaments; the complexity of celestial bodies borne out by astronomical observation merely made their divine creation and sustenance all the more miraculous.

Our modern relationship to space has lost much of that sense of sacred transcendence that marked our ancient, and to a somewhat lesser extent, our medieval ancestors. Outer space has become less a tool to marvel at the work of a supreme being to becoming increasingly defined by its practical usefulness to further our science, our engineering, and our entrepreneurial pursuits. Replacing the once transcendent meaning of space with the ordinary or profane, conquest of technology and profit has inevitably and, perhaps irrevocably, altered our relationship with the cosmos that surrounds us, and, likely, our relationships with each other as well. In the 2014 edition of *The Space Report: The Authoritative Guide to Global Space Activity*, the Space Foundation reports:

> The past year [2013] has seen substantial growth in space technology and capabilities. A vibrant commercial sector has led the way with compelling products that provide significant value to customers around the globe. Despite budget constraints in some countries, governments have continued to invest heavily in space agencies, exploration programs, and the further development of commercial capabilities. Interest in the space industry has increased and has created a surge of young excited talent, providing the building blocks for future success. Venture capital firms and other investors are demonstrating interest in the potential of space to introduce world-changing technologies. For all of these reasons, the outlook for the space sector is very bright in the years to come. [p. 4]

The numbers support the Space Foundation's boosterish optimism. With over 75% of revenues generated by commercial space products, services, infrastructure, and other support industries, the US "Space Economy" rings in at a stellar $315 billion (Space Foundation, p. 4). The biggest publicly traded players comprise the Space Foundation Index (SFI), an economic indicator charting stock fluctuations similar to the S&P 500 or NASDAQ. While many names on the Index are long-standing government contractors and manufacturers (Northop Grumman, Lockheed Martin, Boeing, etc.), others represent corporations with heavy investments in cutting-edge satellite components, launches, and leasing (Globecomm, ViaSat, DirecTV, DISH Network, etc.). Absent from the Index are some privately-held, high-profile names in the popular media such as Virgin Galactic, Space X, and Bigelow Aerospace who are investing in space tourist vehicles, reusable rockets, and lunar habitats, respectively. Overall, the Index is performing on par with other more traditional stock indices, with 2013 gains in the range of 34-48% (Space Foundation, p. 5).

These numbers represent more than a burgeoning new economic sector. They also betray a deep-seated shift in humanity's relationship with space. While there will always be individuals and organizations intent on space exploration for knowledge's sake – and to answer the age-old question of whether we are alone in the universe – the growing focus on space as "assets" or as the raw material of a new extraterrestrial Gold Rush constitute a new, almost sacrilegious posture. Sacred space has become profane not only in the religious sense, but also in the more neutral sociological sense of being ordinary, everyday, and routine. Living on space stations or on the Moon, extracting resources from asteroids, taking tourist jaunts to the edge of outer space and back may seem quite amazing to us now, but in the span of one hundred years or so, they all may be quite commonplace. As Captain Kirk (William Shatner) corrects Dr. Gillian Taylor (Catherine Hicks) in *Star Trek IV: The Voyage Home* (1986), when she asks him if he's from outer space, he modestly defers, "No, I'm from Iowa. I only work in outer space." Only. We are on a bold trajectory, and not just to build the Enterprise or to reach Europa or even Alpha Centauri; we are also on a path to a new relationship with space in which the extraordinary is becoming as mundane as the place we merely work everyday. The implication, of course, is that if the universe is no longer extraordinary – either in origin or in teleology – then perhaps, and I would say quite likely, neither are we. And, in the long run, that may be the scarier part of the equation.

Letting go of the sacred in space need not, in itself, be a negative. It does not portend doom and gloom for humanity's sense of the spiritual, whether defined parochially or in cosmological terms. Humanity has survived paradigm shifts before; sometimes, we actually embrace them. In the Western world alone, Greco-Roman polytheistic worldviews gave way to a European medieval monotheism, which later shared influence with Renaissance humanist and Modern individualist or legalist perspectives. Add in contemporary corporate and globalist perspectives along with the philosophical overlays of fundamentalism, conservatism, and liberalism – both old and "neo" – and human worldviews present a buffet of choices. Over time, worldviews overlap, merge, fade, and sometimes re-emerge like the mythical Phoenix to entice new generations or new places on the planet. Our increasingly secular worldview of space presents no fundamental challenge here. Perhaps seeing space for what it really is – an amazing and still largely unknown and unexplored locus encompassing both womb and grave within which galaxies, solar systems, and our own Earth are born, mature, and themselves die – is itself a realization of the extraordinary nature of the universe in which we find ourselves. For many of us, that sense of awe that one encounters looking up at the milky arms of our galaxy satisfies, in itself, whatever need we have for the sacred, sanctified, or blessed. Carl Sagan's oft-quoted observation, "We are made of star-stuff," elevates humanity to the level of the stars and resonates in the traditional Ash Wednesday prayer, "Remember thou art dust, and to dust, thou shalt return." Returning to "star-stuff" or "stardust" loops the beginning and end of both my individual life as well as my part in the larger totality of human existence, and somehow I find this comforting, as I do Van Gogh's sigh that "For my part, I know nothing with any certainty, but the sight of the stars makes me dream." Simple. Direct. Honest. And, for me, sacred enough.

From a more vantaged viewpoint, however, perhaps this perceptual shift is more than merely transferring a sense of the sacred from formerly deified to now scientifically secular ideas of space. In other words, perhaps humanity is simply and gradually outgrowing the need for any sacred heaven-space and an awe-struck response to it. Perhaps the worldview of space as sacred has simply run its course. If so, the secularization of space, and even the commercialization of it, diminishes nothing of what space has always objectively been – long before humanity superimposed itself on it and alternately feared and admired, or tried to tame and monetize it – but only what we have tried to make it out to be. If we are honest with ourselves, we might agree with Sagan that, "The tidy anthropocentric proscenium of our ancestors has been replaced by a cold, immense, indifferent Universe in which humans are relegated to obscurity" (1997, p. 256).

Perhaps we can finally ponder humanity's relative insignificance and concede that we have been trying to fit a square peg into a round hole, or more precisely, a finite Earth and frail human existence, into a potentially infinite – and possibly unknowable – multiverse. Thus, what is lost from our casting down of the heavens is our illusions and, depending on an individual's personal psyche, that could trigger a multitude of responses ranging from comfort to resignation, and, more profoundly, from dread to existential angst. Foundational challenges to worldviews are not lightly dismissed, and the transition from one worldview to competing or succeeding ones is often fraught with internal and external conflict. Psychologist and astrosociologist Albert Harrison's observation that "worldviews are complex, dynamic systems such that an attack on a particular manifestation of the worldview sometimes threatens the worldview as a whole," means that losing the sense of sacred heaven-space may open a Pandora's box, questioning the religious fundamentalist tenet that "considers people as the core purpose of the universe" (2015, pp. 20-21). In short, we cannot change our beliefs about the cosmos without – intentionally or not – changing our beliefs about ourselves.

Ironically, perhaps, in the end, humanity will gain far more than it loses in recalibrating its place in what was once a sacred universe. In her Editor's Introduction to Carl Sagan's posthumously published essay anthology, *The Varieties of Scientific Experience: My Personal View of the Search for God,* Sagan's widow and scientific collaborator Ann Druyan (2006) recounts that the famed Cornell astronomer had repeatedly asked NASA to program one of the twin Voyager probes to sneak a turn-around look at the Earth and snap a photo. Sagan had spearheaded the creation of the twin LP-like Golden Records that were affixed to each of the identical probes, and, with his wife and others, had created a compilation of images, sounds, and music representing the diverse people and history of Earth. These images, anticipated to last a billion years, were – and are – as close to an immortal presence that humanity might ever achieve in the universe. That Sagan pressed NASA for a "rear-view-mirror" shot of the Earth – finally taken in February 1990 as Voyager 1 buzzed the edges of the solar system on its way to unanticipated discoveries in the interstellar medium – reveals his belief in our emotional connection to our "pale blue dot" and its place among the stars (Voyager 1 snapped the iconic Pale Blue Dot photo, not its twin, Voyager 2, as Druyan implies in her Editor's Introduction):

> [He] asked us to meditate on that image and see our home for what it is – just a tiny 'pale blue dot' afloat in the immensity of the universe. He dreamed that we might attain a spiritual understanding of our true circumstances. Like a prophet of old, he wanted to arouse us from our stupor so that we would take action to protect our home. [p. xii]

Sagan, who worked tirelessly to demystify and demythologize outer space, was also instrumental in shaping a contemporary social construct of the Earth itself – apart from the totality of the heavens or the universe – as extraordinary and unique, not least in the sense that it remains to date our only planetary home and the only known home to life in the universe. Noting human-made threats posed by war, overpopulation and the abuse of natural habitats through deforestation, chemical pollutants, and the like, Sagan echoed the calls of fellow scientists (Rachel Carson's pleas in her classic *Silent Spring* come to mind here) to forsake a utilitarian relationship with the planet for one based on respect and stewardship (Sagan, in Druyan, 2006, pp. 195-205; Sagan, 1994, pp. 77-79). In many ways, it is a call to action that still remains unheeded. But, more importantly from a sociological perspective, it is a call predicated on a new collective worldview of our own physical world. That which is both rare and threatened often takes on inordinate meaning and value, and in this case, I would argue, sacredness. However prescient Sagan might have been a generation ago about the political, climatic, and environmental challenges facing our home planet, his vantage point was still that of a man with his feet tethered by gravity. In the end, it may be the literally breathtaking view of the Earth while looking "down" from space that provides the greatest counterpoint to the awe first experienced by our ancient ancestors looking "up" so many millennia ago.

The vanguard of this new sense of awe has, somewhat surprisingly, been the scientifically trained men and women who were this planet's first travelers to space.

Throughout the previous five decades of spaceflight with humans aboard, astronauts and cosmonauts have reported that their direct perception of space, and the Earth hanging in it, produced unexpected emotional reactions and intellectual, perspective, perceptual and paradigm shifts.

> These shifts naturally included a greater and more accurate sense of the reality of the universe and the nature of the Earth as a planet in space. But it often included new or intensified insights into how this re-contextualizing from 'life in the world' to 'life on a planet' changed their understanding of many other aspects of life, from the environment to politics to resources, energy and humanitarian issues in general. [The Overview Institute, 2012]

Frank White (1998/2014) first analyzed what he later called the "Overview Effect" in the 1980s, interviewing former American and Soviet flight personnel who had each experienced a uniquely personal transformative understanding of the relationship between Earth, outer space, and humanity during their respective space missions. Earth, as seen from space, is void of nationalist borders; the religious, political, and economic boundaries dividing humanity grow increasingly obscure and vague as astronauts travel from low Earth orbit to the Moon, and thus, reveal themselves for what they truly are: transient constructs of fallible human societies.

Michael Collins, veteran of the Gemini 10 mission and command module pilot for Apollo 11, observed:

> I really believe that if the political leaders of the world could see their planet from a distance of . . . 100,000 miles, their outlook would be fundamentally changed. That all-important border would be invisible, that noisy argument suddenly silenced. The tiny globe would continue to turn, serenely ignoring its subdivisions, presenting a united façade that would cry out for unified treatment. . . . [Quoted in White, pp.182-183]

Though lacking the *Pale Blue Dot*'s sense of immense space and distance, we can garner at least a sense of what Collins and the other astronauts saw firsthand in the December 1968 Earthrise photo, taken by the Apollo 8 crew, or the December 1972 Full Earth photo, taken as Apollo 17 embarked on humanity's last crewed lunar mission. (The original orientation of the Earthrise photo was vertical. That it is often mistakenly rotated to place the Earth at the top of the Moon suggests a need to see our planet as "up.")

It is not just what a space-based observation of Earth is missing that makes the Overview Effect so compelling; it is also what can be clearly and unequivocally seen from the unique vantage point of low Earth orbit. Deforestation, receding glaciers, effects of droughts and floods, and raging wildfires are just some of the geophysical and human-made changes that are visible from space. These scarring features transcend terrestrial constructs of nation or society and evoke a sense of global environmental action.

Charles D. Walker, payload specialist on shuttle missions STS-41-D, STS-51-D, and STS-61-B, recalled:

> I found the experience of seeing the world as one distinct entity an enlightening one, and realizing with my own senses the interrelatedness of the environment to have a firsthand feel for the world around us, and it sensitized me to learn as much as I could about the interconnectedness of the environment. [quoted in White, p. 214]

Helen P. Sharman, a civilian who won a contest in Britain with the prize of spending eight days at the Russian Mir station in 1991, summed up her experience of seeing Earth from space:

> It brings out the idea that you are insignificant . . . It really puts things into perspective. You realize that all the arguments and so on are really worthless, when you think about what is really important in life and what we really should be aiming for. [quoted White, p. 258]

White, too, has more recently aimed higher by broadening his understanding of the Overview Effect: philosophically articulating it both as a compass which "may point to humankind's purpose as a species" and as the "foundation for a series of new civilizations evolving on Earth and in space" (p. 3). However, its core tenet of being "the predicted experience of astronauts and space settlers, who . . . have a different philosophical point of view as a result of having a different physical perspective [in this case, orbiting the Earth rather than standing on it] remains (White, p. 2).

White's research, though heavily based on subjective and anecdotal testimony, has inspired more objective and literally down-to-Earth attempts to find collaborative domestic and international solutions to some of humanity's most pressing social, economic, and political problems, just as collaboration was necessary to overcome Cold War distrust to build the International Space Station. In *The Orbital Perspective: Lessons in Seeing the Big Picture from a Journey of 71 Million Miles*, retired astronaut Ron Garan (2015) picks up where White left off, by advocating a "call to action . . . to continue to spread this message of cooperation around the world and to continue working to improve life on Earth, to continue to look for real, sustainable solutions that have the greatest long-term effect . . . Like an asteroid deflection mission, in which a slight force early enough and far enough out can prevent an extinction-causing asteroid from hitting Earth, I want, through my small actions, to nudge the trajectory of our global society" (pp. 169-170).

Garan is not alone in his pursuits. Dr. Mae Jemison, the first female African-American astronaut in space and head of the DARPA-created 100 Year Starship mission to support the "radical leaps in knowledge and technology" needed to launch an interstellar craft within the next one hundred years, speaks of "pursuing an extraordinary tomorrow . . . to build a better world today" (100 Year Starship, 2013). A vision of space inspiring a new vision of Earth.

Idealistic? Definitely. Sacred? Perhaps. Extraordinary goals being pursued by ordinary humans who have themselves experienced – and shared with those unable to make the trip spaceward themselves – an extraordinary vision of the planet. Perhaps this is Sacred Space 2.0, an ideation of outer space as a vantage point from which we can see ourselves, rather than as a window to gaze up at distant stars in dumbstruck awe of elusive gods. The sacred heavens have not been cast down, but simply recast. We are the new ancients on the shore looking up; only now we know that it is a two-way mirror. Those up there can also look down on us, see us stripped bare of our nationalist pretenses, and use what Frank White calls their newly-acquired "universal insight" to inspire our future (White, p. 24). In this sense, I've come full circle to what first intrigued me about space as a youngster, that is, the ways in which space informs us, not about rockets, or stars, or extraterrestrials, but about ourselves. We have challenges and roadblocks ahead to be sure. Nationalism, profit, and intolerance are strong human motivations and will likely hitch a ride to any mining platform, lunar base, or starship mission that we undertake. But there is hope. If looking up at the stars is to see the universe's own past, writ large in eons and light years, then perhaps looking down from them is also the path to imagining an extraordinary future for Earth and all the species that call it home. And I don't know of anything that is more sacred than that.

Bibliography

100 Year Starship (2013) http://www.100yss.org

Campbell, Joseph (1986/2002) *The Inner Reaches of Outer Space: Metaphor as Myth and as Religion.* Novato, CA: New World Library.

Einstein, Albert (1954) *Ideas and Opinions.* New York: Wings Books.

Garan, Ron (2015) *The Orbital Perspective: Lessons in Seeing the Big Picture from a Journey of 71 Million Miles.* Oakland, CA: Berrett-Koehler.

Harrison, Albert A. (2015) "Where Astrobiology Meets Humanistic Inquiry," *Journal of Astrosociology, 1,* pp. 11-30, 21 June.

Overview Institute, The (2012) http://www.overviewinstitute.org

Sagan, Carl (1997) *Billions & Billions: Thoughts on Life and Death at the Brink of the Millennium.* New York: Ballantine Books.

_____ (1994) *Pale Blue Dot: A Vision of the Human Future in Space.* New York: Random House.

_____ (2006) *The Varieties of Scientific Experience: A Personal View of the Search for God*, ed. A. Druyan, New York: Penguin Books.

Space Foundation (2014) *The Space Report: The Authoritative Guide to Global Space Activity.* http://www.spacefoundation.org/programs/research-and-analysis/space-report/

White, Frank (1998/2014) *The Overview Effect: Space Exploration and Human Evolution.* Reston, VA: American Institute of Aeronautics and Astronautics.

-=-

Kathleen D. Toerpe, Ph.D., is a social and cultural historian, researching the human dimension of outer space through an emerging field called "astrosociology." She is the Deputy CEO for Programs and Special Projects with the Astrosociology Research Institute, is an Executive Editor for the *Journal of Astrosociology*, and edits the newsletter, *Astrosociological Insights.* She directs the Education Special Interest Group for 100 Year Starship, preparing for future human travel beyond our solar system. She curates youth.100yss.org, serves as a 100YSS Track Chair, and volunteers as a NASA/JPL Solar System Ambassador. She provides space outreach consulting through Stellar Outreach, LLC, and teaches social sciences and critical/creative thinking courses at Northeast Wisconsin Technical College. She is on Twitter at @ktoerpe and email at stellaroutreach@gmail.com.

The Heavens Declare the Glory of God

Michael Waltemathe

Up until today all human space exploration has essentially been confined to the immediate surroundings of our home planet. While robotic probes like Voyager have been sent out into deep space, every human mission was planned to return the human explorers to the home planet. When religion was involved in the space program, as it was frequently done during the history of human space flight, all these instances thus far had been aimed at religion and religious authority here on planet Earth. Astronauts have read biblical texts from and in outer space and asked for blessings for Earth and their fellow human beings. Astronauts have performed religious ritual in space and on the surface of the Moon. Astronauts have returned to Earth changed in a spiritual way by their space experience. This phenomenon has been described by Frank White's (1987) coining of the term "The Overview Effect" and is perhaps one of the most space-specific aspects of the relation of spaceflight and religion.

Until now religion has been something humans have taken into space and/or brought back from space in a transformed way to influence religious culture here on Earth. Religion has played little role in motivating space flight until now.

With commercial space ventures entering the area of human space exploration and public and commercial initiatives to start mining asteroids and other celestial objects, we are now entering a new era of human space exploration. One sign of the advent of this new era is the recently passed "Space Resource Exploration and Utilization Act of 2015" in the USA.

These new space ventures aim at slowly extending our resource base into space and turning humanity from being an Earth-based civilization into a solar-system-based civilization and possibly over centuries causing it to spread out into the galaxy. This is literally new territory for humanity, untrodden ground, or, as it has been put rather poetically: leaving the cradle of humanity. But leaving the cradle needs an extraordinary act of motivation for humanity, and religion has played a crucial part in similar endeavors throughout human history.

What possible connection between human space exploration and religion can be imagined now that humanity may finally leave the place that religions understand as its God-given location in the cosmos? What religious perspectives are there that will enable human space exploration from the perspective of religion? What role can religion play in human space exploration when humanity will finally leave Earth for the stars? What role will religion play in the change of humanity from an Earth-bound species to a solar-system-bound, even a galaxy-bound civilization?

On the one hand, there are several examples of religion being in opposition to human space exploration, among them certain Christian groups with a strong eschatology that understands Earth as the only place for humanity to live. Also, as Rojas (2014) reports, there is a religious ruling against the Mars One Mission from an Islamic religious authority on the grounds that one-way missions to other planets are comparable to suicide and thus forbidden in Islam. This ruling essentially makes leaving Earth for other planets quite problematic.

On the other hand, aside from religious opposition, there should be other religious perspectives that foster space exploration, as religion has fostered other exploration during the history of humanity. One possible and rather obvious connection is understanding the change from Earth to solar-system-civilization as a religious journey, a voyage of faith and thus making space exploration an endeavor connected to a religious perspective.

A Voyage of Faith

There are many examples of religious texts that describe voyages of faith leading to the promised land, the holy kingdom, and so forth. These voyages have different motivations and phases. The basic structure of a voyage can be described (quite trivially, really) to have three aspects:

1. The start of a voyage is a point from which the voyager is going away.
2. The voyage itself is a process on which the voyager embarks. Usually the voyage comes with transformation.
3. Finally the voyage ends. There is a point, a goal the voyager wants to, needs to, travel to.

While religious myths know all of these and many more aspects (see Campbell 1968; Propp, 1975) (Vladimir Propp approaches the structure of fairy tale from a formalist point of view -- these ideas could be useful in analyzing a mission statement for interstellar spaceflight, but for the scope of this essay the trivial description above will suffice), this essay will take a closer look at the mythological aspects of the starting and end point of the voyage on the one hand and the process of the voyage as a religious means on the other hand, concluding with an astro-theological look at a possible connection of these aspects as a motivation for space-exploration.

First let us take a look at mythological aspects of religious voyages.

Flood mythology from different religious traditions, for example, emphasizes the religious traditions that deal with traveling away from a threat of extinction. The story of Noah's Ark is an example for just such a voyage. It even involves building a specific hermetically sealed craft for just this voyage.

Other religious traditions tell stories of persecution and oppression which need to be overcome by a similar voyage that leads the oppressed away from these circumstances. These stories usually have a specific goal in mind, a promised land, a heavenly kingdom given to the oppressed people by divine mandate or prophetic revelation.

Exodus - Going Away

Just as Noah built the Ark to evade extinction of the human race, a spaceship could serve just the same purpose. (Actually this is one of the most prevalent arguments for building an interstellar spaceship that can be found in the literature. Building such a ship is so immensely expensive that the only acceptable reason to build it is to stop the possible extinction of humanity.)

In such a situation, all religious opposition I have mentioned previously would probably become void. If the survival of humanity is at stake, religions will have to deal with that situation and not with the flight itself. Some religions may still be opposed to spaceflight, especially if they frame an extinction event as an eschatological part of their religion. Religious opposition in this instance will probably be restricted to converting nonbelievers to their own way out.

An alternative scenario would be to flee from oppression with the help of religious motivation. Just as the Pilgrim Fathers described the voyage to the New World as the voyage to the Promised Land and in which England represented Egypt and even King James I was referred to as Pharaoh, such an analogy could motivate a journey into outer space.

Tworuschka (2002) gives the following illustrating example by William Clayton, in his Hymn "Come, Come, Ye Saints".

> "We'll find the place which God for us prepared,
>
> Far away, in the West,
>
> Where none shall come to hurt or make afraid;
>
> There the saints, will be blessed." [p. 131-132]

This could easily be applied to any space exploration scenario.

The Promised Land - Going Towards the Divine

The "going-to" analogy instead of the "fleeing-from" analogy offers a lot of merit but also a different set of problems. If an interstellar space flight leads into what is thought to be the transcendental realm, opposition by religious groups is to be expected. Announcing that the ship is traveling to God or to Heaven is a sufficient analogy to the story of the Tower of Babel and will therefore guarantee at least some opposition. Those groups who will not oppose such a mission because of possible damage to God's glory or overt display of human hubris will just consider it foolhardy.

One other aspect of going to a "promised land" may need direct transcendental interference. Just as with Abraham, Noah, and Moses, a space mission might also profit from being supplied with a divine mandate.

Obviously the strategy for human space-exploration can not wait for divine intervention on its behalf. Should this happen, however, funding and motivation would still not automatically follow, as the story of Abraham shows.

On the other hand, traveling into a creation that is made for discovery is a concept that is in line with a lot of religious traditions, especially those with a strong tradition of natural theology. If one can experience the Glory of God through creation, why not go explore and learn more about the nature of God. This is probably the strongest direct religious motivation a space mission can achieve and will need to be discussed further in the light of the aspects of an individual perspective on religious voyages.

Pilgrimage – Going Out There

The aspect of traveling as a means in itself is alive in the phenomenon of pilgrimage. A pilgrim travels to a holy site or a shrine and then back home, having aimed at a religious transformation while being on the way. This aspect of religiously motivated travel can be distinguished in two forms.

On the one hand, there is the voyage to a shrine, a holy place and back, where transformation is relevant in regard to the starting position to which the pilgrim returns.

On the other hand, the pilgrimage itself becomes the whole process. Transformation is the goal in itself. The German language knows the distinction between "Pilgerfahrt" and "Wallfahrt". One could try and describe this as the difference between pilgrim (traveler) and peregrine (alien).

Pilgrimage as such is the distance one travels to transform oneself, without a necessary geographical goal, while peregrinage is the voyage one undertakes to a shrine and back, being the stranger at the holy site as opposed to being at home and not being at the holy site (for a discussion of this aspects see Tworuschka, 2002).

Certain aspects of religious voyages, of pilgrimage or peregrinage, might be useful in describing a possible connection between religious motivation and human space exploration.

Probably the most powerful aspect of motivation for human space exploration is pilgrimage. As mentioned above, this idea takes the religious aspect down to the individual level. A pilgrim is basically alone, trying to achieve transformation on an individual level. If one's personal beliefs are in accordance with the parallels between religious ideas and space travel, individual motivation in a religious sense can thus easily be achieved.

But how can this be achieved by including religious traditions that do not share this personal belief?

A feasible concept could be to concentrate on the individual pilgrim's relation to religion. Even if the pilgrim is alone on his or her voyage, seeking individual transformation, the voyage itself usually follows the footsteps of giants, of religious traditions, religious leaders and such. This dichotomy between individual religion and religious tradition can be further explained and broken down by taking a look at a theory of religious experience which focuses on the individual's construction of faith: Peter Berger's (1997) idea that religion is socially constructed and transferred on an individual level.

Humility and Simulated Religion

Berger argues that both the religious experience and the comical relieve us from the tension and fundamental anxiety of our paramount reality and enable shifts in the "accent" of reality. Relying on Alfred Schutz's analysis of *Don Quixote*, Berger points out that the act of faith brings about a shift in the accent of reality due to what Berger calls the epistemological reversal:

> The paramount reality of everyday life is relativized; conversely, the specific finite province of meaning to which faith pertains is absolutized. Needless to say, it is finite only in the perspective of the paramount reality. As the epistemological reversal occurs, it is, on the contrary, the threshold of infinity; conversely, the empirical world, far from being paramount, is disclosed as being very finite indeed.[p. 205]

Berger goes on to argue that humor and religion enable us to look at ourselves and our problems from a perspective well outside the world of working in daily life and can thus be seen as structurally equivalent in regard to the life-world. Now, the act of faith is usually a lot more consequential than just telling a good joke, but still, the similarities are obvious. As does religion, the comic can provide us with a sense of epistemological humility. The act of faith is what distinguishes the religious sphere from the secular. Once one has taken that leap, one will regard the world of religion as the paramount reality and all the other worlds of the life-world as being grounded in it. Humor can provide the individual with a certain humility, that is, the ability to look at different systems of faith and play with them, recognize their ultimate value for their followers, and simulate what it would be like to take this system for granted.

It can thus be argued that pilgrimage as a lifelong journey works in analogy to what Berger states as the connection between humor and faith. A pilgrim is on the way, trying to experience transformation. This process is ongoing, for some never-ending. Only after or during a long journey will the pilgrim reach transformation and in between have often encountered experiences similar to humor, where suddenly everything turned out to be different than it seemed, where former knowledge was cast into doubt. While religious knowledge and the perception of religious tradition may change during such a journey, the existence of the religious knowledge in the first place is what enables the transformation. Religion and humor not only differ through the act of faith and the persistence of the epistemological reversal but also through the existence of socially handed-down knowledge.

The analogy of the pilgrimage for human space exploration understood in this way enables the mission to describe itself in terms that are analogous to religious terms without interfering in the religious domain. Being a pilgrim, a seeker, someone who looks at the world constantly from all possible worlds that make up one's life-world enables one to experience religion as a process not a given fact. Even if Berger is only partially right, as many factors (some possibly transcendental) influence the final act of faith and not one single choice, there is a lot of merit to the idea that religion is a way of giving a new perspective on all other aspects of the life-world.

Motivation for human space exploration needs to draw from just such a perspective. Going away from everything that is familiar into the alien realm of outer space is an act that transforms one's vision of all other aspects of the life-world, even religion as one's personal faith (see the Overview Effect). But in addition to being one's personal faith, Berger points out, religion is socially constructed. The individual chooses themes and patterns of religious content from a symbolic universe that society erected over time (Berger, 1990). Such an understanding of religion is not only reliant on the individual perspective but also on the kind of religious tradition that allows the individual to draw ideas for personal choice.

Some of the content of religious universes already is used in popular culture and in civil religion to foster the idea of space travel. The Mormon Trail as a metaphor for the journey of the Israelites to the Promised Land has already been mentioned. Other examples are science fiction stories which draw from the multiple symbolic universes of different religions to construct space travel scenarios ripe with religious metaphor. (As Henderson, 1997, shows, Joseph Campbell's idea of the structure of the mono-mythical story can be used to explain these phenomena and to ground space travel in religious mythology.)

Traveling into Creation

Presenting human space exploration as a symbolic universe with aspects of different religious traditions enables these traditions to relate to the space project, and applies to individuals and organizations alike. But what is the common denominator, the main aspect of such motivation?

While a pilgrimage draws on religious tradition and mythology that give the voyage religious framing, the voyage itself needs purpose, too. I briefly mentioned the idea that a space mission could be understood as a voyage into creation, a voyage that teaches us more about the nature of God. Every pilgrimage – while aimed at individual transformation – knows this aspect. The traveler, the voyager, wants to also learn about his or her relationship to God. If this is an aspect of traveling out into creation and thus learning about God's glory in the larger universe, religion becomes a strong motivating factor for human space exploration. The theology behind this motivation, however, needs to enable the faithful to understand this connection. It needs to overcome the understanding of Earth as the sole place of creation and give humanity the perspective of its place in the whole universe. The necessary humility for this understanding should come, one hopes, from an understanding of religion as a perspective from well outside this world!

If indeed the heavens declare the glory of God, as the Psalmist says, it seems to be our destiny to go out there and try to discover more about the heavens and the divine nature to which they testify.

Bibliography

Berger, Peter L. (1990) *The Sacred Canopy*, New York, NY: Anchor Press.

_____ (1997) *Redeeming Laughter: The Comic Dimension of Human Experience*, New York: Walter de Gruyter.

Campbell, Joseph (1968) *The Hero with a Thousand Faces*, Princeton, NJ: Princeton University Press

Henderson, Mary S. (1997) *Star Wars - The Magic of Myth*, New York: Spectra.

Propp, Vladimir (1975) *Morphology of the Folk Tale*, Austin, TX: University of Texas Press.

Rojas, Alejandro (2014) "Islamic Leaders Issue Fatwa Prohibiting One-Way Trips to Mars," retrieved 9 December 2015. http://www.huffingtonpost.com/alejandro-rojas/fatwa-prohibiting-mars-trip_b_4833445.html

Tworuschka, Udo (2002) *Heilige Wege: Die Reise zu Gott in den Weltreligionen*, Frankfurt, Germany: Lembeck.

White, Frank (1987) *The Overview Effect: Space Exploration and Human Evolution.* Boston: Houghton Mifflin.

Space Exploration as a Religious Pilgrimage

Juan Pablo Marrufo del Toro, SJ

Space exploration and religion have more in common than one may think. In the Christian religion, we often say that the universe is a manifestation of God's love. The more we know about the universe, the more we learn about God, its creator. Scientific enterprise and space exploration give us knowledge about the universe. But we gain more than knowledge when we explore space: we embark on a journey to the deeper sense of the Holy. We embark on a pilgrimage.

A pilgrimage is a journey to a Holy place. Famous pilgrimage sites include Mecca in Saudi Arabia, Santiago de Compostela in Spain, St. Peter's in the Vatican, Our Lady of Lourdes in France, and Our Lady of Guadalupe in Mexico City. These places, among many, are visited by millions of people searching for deeper meaning, healing and answers to their questions. Those of us who have embarked on pilgrimages may or may not find the answers to our questions; regardless, the journey is what matters. It is in the journey that we find the holiness within us. We have many examples, both in real life and in movies and novels, of space exploration as a religious pilgrimage:

Astronauts in the Apollo VIII mission prayed with the Book of Genesis; astronaut Buzz Aldrin of Apollo XI took Holy Communion on the Moon. Islamic holidays, Chanukah, and Christmas have been celebrated on the International Space Station.

There are many examples in the entertainment industry of the intersection between space exploration and religion, such as in the movie *Gravity*, in which Dr. Ryan Stone (Sandra Bullock) was asking whoever was on the radio to pray for her, saying that no one had ever taught her to pray. There is also an icon of St. Christopher on the dashboard of Stone's space capsule.

In ABC's TV series *Defying Gravity*, astronaut Paula Morales was a devout woman who wore a religious necklace. The popular series *Star Trek* has several examples of the intersection between religion and space exploration, such as in the movie *Star Trek V: The Final Frontier* in which the Enterprise is hijacked by Spock's charismatic half-brother on a quest (a pilgrimage) to meet God at the center of the galaxy. C. S. Lewis' "Space Trilogy" of fantasy novels *Out of the Silent Planet*, *Perelandra*, and *That Hideous Strength* portray an English language professor who finds himself swept up in a spiritual war that takes him to Mars, Venus, and back to Earth. And let us not forget *The Sparrow* and *Children of God* by Mary Doria Russell (1996; 1998), in which Jesuit priests go on space missions to other civilizations in the galaxy.

As we can see, space exploration can be interpreted as a religious experience. Besides the gathering of information and research that can be done in space, what makes it a religious experience is that the universe is a Holy place: it can place us in contact with the divine. According to Christianity, the whole of creation is made by God with love. The universe is fundamentally good and blessed by God. (Gn. 1). Space is a place where many people are able to have a religious experience.

Many people define themselves as "spiritual but non-religious;" this indicates a break from organized religion but still a belief in the divine. Also, many people express that they do not go to church but, rather, worship God in nature. God makes Godself manifest to people as God seems most fit. For many, finding God in nature and the universe is sufficient. As they are on a journey toward the divine, space exploration can be a way of strengthening this relationship with the divine. Either way, we all are in a journey, a spiritual journey. Space exploration is part of that. Space exploration is the journey of our civilization.

When we explore space, we are trying to answer our deepest questions: Who are we, where do we come from? What is our purpose and the purpose of the universe? These questions also have a place in religion. We are a species that believes, that hopes, that dreams. We define ourselves, most of the time, by those characteristics and attitudes: our hopes, dreams and beliefs are what make us unique. They are what make us human.

Space exploration has allowed us to see our planet, our world, from a very different lens. We can see our planet as part of the creation, as part of this holy place, thanks to the pictures taken by the Apollo and voyager missions. As Carl Sagan (1997) says in his famous *Pale Blue Dot*:

> From this distant vantage point, the Earth might not seem of any particular interest. But for us, it's different. Consider again that dot. That's here. That's home. That's us. On it everyone you love, everyone you know, everyone you ever heard of, every human being who ever was, lived out their lives. The aggregate of our joy and suffering, thousands of confident religions, ideologies, and economic doctrines, every hunter and forager, every hero and coward, every creator and destroyer of civilization, every king and peasant, every young couple in love, every mother and father, hopeful child, inventor and explorer, every teacher of morals, every corrupt politician, every "superstar," every "supreme leader," every saint and sinner in the history of our species lived there – on a mote of dust suspended in a sunbeam.

Our civilization keeps dreaming. We keep believing. Space exploration has allowed us to see our civilization and ourselves in a deeper, more meaningful and challenging way. This is the wonder of our journey, of our pilgrimage, which we just have begun.

Space, being also part of the creation of our loving God, is a holy place. A place that brings us closer to the reality of our hopes, of our dreams, of our beliefs. That is why space exploration is a religious experience too; it places us in contact with our deepest questions and our deepest fears. It places us in contact with the places in which God dwells in our hearts.

We may find what we look for as we explore space; we may not, but, as in every pilgrimage, it is in the journey of our exploration that we can learn more about us and about God. We find God simply by being on the pilgrimage toward the depths of the universe.

Bibliography

Cuaron, Alfonso & Cuaron, Jonas (directors) (2014) *Gravity*, motion picture. Warner.

Gerber, Fred (director) (2009) *Defying Gravity*, television series. 20th-Century Fox Home Entertainment.

Lewis, C. S. (1938, 1943, 1945) *Space Trilogy* London, UK: Bodley Head.

Russell, Mary D. (1996) *The Sparrow*, New York: Villard Books.

_____ (1998) *Children of God*, New York, NY: Villard.

Sagan, Carl (1997) *Pale Blue Dot: A Vision of the Human Future in Space*, New York: Ballantine.

Shatner, William (director) (1989) *Star Trek V: The Final Frontier*, motion picture. Paramount.

-=-

Fr. Juan Pablo Marrufo del Toro, SJ, is a native of Guadalajara, Mexico, where he studied physics and business graduating in 2001. He joined the Jesuits in 2003 and was ordained a Roman Catholic Priest in 2015. As a Jesuit, he earned an M.A. in philosophy in 2009 from Loyola University Chicago where he was a telescope operator for the Adler Planetarium. Upon completion of his degree, Fr. Marrufo-del-Toro has worked as a teacher of mathematics and physics and was also a campus minister at Jesuit schools in the USA and Colombia. He has also worked for the Vatican Observatory doing stellar photometry and Public Relations. Currently, he is studying spirituality and science at the Jesuit School of Theology of Santa Clara University in Berkeley, California.

Did Jesus Die for Klingons, Too? Christian Faith and Extraterrestrial Salvation

Christian Weidemann

Alien Sinners

Suppose the universe teems with civilizations. Are we to expect that most or all other rational species are, like us, 'fallen'? Do members of these species commit murder, theft and (if sexually reproducing) rape? Are they often or at least sometimes greedy, envious, lazy, lying or coward?

It might seem that, unless you are a science fiction writer who needs to make a living, the most sensible reaction to this kind of questions is suspending judgment. Without contact, how are we supposed to know anything about extraterrestrial psychology? Closer analysis, however, reveals that taking such an agnostic stance is mistaken for at least two reasons:

1. If there are life forms on other planets at all, they, very probably, have been gradually shaped by natural selection in just the same way as terrestrial organisms. Natural selection, however, favors the development of "selfish" traits aimed at reproductive success. Therefore, everyone who accepts common descent on Earth and who ascribes an important role to natural selection within the evolutionary process seems forced to concede that, very probably, extraterrestrial intelligent beings inherited a strong inclination to certain immoral activities from their phylogenetic ancestry. Surely, terms like "selfish" or "immoral" only make metaphorical sense when applied to life forms that cannot discriminate between right and wrong. However, this clarification is perfectly compatible with the claim that biological traits responsible for the human or extraterrestrial proneness to literal selfishness already originated in phylogenetically earlier life forms. You might object that members of terrestrial species occasionally display extreme forms of "altruistic" behavior as well, e. g., when sacrificing their own life for the benefit of their kin or group. Darwinists had a hard time to explain the evolution of "altruism," and with respect to the emergence of complex ethical thinking in humans it is, arguably, still an open question whether evolutionary explanations will prove sufficient. On the other hand, no evolutionary psychologist would deem it worthwhile to start a research program on whether killing a rival or cheating has sometimes fitness-enhancing effects. The answers are just too obvious.

2. The Principle of Mediocrity tells you, roughly, to reason as if you were a random sample from the set of all intelligent observers at stake. If we ask ourselves what extraterrestrial intelligent beings may be like, we should assume – unless we have made some kind of contact – that most of them are not radically different from us.

Why is this a sensible advice? Imagine the following two thought experiments:

1. An opaque urn contains 1000 balls. A tombola is arranged and 1000 tickets are sold. Peter buys a ticket. He knows that there are only black and white balls in the urn and that the winning ball is the only one of its kind. He does not know, however, which color the winning ball is. He draws a black ball. He concludes that, very probably, the winning ball is white.

2. Ms. X awakens in an empty and windowless room suffering from retrograde amnesia. She has lost all her personal memories; she does not even remember what the language she speaks is called. Her demographical knowledge, however, remained intact. To start somewhere, she begins wondering what her nationality might be. She concludes that there is a great chance of her being Chinese or Indian.

These inferences are perfectly reasonable, notwithstanding that someone might insist: "But couldn't it be that Peter actually drew the winning ball or that Ms. X was born in Liechtenstein?" It could be, of course, but it is highly unlikely. In the same vein, human sinners who lack any empirical evidence on the moral character of extraterrestrial intelligent observers in the universe must not suppose that evildoers are members of a highly exclusive group in the cosmos (like lottery winners and Liechtensteinians on Earth).

Alien Salvation

Christians believe (i) that a person who has done morally wrong is in need of divine salvation and (ii) that God will save many (according to universalism: all) human sinners. Now, given God's omnibenevolence and omnipotence, it is extremely plausible to suppose that He will save many extraterrestrial sinners, too. Even if the Christian theist denies that God is morally perfect and/or omnipotent or if she thinks that God has no moral reason, let alone obligation, to save anybody, the principle of mediocrity cautions her not to assume that among the myriad of sinful species in the universe only members of *Homo sapiens* are recipients of God's unmerited grace.

Finally, traditional Christians believe (iii) that Jesus Christ plays an essential part in God's terrestrial work of salvation: Jesus was a divine incarnation whose atonement (suffering, teaching, good example ...) will ultimately reconcile many (or all) human sinners to God. The crucial problem is how God is supposed to save extraterrestrial sinners. There are three jointly exhaustive alternatives: Either a) Jesus died for them as well, or b) they will be reconciled to God by another divine incarnation, presumably on their home planet, or (c) they will be saved by means different from a divine incarnation.

I shall now argue that all three alternatives lead to highly problematic consequences. Traditional Christian faith and belief in multitudinous extraterrestrial civilizations are in deep conflict. My argument is unaffected by how the alleged reconciliation to God via the life and death of Christ is supposed to work exactly – a complex and hotly debated topic among Christians. What seems uncontroversial to me, however, is that all traditional Christians agree that the incarnation of Christ somehow does the soteriological trick for human beings.

Soteriological Geocentrism Rejected

Suppose a biblical literalist endorses the Epistle to the Colossians 1, 20 – "And, having made peace through the blood of his cross, by him to reconcile all things unto himself; by him, I say, whether they be things in Earth, or things in heaven" – as a statement on exotheology. What would be wrong with that? It is tempting to charge the literalist with anthropocentric hubris or "intergalactic chauvinism". This would be a premature objection, however, since the soteriological geocentrist need not think that human or planetary grandeur persuaded God to incarnate, of all places, here on Earth. Consider, for instance, the humble rhetoric of 19th century theologian and geocentrist Joseph Pohle:

> God descended to Earth, although, from a cosmic standpoint, it is one of the most insignificant and most miserable celestial bodies. Therein lies the truly divine character of this salvific act; God does not choose the great and powerful, but takes care of the weak and tiny with a loving eye. Not in a royal palace the word incarnate was born, but in a barn; not on a magnificent planet of some handsome binary star system God became human, but on this tiny grain of sand, Earth.

The problem with soteriological geocentrism is not ethical or psychological, but epistemological in nature. Like the Ptolemaic brand of geocentrism, it blatantly violates the principle of mediocrity. True enough, the epistemological weight of the principle, which teaches us to deem our position average, decreases the more information on our actual situation we possess. When a player missed the lottery results she should, until further notice, assume that her position among the fellow-players is average, i.e. that she lost her wager. However, through reading her winning numbers in a newspaper, calling the lottery company that hereupon confirmed her hitting the jackpot, and finally through checking her bank account, she might learn that her position is very special indeed.

Correspondingly, is there any analogous evidence that Earth plays a special role in God's plan for cosmic salvation, i.e. that God chose our planet among billions of candidates as the stage for his incarnation? I do not think so.

To begin with, the prior probability of finding oneself on exactly the planet God chose for his unique incarnation among billions or trillions of alternatives is lower than even the chance of hitting a lottery jackpot. There have been some serious attempts to make an inductive case for the historicity of the resurrection of Jesus. Whatever the merits of such arguments, they can, at best, make plausible that miraculous, i.e., naturalistically unexplainable, events happened 2000 years ago in the Near East. However, such arguments are unable to show, in principle, that the protagonist at that time, Jesus of Nazareth, was, though truly human, God himself! The Chalcedonian Christology (Christ as "truly God and truly man") was the result of a subsequent process of theological interpretation and rationalization, which never took into account that God had possibly a myriad of other inhabited planets at his disposal.

It is true that most Christians do not believe in Jesus as the "Son of God," because they have been convinced to do so by inductive or a priori arguments. That Jesus was God incarnate, suffered and rose from the dead, just seems true to them – without elaborated argument. Many Christian thinkers have tried to show that trusting the deliverances of alleged revelation or religious experience can be reasonable even without empirical evidence or philosophical argument. Even if we concede, for the sake of argument, that some religious beliefs can be defended against criticism along those lines, this will be of little help for the geocentrist. First, and most important, it is very doubtful whether a divine incarnation can be experienced as such or whether it could be the subject of a revelation or of "properly basic beliefs" as such. It is one thing to experience a numinous presence, or to form, while reading Scripture, the basic belief that Jesus rose from the dead; it is quite another thing to have the experience or basic belief that a concept as abstract as divine incarnation was exemplified in Jesus. Nobody would accept statements like "I have the impression that string theory is wrong" or "substance dualism just seems true to me" as viable justifications for corresponding scientific or philosophical beliefs, at least if put forward without giving further arguments. Why should Christology that involves similarly difficult and opaque concepts be different? Second, even conceded that, per impossibile, belief in a divine incarnation could be warranted on the basis of religious experience, education, or revelation alone, it thereby does not gain incorrigible or infallible status. Even my (putatively self-evident) basic belief, that there is a desk in front of me, would be defeated if I learned that my wife had dropped some LSD in my morning coffee.

Traditional-minded Christians at least implicitly accept the idea that their basic theistic beliefs are subject to correction. This can best be seen in cases of religious lunacy: Suppose a Christian believer declares, "It just seems true to me, that God told me to blast the schools of infidels." Every sane person, theistic and atheistic alike, would consider it a good thing to dissuade that individual from his or her corresponding basic theistic belief (if necessary in a mental institution).

Once this is admitted, there is no longer room for denying a priori that the basic theistic belief that God incarnated himself on Earth, if there is such a basic belief at all, might be defeated by learning that a myriad of extraterrestrial civilizations exist. And the argument of the present paper at least provides a strong prima facie case that it would indeed be defeated.

Multiple Incarnations Rejected

The Confession of Chalcedon (451 AD), which is still binding for most Christian denominations, determined the famous phrase according to which Jesus Christ was "truly God and truly man," but as "one and the same" person, though "in two natures." Now, obviously, the proponents of multiple incarnations have to suppose that corresponding statements hold for incarnations on other planets. Otherwise, the outstanding soteriological status of humankind would just be reinstalled through the back door, again blatantly violating the principle of mediocrity. So let us assume that there are, besides Jesus, incarnations who are "truly God and truly Klingon," "truly God, and truly Alpha Centaurian," and so on. Then the following problem immediately crops up: According to Chalcedon, Jesus of Nazareth is personally identical with the second person of the Trinity; the latter in turn is personally identical with the redeemer of Alpha Centauri, the Klingon savior, and so on. Since the relation of identity is transitive (the Morning Star is identical with Venus; Venus is identical with the Evening Star; therefore, the Evening Star is identical with the Morning Star), Jesus of Nazareth is personally identical with his counterparts at Alpha Centauri, Kronos, and at innumerous other places.

That members of completely different biological species ("truly man," "truly Alpha Centaurian") are supposed to stand in a relationship of diachronic personal identity is already something most people will find too hard to stomach. Even worse, if the number of sinful species in the universe exceeds a certain threshold, God (the second person of the Trinity) would be forced to incarnate himself simultaneously. (The purported difficulties that the Special Theory of Relativity poses to the notion of cosmic simultaneity will be ignored here). For instance, given, say, 100 billion extraterrestrial civilizations in need of salvation so far, an average incarnation time of 30 years, and roughly 12 billion years since the first emergence of habitable planets, God's incarnations would on average have had to live at 250 places simultaneously, in order to accommodate all sinful civilizations! If these numbers strike you as far-fetched, reflect on the more than 100 billion stars in our galaxy, on the more than 100 billion galaxies in the visible universe and on the idea of an enormously (perhaps infinitely) big multiverse, advocated by many prominent cosmologists.

It is obvious, I think, that no matter which reasonably serious position in the philosophy of mind one may adopt, the conclusion will always be the same. No single person who is an embodied being, a "truly" biological organism, can be more than one such being at the same time. The same corporeal being simply cannot exist at many distant places simultaneously.

Other Means of Salvation Rejected

May extraterrestrial sinners have been reconciled, or are they going to be reconciled, to God by means different from a divine incarnation? C. S. Lewis speculates: "To different diseases, or even different patients sick with the same disease, the great Physician may have applied different remedies."

Would it not still be implausible in the extreme to suppose that on Earth, of all places, God's unique incarnation took place? Let us consider the following argument to the contrary: If God wanted to save humankind he had to choose some means. If he chose a different way of redeeming the human race, this soteriological alternative would have struck the critics as just as improbable or exceptional as did his incarnation. These people behave like the conspiracy theorist who proclaimed after watching the roulette table for a while: "Isn't it amazing. The last numbers have been 12, 34, 5, 18, and 27. You know what the probability for this sequence was. 1: 69.343.957." True enough, but some numbers had to fall. Some way of salvation God had to choose. The actual outcome is nothing to be amazed at.

Admittedly, not every improbable event is in need of explanation. The roulette sequence does not become remarkable by the sheer fact that one would have to wait many lifetimes in order to see it again. Nor is my existence rendered remarkable by how my parents' genes might have combined in trillions of ways that did not yield me.

Suppose I have made an astonishing discovery while searching a genetic sequence database: a certain Peter seems to have a genome almost identical to mine. I ask the database officials to explain this coincidence. My suspicion is that Peter is either my forgotten twin, or a clone, or, most probably, that someone screwed up the data. The officials' answer, however, denies all these possibilities: "The sheer fact that you have the genome you have and Peter has the genome he has, is nothing to be surprised about. Every other combination of your two genomes would have been just as improbable. Please don't waste our time."

Of course, nobody would accept such an answer. The actual combination of Peter's and my genome is not just improbable; it stands out against almost all other possible combinations and therefore cries out for an explanation.

In just the same vein, God's incarnation stands out against other means of redemption. The reason for this is not that God's becoming human constitutes a special act of his love. God is morally perfect; everything he does is informed by his unsurpassable holy nature. Of course, not everything God does or refrains from doing is equally recognizable as proof of his love (problem of evil). However, if God aimed for clarity, he would have had more unambiguous proofs of love at his disposal than an incarnation whose authenticity was, and is, rejected by so many people, this rejection not being obviously unreasonable. Christians themselves usually believe that only after death will they experience indubitable proofs of divine love (visio beatifica).

God's incarnation stands out for a different reason: God could have refrained from creating a world inhabited by beings capable of sin and suffering. It was neither metaphysically necessary to bring about such a world nor would anyone have been wronged by his refraining from creating it. (Nobody can be wronged, unless she exists.) That means that God is at least co-responsible for all the suffering in the world. Therefore, it seems appropriate (and perhaps even obligatory) to share the misery of his creatures at least at one occasion. Thus, he incarnates himself. Such a presumably unique (see above) act of solidarity would be one of the most remarkable events in the history of the cosmos. To claim that it happens just 2000 years ago on our planet is therefore, given widespread intelligent life in the cosmos, an extremely strong statement; a statement that needs a correspondingly strong justification. As far as I can see, neither historical evidence, nor Scripture nor ordinary basic theistic beliefs will be able to provide anything as powerful as would be required.

Options for the Christian Believer

I conclude that either a part of the traditional Christian doctrine or belief in the pervasiveness of extraterrestrial intelligence (ETI) has to be abandoned by rational theists.

The most obvious obstacle that stands in the way of reconciling traditional Christianity with ETI seems to be the Christological doctrine of Chalcedon. This doctrine could be modified in two ways that unfortunately both have been deemed heretical by the early church. First, it could be denied that Jesus was "truly God," as e.g. Arians, Unitarians and Deists have done. According to such a conception, God is neither personally identical with Jesus nor with any other corporeal being in the cosmos, which would make it unproblematic to assume that the Klingons and Alpha Centaurians had their own messiahs.

Second, it could be denied that Jesus was "truly man," as the ancient Docetists did. According to such a conception, Christ was only disguised as man, a human only in appearance, which would make it unproblematic to claim that all the cosmic redeemers, whether they live successively or simultaneously, are the same person with the same single divine nature.

Alternatively, the Christian believer could stick to the doctrine of Chalcedon by rejecting the ETI-hypothesis. At least as long as no infinite multiverse theory will be established, and given the highly speculative character of astrobiology, even a radical skepticism with respect to ETI is not wholly without merit. Note, for instance, that the fact that our planet teems with organisms tells us very little about the frequency of life in the cosmos. If the preconditions for intelligent life were such that only one planet in the universe meets them we would find ourselves on just that planet (weak anthropic principle).

Suppose my argument has convinced a traditional Christian believer that there are no (or at best, very, very few) other civilizations in the cosmos. This will have interesting consequences for her belief system. I will briefly mention two of them.

Indeterminism and Divine Providence

According to the standard Copenhagen interpretation of quantum mechanics, events at the quantum level are ontologically indeterminate. According to the standard cosmological model, what comes out of the Big Bang singularity was ontologically indeterminate as well. If so, how can God make sure that his providential aims, like the emergence of intelligent life, will be realized? There are, roughly, three kinds of answers available for the theist. First, she can maintain that God infallibly foreknows even ontologically indeterminate events. It is, however, very difficult to see how such an ability is supposed to be possible. Second, she can claim that God miraculously intervenes during cosmic history. The main problem here is that such subsequent repairing looks more like an inefficient kludge than like the work of a perfect designer. Why did God not create a universe that inevitably leads to intelligent life in the first place? Or third, the theist can hold that—even if, say, the emergence of life on Earth-like planets is extremely improbable, and even if it was extremely unlikely that the fundamental physical constants of our universe fell into a life permitting range—God (almost) made sure that life will emerge, simply by arranging for an enormous quantity of Earth-like planets and/or universes.

Here is the problem with this proposal: If the probability of the emergence of intelligent life via random means in the cosmos is very close to one, very probably, intelligent life forms have emerged multiple times. (Given the emergence of intelligent life somewhere does not inhibit the emergence of intelligent life everywhere else.) You can easily see this as follows: Suppose a mad scientist has kidnapped Ann. The lunatic is going to kill her, unless a fair coin is flipped and tails comes up. Ann can choose in advance how many successive flips are made. If none of the coin flips comes up tails she will be shot, if at least one comes up tails she will be released after the last flip. Every day just one coin will be flipped.

Understandably, Ann is not eager to share the mad scientist's company any longer than necessary. On the other hand, she very much wants to survive the episode. How many coin flips should she demand? There is, of course, no single correct answer to this question. Ten coin flips, e.g., will leave Ann with a risk of dying of roughly 0.1 %; 25 coin flips would give her a chance of survival of roughly 33 million to 1. For all practical purposes, this might be enough. However, with 25 coin flips it is exorbitantly probable that tails will come up more than once. Moreover, for God who aims at realizing his central providential goals by indeterministic means, even a chance of 30 million to 1 might nowhere big enough. Therefore, a theist who believes in the uniqueness of intelligent life in the cosmos should be very skeptical with respect to the third option mentioned above. Given the problems of the other two alternatives, it might be a good idea for her to re-evaluate the standard interpretations of quantum mechanics and Big Bang singularity.

Christianity and Interstellar Spaceflight

There is yet another problem for a (scientifically educated) theist who believes in the uniqueness of (intelligent) life. If God made nothing in vain, why is the immensity of space almost devoid of complex life or other similarly interesting things? From the perspective of a divine creator, there seems to be no point in repeating the same dull cosmic structures over and over again. Even the inner workings of a worm or of a blade of grass are more intricate than the life cycle of a star. It is true, we got used to the fascinating pictures taken by the Hubble-telescope, but here clearly is an aesthetic bias at work. We got to see only a small and very carefully polished part of reality. Closer to the truth seems the remark of one of Stanislaw Lem's characters, "A dotted nothingness going on and on into infinity – who would contrive such a witless thing if it had yet to be created? Only a cretin, surely."

If God is no cretin, what is the universe all about? For a theist who thinks we are and will remain alone, one answer suggests itself: The empty cosmos is intended for human flourishing, i.e., for exploration and colonization. This is a surprising result. Careful reflection on the problem of extraterrestrial salvation will tend to turn traditional Christians into interstellar flight enthusiasts (given they do not believe in near doom and are amenable to rational argument). Moreover, unlike most atheist or agnostic proponents of space exploration, the Christian theist need neither be bothered by close relatives of the Fermi-paradox—"If space colonization is technically feasible, why don't we see anybody else doing it?"—nor by ethical concerns of a certain kind—"Are we going to harm the habitats of extraterrestrial persons?" Perhaps, in the end, only religious motivations will be strong enough to overcome the numerous obstacles of interstellar spacecraft.

Acknowledgments

Work on this paper was part of a project on "Randomness and Divine Providence," generously funded by the John Templeton Foundation. Thanks to Christoph Jäger, Christian Tapp and Michael Waltemathe for helpful discussion.

Bibliographical Remarks

The first six paragraphs of this essay are largely based on a more technical paper: "Christian Soteriology and Extraterrestrial Intelligence," *Journal of the British Interplanetary Society, 67/11* (2014), pp.418-425. A different German version that includes some historical discussion can be found here: http://www.theomag.de/89/cw2.htm.

I first held a talk titled "Did Jesus Die for Klingons too?" at the 100 Year Starship Study Conference in Orlando, Florida, in 2011.

Arguments for the incompatibility of Christian soteriology and extraterrestrial intelligence have a fascinating history. They can be traced back to Melanchthon and, arguably, the Middle Ages. See the excellent historical monographs by S. J. Dick (1982) and M.J. Crowe (1986).

Author of the argument's most famous (and infamous) version is American Founding Father and enfant terrible Thomas Paine (1974) in his work *The Age of Reason*, 1794:

> From whence, then, could arise the solitary and strange conceit that the Almighty, who had millions of worlds equally dependent on His protection, should quit the care of all the rest, and come to die in our world, because, they say, one man and one woman had eaten an apple?
>
> And, on the other hand, are we to suppose that every world in the boundless creation had an Eve, an apple, a serpent and a redeemer? In this case, the person who is irreverently called the Son of God, and sometimes God Himself, would have nothing to do than to travel from world to world in an endless succession of deaths with scarcely a momentary interval of life.

To my mind, the best version of the anti-Christian argument so far is due to an anonymous German deist:

Anonymus: *Theologischer Briefwechsel eines Laien über die Versöhnung unsers Planeten und anderer Welten mit Gott durch Christum [Theological Correspondence of a Layman on the Reconciliation of Our Planet and Other Worlds to God through Christ]*, Leipzig 1782.

The almost forgotten text and some (German) speculations about its author can be found here: http://www.theomag.de/89/cw1.htm

C. S. Lewis provides an elegant, though too simplistic, overview of the problem: *Religion and Rocketry* (1958). Lewis has also pursued the topic in his *Space Trilogy.*

My argument against multiple incarnations is indebted to R. Puccetti (1968) especially pp. 137 ff.

To my knowledge, the term "Principle of Mediocrity" has been coined by astrophysicist Alexander Vilenkin (2006). Another similar "Copernican" principle can be found in Gott (1993).

For intriguing philosophical discussions of "anthropic reasoning,' consult J. Leslie (1989) and Nick Bostrom (2002).

Quotes are from J. Pohle (1906) [my translation] and Stanislaw Lem (1977) from his story "King Globares and the Sages".

Bibliography

Bostrom, Nick (2002) *Anthropic Bias: Observation Selection Effects in Science and Philosophy.* New York: Routledge.

Crowe, Michael J. (1986) *The Extraterrestrial Life Debate, 1750-1900: The Idea of a Plurality of Worlds from Kant to Lowell.* Cambridge, UK: Cambridge University Press.

Dick, Steven J. (1982) *Plurality of Worlds: The Origins of the Extraterrestrial Life Debate from Democritus to Kant.* Cambridge, UK: Cambridge University Press.

Gott, J. Richard (1993) "Implications of the Copernican Principle for our Future Prospects," *Nature, 363*, pp. 315-319.

Lem, Stanislaw (1977) *Mortal Engines.* New York: Seabury Press.

Leslie, John (1998) *The End of the World the Science and Ethics of Human Extinction.* London: Routledge.

Lewis, C. S. (1960) *The World's Last Night, and Other Essays.* New York: Harcourt, Brace.

Paine, Thomas (1793-1794) *The Age of Reason*, reprint ed., 1974. Secaucus, N.J.: Citadel Press.

Pohle, Joseph (1906) *Die Sternenwelten und ihre Bewohner zugleich als erste Einführung in die moderne Astronomie.* Köln: J.P. Bachem.

Puccetti, Roland (1968) Persons: A Study of Possible Moral Agents in the Universe. London: Macmillan.

Vilenkin, Alex (2006) *Many Worlds in One: The Search for other Universes.* New York: Hill and Wang.

-=-

Christian Weidemann, Ph.D., is a philosopher and Assistant Professor (Wiss. Mitarbeiter) at the University of Innsbruck. His main areas of interest are philosophy of religion, philosophy of science, and Enlightenment thought. He is author of an award-winning monograph on "The Indispensability of Natural Theology" (in German: Freiburg 2007). Recent talks and papers include: "Analytic Philosophers on 'Why is There Anything Rather than Nothing?'," "The Origin of Life: Why the Chance Hypothesis Should Not Be Dismissed Too Easily," "Sex with Someone I Love. The Ethics of Masturbation," and "Why are More Boys Born than Girls? A Short History of the Problem."

Anticipating the Contours of Extraterrestrial Religion

Peter M. J. Hess

Let's imagine a group of space farers relaxing in the lounge of their starship heading toward Gliese 581-d, Kapteyn-b, or some other relatively nearby star with a potentially habitable planet in the "Goldilocks zone" (Dvorsky, 2014) As they hurtle through interstellar space, our astronauts speculate with a mixture of uncertainty, apprehension, and excitement about a host of practical and theoretical issues facing them. Will they find the planet already inhabited by intelligent life? What physical, chemical, or meteorological conditions might have shaped the contours of that species' experience? (Huston Smith, 1957, pp. 7-19, intriguingly sketches how geography and climate might have influenced the three great families of terrestrial religious philosophies.) Will alien intellectual life be based on biochemistry similar to ours, or so different from our own that it will scarcely be recognizable to humans?

Of particular interest to me is the question of extraterrestrial religious experience. Some might argue that this is so entirely hypothetical as to be of no practical value: why speculate about the putative spiritual experience of beings whom as yet we have no reason even to believe exist? It is important to consider the implications of the possible religious experience of an extraterrestrial species for two reasons: (1) In preparing for first contact we should naturally be interested in and sensitive to every aspect of an extraterrestrial's physical, emotional, intellectual, moral, and spiritual life. (2) Recognizing that understanding the universe does not revolve around adherence to the archaic terrestrial worldview of one tribe of Homo sapiens is essential to the continuing relevance of religious belief on Earth in the third millennium.

ET in Western Thought: Speculation and Clichés

Speculation about life on other worlds dates back at least to the Greek and Roman Atomists—Leucippus, Democritus, Epicurus, and Lucretius. They argued for a plurality of worlds from their premises of the "uniformity of nature" and of an infinity of atoms moving randomly in infinite space. However, this atomist idea was submerged for nearly two millennia by the dominant Aristotelian-Ptolemaic cosmology, based on a physics of elements having a "natural place" within the sphere of fixed stars. Aristotle (384-322 BCE) held that only one world is possible, a view reaffirmed by the medieval Catholic philosopher Thomas Aquinas (1225-1274).

But overconfident Aristotelians provoked a backlash when they declared on the authority of Aristotle that other worlds could not exist. In 1277 Bishop Stephen Tempier of Paris issued a series of condemnations limiting the self-proclaimed authority of arts masters of the University of Paris, asserting that "one may not hold that the first cause cannot make more than one world." The effect of this condemnation was to permit speculation in non-Aristotelian directions, including the theoretical consideration of a plurality of worlds, leading ultimately to the modern debate. (See Grant, 1986; Steven J. Dick, 1982, p. 23, notes that "It is one of the great ironies of the history of ideas that while the passionate Atomist espousal of the idea of plurality of worlds fell on deaf ears with the rest of the Atomist system until the end of the sixteenth century, the rejection of the idea by the dominant Aristotelian worldview inspired critical discussion of plurality of worlds as early as the thirteenth century in the Latin West.")

Cardinal Nicholas of Cusa (1401-1464) speculated that "in the area of the sun there exist solar beings, bright and enlightened intellectual denizens, and by nature more spiritual than such as may inhabit the Moon—who are possibly lunatics—whilst those on earth are more gross and material" (Cusanus 1954, pp. 114-115). Nehemiah Grew (1641-1712) thought that every fixed star is a sun surrounded by planets, "which we assume to be inhabited in order for their respective suns to serve some purpose," (Grew, 1701). Countless other figures joined the debate in the modern period, as Crowe (2008) points out.

It would of course be extraordinarily anthropomorphic to import the details of human religion into our imagining of extraterrestrial life. (Frank Herbert seems to have done this in his novel, *Dune*, 1965.) Religion is treated syncretistically and not in a particularly evolutionary way. "Zenshiism" is a hybrid of the religious principles of Zen Buddhism and Shia Islam; "Navachristianity" is a blend of Navajo and Christian spirituality.) Nevertheless, a reasonable working assumption is that if extraterrestrial religion exists it will be in some essential respects analogous to our own experience. Terrestrial religion is, after all, a product of human evolutionary history, as Bulbia (2008) points out, and presumably ET religion would likewise be a product of the evolutionary history of its respective planets. Ritual, belief, prayer, doctrine, artistic creation, and other aspects of what we broadly conceive of as "religion" are artifacts of human experience and culture. Current scholarship does not support the primacy of either myth or ritual, but sees them as sharing common paradigms (Meletinsk, 2000). Theologian Linda Gibler, O.P. (2010) offers a fine example of this in her exploration of the scientific and religious history of oil, fire, and water central to the Roman Catholic sacrament of baptism. Her work integrates the liturgical and theological significance of the sacramental elements into their 13.7 billion year cosmological and evolutionary history.

We need at this point to dispel one impediment to thinking theologically about ET, namely, the clichéd categories imposed on alien beings by science fiction. Too often ET is portrayed stereotypically either as evil or demonic on the one hand, or as benign or morally superior on the other. Examples include cardboard-cut-out evil aliens such as those in *Independence Day*, the arthropodic Sarris or reptilian Xindi in *Galaxy Quest*, the "chest bursters" in *Alien*, or the ant-like invaders in *Battle, Los Angeles.* On the opposite extreme we have the benevolent Klaatu from *The Day the Earth Stood Still*, the angelic healer in *E.T.*, the peaceful genetic shape shifter in *Starman*, and the wise teacher Yoda in *Star Wars.*

However, a more nuanced reading suggests that if extraterrestrial life has followed a similar evolutionary trajectory in the heavens as it has on Earth, it will be characterized similarly by moral ambiguity. Examples include the Klingon Worf in *Star Trek: The Next Generation*, the Drac Jeriba Shigan in *Enemy Mine*, and the alien beings derogatorily referred to as "prawns" in *District Nine.* For theologians, the broadly accepted Neo-Darwinian evolutionary framework necessarily changes our theological understanding of "sin" to include the evolution of moral ambiguity. Daniel Dennett (1996) notes that the theory of evolution is transformative of every traditional concept, an idea certainly not lost on theologians. The theory of evolution is a universal acid that "eats through just about every traditional concept, and leaves in its wake a revolutionized world-view, with most of the old landmarks still recognizable, but transformed in fundamental ways" (p. 63). This is not news to theologians sophisticated enough to place theology in its scientific context, but it is worth bearing in mind.

Let us consider one of the foundations of morality to be the physical parameters of a planetary environment, and organisms' response to the constraints imposed by that environment. All planets have finite energy resources that are competed for by any evolving life forms. As life expands into every available ecological niche, predation between species and competition within species inevitably arises. Prior to the evolution of self-consciousness, competition and predation are ecological but not moral issues. However, with self-consciousness comes moral awareness: the recognition of the possibility that I could choose a different path; that, for example, rather than hoarding all our wooly mammoth meat in a time of famine, we could share it with a neighboring tribe.

Life developing in an ecological web of predator-prey relationships will thus reflect an evolutionary morality in which a range of moral ambiguities compete within a gradually widening circle of ethical inclusion. Robert Russell (2001) has summarized the probable character of ET nicely: if and when we meet alien intelligent life, it will be neither angelic nor demonic, but in theological terms *simul iustus et peccator* —at "once justified (redeemed) and a sinner". Human space-farers must be alert to the importance and the difficulty of recognizing the stages of moral development in alien species.

An example of such a morally ambiguous landscape is painted by Mary Doria Russell (1996) in her fine but darkly disturbing novel *The Sparrow*, recounting the story of a Jesuit mission to the fourth planet in the Rakhat system. The moral world of Father Emilio Sandoz, S.J., crumbles when he learns that on this planet two species—evolutionarily locked in a primordial predator-prey relationship—have co-evolved into rationality. The Runa species that historically has been the prey species continues to serve as food for the predator Jana'ata species. From within his Roman Catholic moral tradition Fr. Sandoz has no theological language through which to interpret this situation so opposite to the refined morality of most human religious traditions. The context of Rakhat 4 seems to contradict the assumed moral ends designed for rational creatures on the part of a loving creator

The Contours of ET Religion

It is in this context of the evolution of religion that I will reflect on the possible religious experience of ET. If we discover that life has evolved elsewhere in the universe, might we find that intelligent beings like us have also evolved a spiritual and ritual imagination? Might this imagination include any of the following elements found in different forms throughout terrestrial religions?

- Creation stories, narratives of salvation from floods or other primal catastrophes
- Rituals to celebrate planting and harvest, birth and death, coming of age and marriage
- God or gods, spirits and angels, demons or devils, saints
- Relationship between spirit, soul, mind and body
- Saviors, sacrifice, salvation
- Logos, Incarnation, divine involvement with the world
- Prayer, worship, consecration, commemoration, sacraments
- Morality, sin, original guilt or perfection
- Forgiveness, retribution, expiation of sin
- Problem of natural evil, redemptive suffering, theodicy
- Church, temple, priesthood, theocracies, evangelization
- Eschatology, heaven, hell, reincarnation, the ultimate fate of the universe

I propose that the evolution of morality, religion, spirituality, or theologies in an extraterrestrial context raises a host of questions that fall into a number of broad categories. Each of these sets of questions naturally constitutes a research area in its own right, but together they convey a sense of the magnitude of the task of evaluating theology in a context that takes the rest of the universe seriously. This essay will conclude with a briefly expanded consideration of two of the following categories as examples of the task of inter-planetary theology:

1. Belief, faith: Is belief in a transcendent dimension of reality an artifact of the evolution of human consciousness?

2. Theism: Will God(s) be thought of as acting in the world? Will monotheism be found to have replaced polytheisms in ET religions? Is monotheism an artifact of our own religious experience in a mono-solar cosmology? How might God be conceived of in a binary star system?

3. God as Trinity: God is triune in Christian experience and theology, but not in other human religions, although Hinduism addresses plural manifestations of the One. How might a multi-faceted experience of the divine be expressed elsewhere in the universe?

4. Incarnation: Could the Logos or "Christ principle" that is foundational to Christianity become incarnate/enfleshed/embodied elsewhere in the universe than Earth, perhaps multiple times?

5. Salvation: What does "salvation" mean in an extraterrestrial context, and is the idea relevant to every biological species? From what and to what should the word "salvation" be understood as referring?

6. Salvific death: Is the Christian idea of salvation through the death of a savior unique to human religious experience? (Note that it is not even characteristic of all human religions, but only of those who interpret the tragic death of a religious leader in the language and sacrificial economy of First Century Judaism.) If salvation through a salvific death is necessary, would multiple such deaths throughout the universe be necessary? Could salvation be accomplished on other planets without a sacrificial death?

7. Competing or complementary experience: if "the Christ" became incarnate a million years ago on Planet X, would the members of an expedition to Earth from that planet recognize Jesus of Nazareth as God incarnate? What might be the interface between an established ET theological doctrine and a human theological system imported from Earth?

8. Gender roles: Would the Roman Catholic argument that the priest—as an "icon of Christ"—must be male be undermined by the discovery of a female-dominant ET species?

9. Suffering and theodicy: How might the problem of unmerited suffering and the search for a cogent theodicy play out in different rational species? The tragedy of 9/11 is a theodicy problem for humans, whereas Thanksgiving would be a theodicy problem for turkeys if that species were rational. Desmond Stewart's sobering short story "The Limits of Trooghaft" (1972) deftly addresses the problem of unspeakable suffering imposed by rational beings on their sentient planet-mates.

10. Religion and evolution: Does religion carry either necessary or sufficient survival value to evolve on another planet?

11. Comparative truth claims: What is the relationship between religious belief as a tool with survival value on Earth, and the claimed truth values of comparative religious doctrines should we someday encounter ET?

12. Future of religion: Is religious belief something a species outgrows, or does it merely increase in sophistication? Would religious belief continue to play a role in the lives of a technologically advanced space-faring people?

The Task of Interstellar Planetary Theology

The discovery of extraterrestrial intelligence would probably not in itself constitute a crisis for any but the most fundamentalist sects in the three Abrahamic traditions. However, the discovery of extraterrestrial religion certainly would challenge our terrestrial religions' claims of exclusivity and the concept of religion itself. But such challenges would be salutary for us. Let me illustrate this with a brief look at two theological challenges that would be raised by ET religion. Both of these issues point to the importance of reexamining our own terrestrial faiths in a broader and deeper cosmological light.

Example 1: Incarnation

Speaking for only one terrestrial religion, Christianity, the central claim is that eternal God, the ground of being and creator of the universe, worked to reconcile the world to Godself by becoming incarnate ("enfleshed") in a particular human person, Jesus. The particular locus (first century Palestine) but universal application of this incarnational claim is already a problem for inter-religious dialogue among humans. How much more problematic might it become in interplanetary religious dialogue? In light of the possibility of encountering ET religion, how might we envision Christianity thinking more universally about the idea of the "Incarnation"?

In *Christ in Evolution*, Ilia Delio (2011) engages precisely this question about the universal significance of incarnational theology. Of the "Christ principle," she writes

On the terrestrial level, Jesus Christ assumes a bodily nature by which all of creation (that is, material reality) is assumed into relationship with God. Similarly, on an extraterrestrial level, incarnation must assume a form that includes the material reality of that creation, in whatever way that creation is constituted. [p. 169]

She notes that although the term "incarnation" might not be appropriate to another world order, since literally it means "taking on flesh," what it means more broadly speaking is embodiment of the divine Word in created reality. Delio sees the primary theological reason for incarnation not so much as the "forgiveness of sin" as the completion of creation in its relationship to God:

> An understanding of the incarnation as an act of love rather than a condition of sin may be more fitting to an evolutionary universe where the understanding of human original sin is under revision.

I find compelling Delio's conclusion that no matter how many times the Cosmic Christ might become incarnate throughout the universe, there is only one spirit and one Christ (p. 168).

Example 2: Eschatology

The second theological gauntlet would be thrown down to any human faith that speaks about the fate of humans beyond this life. Eschatology is the branch of theology that deals with the last things: death, judgment, the end of the world, reincarnation, and heaven or hell. All eschatological ideas—including the recreation of a "new heavens and new Earth"—were developed in a prescientific context that assumed a young, small, geocentric, and anthropocentric cosmos. We now know from physics and astronomy that although our Sun will be around for another five billion years, that macro-life on Earth (plants and animals) will end in about half a billion years, when the increasing luminescence of the expanding Sun will increase the solar winds that gradually strip away our atmosphere and evaporate the oceans, as Ward & Brownlee (2004) describe. Many galactic nebulae will continue to spawn stars with new planetary systems long after our death for billions of years into the future, until the gradual metallization of the galaxies pushes the universe toward an entropic heat death.

How can terrestrial religions speak meaningfully of "the end of the world" or "the new heavens and the new Earth," when we recognize that stars and planets that have not yet even been formed may spawn extraterrestrial religions in our own or other galaxies? What does such religious language mean in a universe in which some ET religions may have gone extinct many millions of years ago, and others may not be born for a billion years to come?

Conclusion

If some day we encounter indigenous religion on Gliese 581-d or another planet, we must be prepared to engage them with a theological sophistication that transcends our Earth-bound experience. And even if we never do make the momentous discovery of extraterrestrial religion, we will have been forced to take the critical examination of our Earthly faiths to a meta-level to which they have not historically been subjected. We forget that our own religions—like the rest of our social structures—have evolved in a brief interglacial window of relatively hospitable conditions on Earth. They also developed in a prescientific era characterized by relative ignorance of the vastness of the universe. (For an engaging panoramic sketch of the human discovery of the vastness of our cosmos, see Timothy Ferris, *Coming of Age in the Milky Way*, 1988.) Discovering ET religion would be a very important moment in humanity's "coming of age," and if religious faith is worth maintaining in the third millennium, it will profit from such theological self-examination.

Bibliography

Bulbia, Joseph et al. (eds.) (2008) *The Evolution of Religion: Studies, Theories, & Critiques.* Santa Margarita, CA: Collins Foundation Press.

Crowe, Michael J. (2008) *The Extraterrestrial Life Debate, Antiquity to 1915.* Notre Dame, IN: University of Notre Dame Press.

Cusanus, Nicolas (1954) *De Docta Ignorantia or Of Learned Ignorance*, Germaine Heron, ed. London: Routledge & Kegan.

Delio, Ilia (2008) *Christ in Evolution.* Maryknoll, NY: Orbis Books.

_____ (2011) *The Emergent Christ.* Maryknoll, NY: Orbis Books.

Dennett, Daniel (1996) *Darwin's Dangerous Idea: Evolution and the Meanings of Life.* New York: Simon & Schuster.

Dick, Steven J. (1982) Plurality of worlds: *The Origins of the Extraterrestrial Life Debate from Democritus to Kant.* Cambridge, UK: Cambridge University Press.

Dvorsky, George. (2014) "The Closest Known Potentially Habitable Planet Is 13 Light-Years Away," 14 June, retrieved December 11, 2015. http://io9.com/the-closest-known-potentially-habitable-planet-is-13-li-1585896900

Ferris, Timothy (1988) *Coming of Age in the Milky Way.* New York: Morrow.

Gibler, Linda (2010) *From the Beginning to Baptism: Scientific and Sacred Stories of Water, Oil, and Fire.* Wilmington, DE: Michael Glazier.

Grant, Edward. (1986) "Science and Theology in the Middle Ages," in D. C. Lindberg & R. L. Numbers, eds. *God and Nature: Historical Essays on the Encounter between Christianity and Science.* Berkeley: University of California Press.

Grew, Nehemiah (1701) *Cosmologia Sacra.* London: n.p.

Herbert, Frank (1965) *Dune.* London: Penguin.

Meletinsk, Eleazar Moiseevich (2000) *The Poetics of Myth*, trans. Guy Lanoue & Alexandre Sadetsky. London: Routledge.

Russell, Mary Doria (1996) *The Sparrow.* New York: Villard Books.

Russell, Robert J. (2001) "Life in the Universe: Philosophical and Theological issues," in *First Steps in the Origin of Life in the Universe*, proceedings, Sixth Trieste Conference on Chemical Evolution, Julian Chela-Flores, Tobias Owen & François Raulin, eds. Dordrecht: Kluwer Academic Publishers.

Smith, Husto. (1957) "Accents of the World's Philosophies," *Philosophy East and West, 7 (1/2)*, pp. 7-19.

Stewart, Desmond (1972) *The Limits of Trooghaft*, retrieved December 11, 2015. http://www.animal-rights-library.com/texts-m/stewart01.htm

Ward, Peter D. & Brownlee, Donald (2004) *The Life and Death of Planet Earth: How the New Science of Astrobiology Charts the Ultimate Fate of our World.* New York: Holt.

-=-

Peter M. J. Hess is a Roman Catholic theologian exploring the dialogue between science and religion, especially the theological significance of evolution, global climate change, and the exploration for life in the universe. His degrees in philosophy and historical theology are from Oxford University and the Graduate Theological Union (Berkeley). He is co-author of Catholicism and Science (2008) and has been on the faculties of a number of Catholic universities. He is a fellow of the International Society for Science and Religion and the American Scientific Affiliation, and serves as a consultant for the AAAS.

Human-Heaven Unity

Wu Jianzhong

Human-heaven unity is the traditional conception of Taoism. From the perspective of the "anthropotropic" principle of Paul Levinson (first presented in his PhD dissertation, *Human Replay: A Theory of the Evolution of Media*, in 1979), this article discusses the unity of intermediaries and the universe.

Human-heaven unity is the highest mental level of Taoism in China. It means the unity of human beings and heaven, in which human being is the heaven and the heaven is the human being. The universe is not illusive; a human being himself is a universe. The highest level that a Taoist could achieve is to well understand the rules of the universe, to obey the rules and get enlightened. So the improvement of universe is the improvement of human being, thus the unity of universe and human being is achieved.

To some degree, this ancient religious concept in China reflects the modern western media theory. The latter justifies the former.

Let's take the evolution of media as an example. According to McLuhan, the medium is the message. What matters is not the messages that the media provide, but the media themselves. This theory is still right even in today's big data era. What has been changed is the users' experience – it has been changed from (a) insights into (b) what the body feels. Insights mean the ability of people to find causal relations in things and objective laws through certain thinking activities; this typified the traditional information era. As for the body's feelings, the large amount of information, sometimes overwhelming, is an obvious characteristic of big data era. So in order to occupy an advantageous position in the fierce competition, people have to find the valuable relations between objects through their body feelings directly, quickly, and even simultaneously. The medium is not only the message, media are data. First, media messages from all levels are expressed in the forms of data. Currently, all the content in different forms and in different platforms, to some degree, are converging into one form – data. Second, every medium is actually an entrance to data, and the data are being dealt with in the cloud; the medium has become one part of the relative data. The relevance of data replaces causal relations. Finally, the difference between different media vanishes via data, and become quantified and materialized via financial tools such as Bitcoin. Therefore, the merge of media is not the merge of functions, but data. So the human-heaven unity, to some degree, already has been achieved in the level of data.

McLuhan also said that media are the extension of human beings. If media are data, then data are the extension of human beings in the big data era. This is because media can be regarded as the extension of vision and hearing. The adoption of the virtual reality technology such as 3D, 4D movies, body-felt games and force-feedback enables the media to become the extension of smell and sensation. All of the organs of human beings are related and interdependent. So media, as the extension of human beings, are actually correlated and interdependent. And under the presumption of media being data, we can presume that data are the extension of human beings; the unity of data is similar to the unity of human organs. Thus, organs are data. The correlations between objects in universe are unified with the correlations between human organs. So between all objects in the universe and between the universe and human beings, all kinds of relations exist. From this perspective, the universe is merely a larger human being, while the human being is a microcosmic universe.

Also, we realize that the universe is the universe reflected in all of our senses. Communication between human beings and all objects in the universe is received by human organs and senses such as vision and hearing. In this process, the users' experience and sensory stimuli are underlined by virtual reality and body-felt feedback, and the users receive them in a form that is similar to biological neural responses. The key to the success of the iPhone and iPad resides in the gestures, and the key to the popularity of 4K television and movies resides in their obedience to sensory stimuli. The trend of the development of media is to simulate human beings' natural biological ways of communication via wearable devices such as intelligent watches and Google Glasses, and to enable simultaneous information stimuli to become a part of human beings via mobile intelligent terminals. They become part of our daily life – what to be seen is what to be gained, and what to be gained is what can be used.

On this basis, Paul Levinson developed McLuhan's theory. He thinks that media are developing, and they are evolving according to the needs of human being.

> The trend of the evolution of humanized media is to represent the continuous development of the real world. Meanwhile, this representation tends to maintain and even increase the extension that the original media has achieved in space and time. So the purpose of the trends of the evolution of humanization is not only to represent the pre-technological environment and to get back to the biological limits of communication in the real world, but also to achieve the extension of technological world. And this extension far exceeds the previous biological limits. [*Human Replay*, 1979]

This thought perfectly explains the general correlations and interdependence between all human organs, between human beings, between human beings and media, and between human beings and the universe in all levels and in different forms. Thus the theory of the unity of an individual and the universe – the human-heaven unity – has been realized.

The evolution of media is involved in the evolution of the universe, and it is just like evolutionary relations between cells and organs. The whole universe is like a human body, and all objects inside of it are correlated and interdependent. They can develop and evolve by themselves. The correlations in the big data are the externalizations of the correlations of human organs.

The current media revolution includes the Internet of Things and virtual reality. The media industry chain just strengthens the unity of Human-Things. Artificial intelligence such as unmanned aerial vehicle and autonomous driving is merely the externalization of human-body system. Reflections in water can evolve itself, but just as the reflections may vary when wind blows, the evolution of artificial intelligence cannot be consistent with the evolution of human beings. However, they share a common ultimate goal, because they all exist in this universe.

With big data, especially with the analyses of big data, the correlations between the objects in the universe have been revealed. And they verify the justifiability of the ancient concept of human-heaven unity in the technological level.

Finally, the exploration of space has realized the "human-heaven unity" concept. The process for human beings to explore outer space is a process to extend human bodies – the interrelations of space are just like the interrelations or organs inside of human bodies. We extend our sight by the Hubble Telescope – we see things that we had never seen before and we embrace the lights from billions of light-years away. We also extend our sight by optical instruments and see infrared rays that cannot be seen by human eyes, and we captured the splendid image of the Orion Nebula. We can hear electromagnetic pulses from billions of light-years away by satellite antenna, and from this voice, which cannot be heart by human ears, we can tell the conditions of planets in space. We extend our legs by satellite probes such as "Voyager 10" and walk out of the solar system – the probe reaches so far, we cannot finish the walking within a lifetime. We use robots and mechanical arms to finish the assignments that cannot be finished by human bodies, and they finish various assignments on comets and Mercury where human beings cannot live. We use sensors to capture the flying data of aircrafts, and they can react to rapidly changing data much faster than human beings.

In the process of exploring the space, astronauts' spacewalks achieved "traveling in the heaven" of "human-heaven unity". Fibers from various instruments transfer all kinds of data including voice in space exploration, and the universal gravitation verifies the interrelations of all things in the universe. Even human emotions can reflect through the universe. We know that emotions are intangible and sometimes emotions vary too fast to be measured. The same situation applies to the universe, such as a wormhole and Black Hole, and they make time and space a comparative concept. Spectrum was originally a concept of vision, but we use it to find out the relations inside of planets, and we are able to analyze the constitution of planets via spectrum analysis. Voice is originally of hearing, but we've learned to use satellites to strike asteroids and analyze the constitution of asteroids by sound, and then we can draw the inner construction of asteroids which cannot be seen by eyes.

In a word, before human beings could leave Planet Earth, "human-heaven unity" was merely a religious belief. Now that human beings can actually leave the surface of Earth, and look back from the universe, we've found verification for this religious concept.

-=-

Wu Jianzhong is Professor of Communication Studies at Sichuan International Studies University. His *Transition of Digital Television and the Research of Industry Development* was published in 2012 by University of Sichuan Press in China. His journal publications include: "The Development Strategy of China's IPTV in the Grand Data Age," *Modern Communication*, 2013; "The Present Difficulties and Transition in the Industrialization of China's TV," *Editorial Friend*, 2013; "Locating Strategies of Chinese Cultural Industry Under the Background of Three Networks' Integration" *TV Research*, 2012; "Cultivating Cross-media Marketing Ability of Students Majoring in Radio and Television," *Journalism Lover*, 2011; and "Brief Analysis of Cultivating Modes of Internet Video Communication Talents in Three Networks' Integration Era," *News Research*, 2011. From 1997-2005, he was director of a television station in Chongqing, China.

Castles in the Air: Young Children Imagine Outer Space

Molly Vozick-Levinson

"What comes after space?" The question rang out with all the force of an unfathomable thought suddenly articulated. It was a bright blue morning in a New York City classroom, and the teachers fell silent for a moment. The speaker was two and a half years old, and she wanted an answer.

The lives of young children, and those who spend time with them, pop with questions at once simple and profound. Good teachers delight in listening to children wondering aloud. In my time working in preschools, I have heard marvelous, thought-provoking questions: "Where do germs come from?" "Do you need a voice to laugh?" "Why did Kafka turn Gregor Samsa into a cockroach?" Point childish curiosity towards vast, complex topics, and the questions that follow can open up new ways of thinking for everyone involved. I have found this to be particularly true when talking with children about the inherently huge subject of outer space.

Preschoolers' understanding of the how the world works is constantly expanding. Thinking about outer space – the fundamental question of what's out there – pushes at those conceptual boundaries just as they are forming. What does outer space look like? What is it made of? Questions like these require children to think in abstract terms and put together new words to express complicated ideas – and, in turn, teachers can witness their students' developing cognitive powers first-hand. Discussions of outer space are a powerful educational tool: We learn how individual children think when we ask them to consider questions without clear answers. Seeing outer space through a child's eyes can also lead us to deeper truths about ourselves. We learn that the idea of space holds a natural pull over the human mind, and heart, too.

This summer (in 2015), I began talking about space with children aged two to five years old at the Children's Learning Center at Morningside Heights, the preschool I run with a group of educators committed to discovering and rejoicing in what makes children tick. Our philosophy of early childhood education is to help nurture children's innate creative abilities in a loving and artistic environment, so that they grow to be present and interested people. Some of my space conversations happened organically, provoked by open-ended explorations of materials like award-winning filmmaker Michael Benson's photography book *Planetfall: New Solar System Visions.* It was while looking at those photos that Parvathi, two years old at the time, first wondered, "What comes after space?" – leading me to wonder what else children were thinking about when they gazed at the stars. Other conversations bubbled up as I asked children further open-ended questions about space. What became clear as I recorded children's imaginings is that when preschool-aged children think about space, they think in ways that many adults have forgotten how to do. They wonder what's out there, and invent all kinds of answers and questions along the way. Powerful visions of both beauty and terror emerge, mixed with the fundamental human desire to understand the unknown.

"What is space?" I asked the children to imagine that I didn't know anything about space, that I had never heard of it. Their answers at first concerned the visual and the geographical.

> Space is a black area. There are planets in it. *-Oscar L.-S., age four*
>
> It's a galaxy like way up, up, up out of the sky. It's like out of the planet. *-Gabriel S., age five*
>
> Oh, it's all around, just everywhere in the night. *-Hagar E.-D., age five*

"What does space look like?"

> Well, it's so dark and crazy. *-Netta E.-D., age three*
>
> It's very beautiful. Like volcano explosions. Space volcanos. *-Gabriel S., age five*

"What is in space?"

> There are lots of little things in space, I think, colorful. They can go 'blup, blup, blup,'and they zoom, zoom, and zooooom back again! *-Umayma B. A., age four*
>
> There are rings made out of rocks. Asteroids, you can call them. Asteroids are beautiful because they have fire and look like a shooting star. *-Alex N,, age five*
>
> The red planet Mars, and, and Saturn. What does Saturn have on his face? A ring! What does space wear on his face*? -Parvathi D., age three*

It was clear from their answers that these children had some prior knowledge of space, and the ability to imagine it vividly. Their words spilled out, eager and natural. Indeed, almost more striking than the content of the descriptions was the sensation behind them. Happy children are usually eager conversation partners, but there was something different in the feeling here – they were talking about outer space with emotion. Casually ask adults on the street "What is space?" and you'd likely get either a scientific answer – learned, not their own – or a dismissal of the question as ridiculous. But the children plunged in excitedly. The fascination was already there. Where does that fascination go when we grow?

The mere mention of space was enough to elicit long and gorgeous soliloquies from some children, their own ideas bringing new questions, imagery, and narratives. I asked four-year-old Oscar L.-S. to tell me what he knew about space:

> I'm trying to think about like what other things are like in space. What's a lightning storm like in space? A lightning storm I think is – you're not going to believe this – it would be sucking up Earth! There's a volcano on Venus, in the thick clouds, and under the thick clouds, animals live inside. Nobody ever noticed. I was the first one to hear it... The weather in space is like raining asteroids... For sunlight to get to Neptune it would take eight hours, that's until 8 o'clock at night, which is my bedtime. It takes a long time because the light gets stuck for 8 hours. How long does it take to get to Mercury? If everybody lived on Mercury I would be, like, 125 years old – or more, a billion 25, because Mercury spins very fast.

Oscar was raising questions and suggesting answers almost faster than my adult's mind could keep up. His words had narrative and poetry: Under the thick clouds, animals lived inside. Nobody ever noticed. I was the first one to hear it. The mix of reality and story was striking, too: Sunlight gets stuck for eight hours on Neptune, and doesn't arrive until 8 o'clock, which is his bedtime! For children, space can feel immediate – its mysteries can exist among regular life. I began wondering more about relationship between space and story for children.

During another conversation about dreams with my colleague Brittany Miller, five-year-old Beals R. said:

> I had a space dream where I had a friend with me and Earth was too small for me and my friend to fit in. Earth was in a little box, up to my waist. There was a dock attached to Earth and some boats. We didn't spend much time on the dock, so we spent a lot of time in space. And we didn't need a rocket ship to be in our space suits. We spent a lot of time fighting an evil space giant. There was someone on the dock who was dressed up as a witch and she kept taking different layers of costumes off.

For Beals, space served as muse. He presented his space visions as authentic dreams he experienced while sleeping. If he did dream this space adventure, we see how ideas about space have crept into his subconscious mind. If he was making it all up on the spot, we see how ideas about space have enlivened his waking imagination. Either way, space serves as a powerful catalyst for story. So is the appeal of space all about fantasy for children?

I asked some of the children to clarify if, when they told me about space, they were talking about real life or pretend. This is a blurry and fascinating distinction for young children – a child's relationship with words and truth can be shadowy, and the ability to concretely distinguish between truth and falsehood doesn't really emerge until children are older. (This is one reason working with the youngest children can be so enjoyable for any sense of humor!) I asked the children if they were talking about real life or pretend, and if in real life, they would travel to space. I asked them what they thought they would find.

> I'm talking about real life, Molly, just above us in the sky. We need to go, but I don't want to scare the aliens away. I want to see some of them. I would take all the people in the planet to see the aliens, but for real. I would take my mom, and [CLC teachers] Gideon, and Ashley, and Taz, and Beth. Everyone." *-Alex N., age five*

> You know Christian said Brittany gave him an airplane that goes to outer space, not just pretend. I could go with Christian. I would explore. I know what could live out there – aliens. *-Gabriel S., age five*

> Yeah. Because you could go out, you wouldn't float away from the ship. Yeah, and you would have a rope that connects you to the ship. And you have to get back to the international space thing. You have to get there before it's out of air so you can get more air. Do you know what we'd find? Aliens – green guys, I've taken a lot of pictures in my mind. With lightning hands. *-Oscar L.-S., age four*

For some children, notes of fear crept in when discussing actual space travel – Hagar thought it might be "pretty scary for breathing" to leave the space ship, and Alex said, "It might be too scary to go alone. If I went to space myself, I would be like, 'I think I'm dead.'" The children were encountering a real complication in the human relationship with space: what's real, what's not, and the fear mingled with pondering the unknown. The kids were quick to dream up ways around the scary parts – they'd bring their teachers with them to space, they'd make sure to bring extra air with them. But what of adults and our space fears? Is the reality or unreality of space too frightening for adults to think about for long? Is that why so many of us stop thinking about space when we get older?

I found myself thinking about what is in some ways the scariest question of all: Parvathi's initial, spontaneous, "What comes after space?" It is a question that defies our logic. Not only can't we explain what comes after space to a child – we cannot truly conceive of a clear answer ourselves, and we often stop trying to imagine one as adults. That the question came from a small child suggests that it is society and the realities of adulthood that stamp this kind of questioning out. Too many school environments teach students to push aside those big questions. As we learn facts, we are all too often taught out of wondering. There's something profoundly human about the pre-school view of life, compared to the one that lives in old, educated minds.

When I am faced with an existential question, I often find it illuminating to ask a young child for an unschooled opinion. "Do you know?" Parvathi asked when I paused after her question. I told her I didn't: "What do you think?" I asked her. "That's the question!"

-=-

Molly Vozick-Levinson is a New York City-based early childhood educator. She is the Director of the Children's Learning Center at Morningside Heights, a Columbia University-affiliated preschool for people aged six months to five years, which emphasizes creative, hands-on exploration of materials and encourages deep thought and feeling. She holds a Master's Degree in Early Childhood Education from Columbia University Teachers College and a Bachelor's Degree in English Literature from Fordham University.

Part II

Stories

The Story of Creation Told from the Moon

Philip Gibson

On Christmas Eve 1968, the largest television audience in history tuned in to see the Apollo 8 astronauts become the first humans to reach the Moon. Halfway through their 6-day historic mission the astronauts broadcast live TV pictures and commentary from lunar orbit.

At that time, no-one had any idea that a mere one minute of their historic journey would cause a nationwide controversy so great that it would end up in a lawsuit to be debated and decided by no less an august body than the Supreme Court of the United States.

The following is an amended and expanded extract from my book #Houston68: Apollo 8 – The Longest Journey. The account is written not in the conventional book format, but in the form of today's social media. While exchanges between the Apollo astronauts and Mission Control in Houston were 95% composed of NASA acronyms and technical numbers incomprehensible to the lay audience, this account imagines that the astronauts, and those following the mission, were able to post their non-technical thoughts to family and friends in real time through an imaginary social media platform of the time – much like our own Twitter, but one with messages not limited to 140 characters.

3 days 13 hours 57 minutes mission time

Walter Cronkite @WCCBSNews
The Apollo 8 astronauts are now able to film the surface of the Moon through the two so-called rendezvous windows, one on each side of the spacecraft. However, the last pictures didn't make a lot of sense to me.
Capsule Communicator @CAPCOMApollo8
Apollo 8 is getting a lot of reflection off the window right now. Hard to make out any detail at all from the TV pictures down here.
Bill Anders @LMPApollo8
I'm going to switch windows to see if we can improve the pictures. I asked Jim not to pitch up but to roll. Roll right and yaw left.
Bill Anders @LMPApollo8
Hopefully, the TV pictures are better now. The large dark crater between the spacecraft and the Sea of Crises, we believe, is Condorcet Crater.
Bill Anders @LMPApollo8

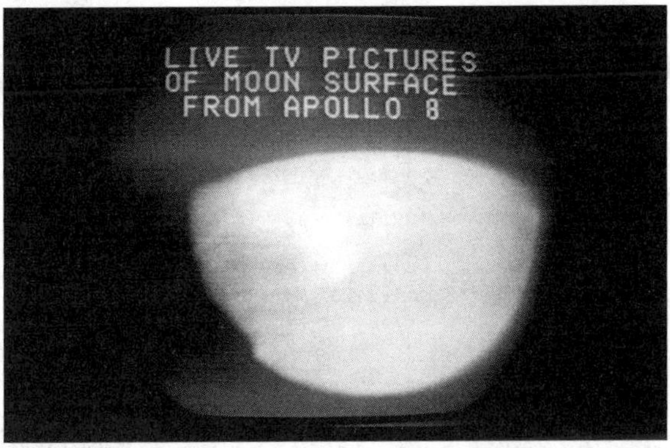

Unlike the high-quality still photos taken by Apollo 8 and developed later on Earth, the live black-and-white TV pictures of the lunar surface were grainy and lacked definition.

The Sea of Crises is amazingly smooth as far as the horizon, past a rather rough mountainous region in front of the spacecraft.

The Sea of Crises

Walter Cronkite @WCCBSNews
The Apollo 8 astronauts are looking up towards the Sea of Crisis. That so-called 'sea' is a large dark flat area between the heavily bombarded surrounding areas.
Frank Borman @CDRApollo8
Okay we can see the crater Picard now.
Bill Anders @LMPApollo8
We're getting a lot of static on the comms right now. Hope they can still hear us. We can see the dark crater Picard towards the middle of the Sea of Crises.

Bill Anders @LMPApollo8
We are now approaching the Moon sunrise (or spacecraft sunset).
Frank Borman @CDRApollo8
We need to yaw a little more to the left. We're over the Sea of Fertility now. It has a mottled look to it, but it is not heavily cratered, so it must be relatively new. It has a strange circular crack pattern around the middle of it.
Bill Anders @LMPApollo8
Looking at the crater Taruntius now. I'd guess it's about 30 or 40 miles across. We need to roll left.
Jim Lovell @JLCMPApollo8
Just to the west of the Sea of Crises, we see an area called the Marsh of Sleep. And to the west of that, the Sea of Tranquility – the proposed landing site for the Apollo 11 mission.
Bill Anders @LMPApollo8
We're yawing a bit too far left. We need to yaw right a little bit.
Bill Anders @LMPApollo8
Okay, we're going over the landing site in the Sea of Tranquility. This smooth area was selected so as to make it easy for the initial landing attempt to preclude having to dodge mountains.

Approaching the Sea of Tranquility

Frank Borman @CDRApollo8
We should start reading the Christmas message now that we are approaching Earthrise. This would be the best place and time to read it, coming up on the rising Earth. I've told Bill to go ahead with the reading.
Bill Anders @LMPApollo8
As we near the point where the Earth will appear above the lunar horizon, and for all the people back on Earth, the crew of Apollo 8 has a message we would like to send to all of you.
Bill Anders @LMPApollo8
In the beginning, God created the Heavens and the Earth. And the Earth was without form and void, and darkness was upon the face of the deep.

Bill Anders @LMPApollo8
And the Spirit of God moved upon the face of the waters and God said, "Let there be light!" And there was light. And God saw the light, that it was good. And God divided the light from the darkness.
Jim Lovell @JLCMPApollo8
And God called the light 'day', and the darkness he called 'night'. And the evening and the morning were the first day. And God said, "Let there be a firmament in the midst of the waters, and let it divide the waters from the waters."
Jim Lovell @JLCMPApollo8
And God made the firmament in the midst of the waters and divided the waters which were under the firmament and the waters which were above the firmament.
Jim Lovell @JLCMPApollo8
And God called the firmament 'Heaven'. And the evening and the morning were the second day.
Frank Borman @CDRApollo8
And God said, "Let the might of the waters under Heaven be gathered together into one place, and let the dry land appear. And the dry land he called 'Earth', and the gathering together of the waters he called 'seas'.
Frank Borman @CDRApollo8
And God saw that it was good.
Frank Borman @CDRApollo8
And from the crew of Apollo 8, we close with "Goodnight! Good luck! A Merry Christmas, and God bless all of you ... all of you on the good Earth!"

Earthrise over the lunar horizon

Walter Cronkite @WCCBSNews
Quite a moving and historic moment we have just witnessed there as we heard first Bill Anders, then Jim Lovell and finally Frank Borman reading from the Book of Genesis, and the moving final words: "God bless all of you... all of you on the good Earth!"

Walter Cronkite @WCCBSNews
The astronauts will now continue around the far side of the Moon as we view it from Earth. They will go around one more time. Then, shortly after one o'clock this morning, they will fire the engine that will, if all goes well, return them to Earth ... the good Earth.
Frank Borman @CDRApollo8
Okay, camera is OFF. How can you beat that? Gees, we just went into the terminator and read out the Christmas message right in time! Perfect! Just hope they got all that back on Earth.
Capsule Communicator @CAPCOMApollo8
Apollo 8 said they were nervous that we might not have gotten their Christmas message.
Capsule Communicator @CAPCOMApollo8
We were happy to tell the Apollo 8 crew that everything came through loud and clear despite the understandable interruptions while they were moving stuff around. I thanked them for a real good show.
Bill Humphries @BHNewcastleUNI
I wonder if the astronauts actually believe the words they just read out from the Bible - that the Earth, indeed the Universe, was created like that. They are scientists of a sort after all.
Jordan Lorence @JLTexasToday
After hearing the astronauts speaking to us from the Moon describing God's wonderful creation, I can go to bed with feelings of seeing ourselves as part of a created order much bigger than ourselves. I thank them for that.
Madalyn Murray O'Hair @MOAmericanAtheists
That was disgusting! A Christian fairy tale broadcast to the entire world by a United States government agency. I'm already organizing a petition to protest this outrageous act on the part of NASA.
Susan Day @SDayBabtistToday
By reading the words of Genesis the astronauts put their incredible achievement in a bigger context. Their words reminded us of the sheer glory and power of the Lord Almighty.
Madalyn Murray O'Hair @MOAmericanAtheists
NASA obviously timed this mission so the astronauts would be going around the Moon during Christmas when they would be able to broadcast their Christian propaganda to the biggest possible audience.
Walter Cronkite @WCCBSNews
Hmm ... As if, when calculating launch dates and suchlike, NASA does not pay close attention to limited launch windows, trajectory and the relative orbits of the Earth and the Moon.
Madalyn Murray O'Hair @MOAmericanAtheists
I'm now in contact with our lawyers. Something has to be done about this and we at American Atheists are the ones to do it.
James Field @JFieldbeingJField
I'm theophobic and would really rather not hear about anything to do with

religion, but I have absolutely no problem with the Genesis reading from Apollo 8.
James Field @JFieldbeingJField
I think the reading was completely appropriate for Christian astronauts, reading to a predominantly Christian nation. It made people think about what it is to be a human on this little blue ball we call home.
Madalyn Murray O'Hair @MOAmericanAtheists
That broadcast was a violation of the United States First Amendment, and the separation of Church and State. I am now instructing our lawyers to sue NASA and the U.S. government all the way up to the Supreme Court.
Dr. Thomas Payne @TPayneNASA
As Chief Administrator of NASA, I can state with absolute certainty that the decision to read from Genesis was entirely the decision of the astronauts themselves. It was not a decision made by NASA.
Madalyn Murray O'Hair @MOAmericanAtheists
Tom Payne can say what he likes, but scheduling this mission for Christmas and the broadcast on Christmas Eve shows that it is NASA's attempt to establish Christianity as the official religion of the United States.
Jordan Lorence @JLTexasToday
I think this Madalyn O'Hair person would be a good candidate for the Antichrist.
Harry Peabody @HPnowandforever
The astronauts have every right to read the Bible to themselves during their downtime. But those religious statements were part of a government broadcast in their capacity as agents of the government – an action prohibited by the First Amendment.
Madalyn Murray O'Hair @MOAmericanAtheists
Our petition now has more than 28,000 signatures demanding that astronauts (or any other government employee) be prohibited from citing Scripture while on duty.
Jeffrey Liggett @GLiggettnowhereyouknow
Some astronauts are religious. If they want to say a prayer while in orbit, I think they should be free to do so. Similarly, if an astronaut wants to read aloud a sci-fi or fantasy story, I see it as a similar act.
James Ganner @JGannerXD556
Maybe the next mission should name the rocket 'Mohammed', the command module 'Jesus' and the lunar lander 'Buddha'. These religions have nothing to do with scientific advancement. Sky genies and science do not mix.
Patricia Holmes @PatHolmestoday
I think it was wrong of them to read from Genesis. Whether it was NASA or the astronauts themselves is irrelevant. They are representatives of the entire human race, of which religion divides rather than unites.
Harry Peabody @HPnowandforever
O'Hare and American Atheists are absolutely right. NASA's claim that it was a free personal action of the astronauts is sidestepping the issue. There is no

difference between this and a school ordering a service during class and a teacher reading from Genesis.

Jason Shutterfield @JSAgnosticslocally

Personally, I see nothing wrong with the reading. I say this as an agnostic who believes Christianity to be one of the more flawed religions. If it is okay for me to denounce a religion in public, then it's also okay for others to promote their own beliefs.

Brian Williams @BWilliamspoetrylover

If I were faced with making a statement after being one of the first humans to witness an Earthrise from the Moon, I would be unable to produce poetry up to the value of the awe-inspiring experience.

Brian Williams @BWilliamspoetrylover

Instead, I would turn to age-old poetry such as that in the Bible. Just as the Apollo 8 astronauts did.

Philip Gibson @philiplaos

^ This! I think Brian nailed it. The astronauts were reciting incredibly moving poetry, not (I assume) what they believe to be literal astrophysical fact. It certainly moved me even though I view the Genesis account of Creation as entirely metaphorical.

###

The Supreme Court of the United States later rejected the case against Thomas Payne, NASA and the U.S. government, ruling that, "The religious statements of the astronauts while on television were made by the astronauts as individuals and not as representatives of the United States government. Furthermore, to have prohibited the astronauts from making these statements would have been a violation of their own religious rights."

-=-

Philip Gibson is author of the *Hashtag History* ebook series, including *#Berlin45: The Final Days of Hitler's Third Reich (European Theater)*, *#Tokyo45: The Final Days of World War II (The Pacific War)*, *#Havana62: The Cuban Missile Crisis-To the Brink of Nuclear Apocalypse*, *#Houston69: Apollo11-When Men Walked on the Moon*, and *#Houston70: The Miracle Journey of Apollo 13.*

Biblical Literalism in the New Jerusalem

James F. McGrath

Bill Larsson double-checked the co-ordinates again. This was his first visit to the New Jerusalem space station, and as the deadline for his story was the beginning of next week, he didn't want anything to go wrong. Bill still hadn't quite worked out why the space station followed such an irregular course. No, he thought to himself, irregular is not the right word. *Complicated.* In fact, the course it followed through space *was* regular - it repeated every solar year. But it was nothing like the movements of any space station he was familiar with. Every other station Bill had visited either orbited a particular planet or object, or maintained a constant distance from a particular planet or object. But not the New Jerusalem space station - it followed a complicated trajectory relative to both the Earth and the Sun, the logic of which (despite its annual regularity) escaped him. "Is it for the sake of secrecy or privacy?" Bill asked himself. "Surely there were other simpler ways of achieving those goals," he thought. "And of course, being *regular* it is hardly conducive to seclusion. I must remember to ask the station director about it".

The station came into view, first as a faint glimmer of the Sun's reflected light, then as an object whose human-made origins became clearer and clearer as one approached. Its shape was that of a perfect cube, and on every side there were slightly protruding segments with windows that formed a cross - a clear symbol of the station's Evangelical Christian ethos and *raison d'être.* Its style was otherwise quite obviously that of the 2170's, with its old-style plasma-thrusters and glowing purple lighting highlighting the outline of the ship. As Bill began to try to think of ways to describe it that would be appropriate and witty without being directly insulting, the station's director, Morris Roberts, appeared on the ship's communication screen.

"Mr. Larsson? We've been expecting you," came the deep orator's voice that had made Roberts famous as a preacher, just as his father and grandfather had been. "We hope that you will find your stay with us a real blessing. Now before you dock, I'd like to familiarize you with the station rules. Under no circumstances are any alcoholic beverages, tobacco, drugs, pornography, or non-Christian music to be brought onto the station. We hope that you understand..."

"Reverend Roberts," Bill interjected. "I received your message and have familiarized myself with your station and its rules and way of life. I assure you that I have no intention of doing anything or bringing anything on board that you would find in any way offensive."

"We appreciate your co-operation," came Roberts' reply, his warm preachers' voice disarming any annoyance Bill might have felt about being lectured to. "I will be waiting for you in docking bay 2. It should take you another 5 minutes and 13 seconds from your present position if you maintain your current speed. If you like, feel free to set your controls to automatic and our computer will direct your ship in the rest of the way."

"Thank you," Bill managed to say before Rev. Roberts' face disappeared and the New Jerusalem logo came onto the screen. The logo was a simple cross with a star revolving in a diagonally-slanted elliptical orbit around it. Bill switched the controls to automatic and set about checking his portable computer to make sure he had everything ready for the interview. It wasn't a story likely to make or break his career, but he still didn't want to blow it.

###

Inside, the station's décor was much more that of the mid-2180's. Still a bit old-fashioned, but Bill nonetheless liked the inside better than the outside. Otherwise, the crew and residents were dressed in a conservative but contemporary style. As he looked past a small crowd of residents who were heading for docking bay 1, and who were quite obviously were getting ready to leave for a visit to Earth, he caught a glimpse of Reverend Roberts' familiar face through the crowd, heading his way. Not that he had ever met him before, but his evangelistic broadcasts on the New Jerusalem station's own channel were received everywhere in the solar system, and he doubted whether even the miners working on Pluto would not immediately recognize him.

"Welcome, Mr. Larsson," said Roberts, as he extended his hand through the parting crowd.

"Please, do call me Bill," came the reply as the two shook hands.

"Ok, Bill," Roberts said, making no effort to allow himself to be addressed on a first-name basis. "Let me show you around a bit. Then you can come with me to my office and I'll give you that interview you asked for."

"Sounds great," Bill replied. "In fact, as I know you're a very busy man, we can probably discuss a lot of things while you show me around, if that's OK with you."

"Sure," said Roberts, turning to give instructions to a few members of the station staff who had accompanied him to the docking bay. "Just follow me - but only inasmuch as I follow the Lord," he said, followed by a laugh that Bill tried desperately to join in on out of politeness. And with that, they set off around the ship.

###

The preliminaries were fairly straightforward and were over with quickly. Rev. Roberts then began to summarize the history and current statistics about the station. Much of the information was common knowledge and had already become familiar to Bill in his preparations for his visit. There were well over 10,000 inhabitants on the New Jerusalem space station, and the number was constantly growing. In addition, thousands more flew in for Bible studies or Sunday church services, and an additional 4,397 children were flown in from around the solar system to attend school on the station. The station contained all the facilities one could desire - work opportunities, shopping, recreation - but without the crime that one inevitably found in pretty much any other city or space settlement. Numbers were constantly growing, and there were plans to open a new station, New Jerusalem II, which would house a seminary. The new station would travel alongside the old following the same trajectory, and this would allow seminarians seclusion and at the same time proximity to 'city life' and to a large community of worshipping believers, in a manner that it was nearly impossible to accomplish at a terrestrial seminary without having a large number of expensive hypersonic transports always on call. "Our community is happy and blessed, and is growing all the time," Roberts added to the statistics and other details he had been providing.

Not everyone is happy here, Bill thought to himself. There had been several outspoken critics of the New Jerusalem station, its beliefs and its ethos, most notably by disillusioned former residents. Their criticisms focused mostly on intolerance of anyone who held slightly different views on what they considered peripheral matters. However, most of those who came to live here clearly *were* happy here, and the numbers genuinely were constantly on the increase.

"So, Rev. Roberts," Bill said, seizing an opportunity afforded by a pause in Roberts' tour guide style monologue about the station. "I suppose what our audience will want to know is whether the recent agreement will in any way affect the station's goals and objectives, or perhaps even render it unnecessary."

"Not in the slightest," Roberts replied with a smile.

"Perhaps you could explain a bit more about this," Bill said. "As far as what I've heard and read, the station was founded when several outer-world settlements outlawed religious proselytizing. I was under the impression that one of the station's initial purposes was to provide a base for broadcasting to and refuge from such settlements. Now that the U.N. and Commonwealth of Independent Settlements have published their joint declaration on the free market of religious beliefs, ensuring everyone's right not only to practice but also to share and change their beliefs, won't this lead your station and its community to move in a new direction?"

"No, not at all," Roberts quickly replied. "It is true that intolerance and restrictions in the outer-world settlements were the initial factors that led to the setting up of our station. However, Christians have from the beginning been persecuted for sharing their beliefs, and so there was never really the expectation that such suffering for the faith would be stopped by the establishment of the New Jerusalem. No, the main reason for our station's existence has to do with the fact that we provide a setting in which believers can take the Bible literally, in a way they cannot anywhere else in the solar system, even on Earth."

"A space station allows you to take the Bible literally?" Bill's bemusement was not completely hidden by his journalistic professionalism at this point, and he hoped he would not end up regretting the slip.

"Why, yes," replied Roberts, either not noticing the tone of Bill's question or willing to let it slide. "I thought surely you must be aware of this aspect. After all, you couldn't have got here without being aware of our station's unique trajectory."

"Yes, I did want to ask you about that," Bill replied, this time genuinely interested.

"Why, surely the purpose of our trajectory would be plain even to a schoolchild with even only a rudimentary knowledge of space navigation."

Bill felt slightly insulted, but his curiosity overrode any offence he might have otherwise taken. He turned to look at a nearby computer console, and called up the station's annual trajectory on screen. There was a logic to it, but he hadn't quite grasped it. The station seemed to remain essentially equidistant from the Earth throughout, but there were much easier and more straightforward ways of maintaining a constant distance from the Earth. There was also a cyclical pattern in the distance from the Sun. What did it all mean? Bill continued to stare at the screen. A few moments later, the screensaver appeared, the New Jerusalem logo of a cross with a star in a circular orbit around it.

"Oh, of course!" Bill exclaimed, staring at the screen, wondering how he could have missed it. He looked towards the window, at the Earth and Sun, both specks to the naked eye. Now at last he understood.

From the vantage point offered by the New Jerusalem space station, any observer could clearly see, or work out for his or her self, how *the Sun orbits around the Earth.*

-=-

James F. McGrath, Ph.D., is Clarence L. Goodwin Chair in New Testament Language and Literature at Butler University in Indianapolis, Indiana. He is author of three books: *The Only True God: Early Christian Monotheism in its Jewish Context* (2009), *The Burial of Jesus: History and Faith* (2008), and *John's Apologetic Christology* (2001). He blogs about religion, the Bible, science fiction, evolution, and lots of other topics at *Exploring Our Matrix.*

The Third Chimp

Gregory Benford

What we observe is not nature itself but nature exposed to our method of questioning. – *Werner Heisenberg*

Interplanetary Diplomacy

Mars sometimes seemed like a graduate seminar for which she lacked the prerequisites.

Such as now.

"Before we go in," Julia said to Victor, "let's have a strategy."

International diplomacy, not my department, Julia thought. They were joining Liang, leader of the Chinese astrobio team, in the spiffy new Chinese rover. They huffed across the messy corral of vehicles and gear between their habitat and the waiting rover, talking on suit comm.

Victor said, "Tell him the truth. Often disarms people."

"Honesty as a startling approach, then?" She chuckled. "We've been married decades now and you still surprise me."

They climbed into the still-shiny blue Chinese rover, fresh down from orbit, and through the lock. They rinsed their suits before entering the surprisingly lush passenger compartment. Liang was a lean, handsome man with graying hair, smiling now as they sat. The purring rover started up on the trip to the Chinese cave emplacement.

"I am happy to greet you in better transport," he said with a thin and somehow sure smile.

"Looking forward, much, to seeing your discovery," Victor said, patting the upholstered bucket seats with appreciation. Their own old rover had hard bench seats that made long trips wearing.

"I hope you are not disturbed by Earthside news," Liang said.

"Had not heard," Victor said.

"More disputes between our countries."

"Since I'm Australian, Victor's Russian and you're Chinese, it's hard to believe we can be antagonists all at once," Julia said wryly.

"Well, we see the Americans as like you Australians," Ling said with a fixed face. "Russians aren't our friends, either."

We always drag our past around with us, Julia thought behind her steady smile, *and so does Mars.*

"But we are scientists here, not nationalists," Victor said.

They all three nodded. "I trust the limited fighting in Korea will not spread," Liang said. Calm words, but his eyes were intense, narrow.

As they lumbered across the red-brown sands she looked out the broad side windows as the human imprint slid by. Humans on Mars had carried the emerging symbiosis of human and machines to new heights. Within a few years of the First Expedition—of which only she and Victor still lived on Mars—wireless sensors lay scattered, to get better local data on the Marsmat's methane releases from subsurface. Robots came next—not clanking metal humanoids, but rovers and workers of lightweight, strong carbon fiber, none looking remotely like people. Most were either stationary, doing routine tasks, or many-legged rovers. The First Expedition was a private enterprise and grabbed headlines for years, so follow-up national expeditions were inevitable. The Chinese chose to send their own, building on their disastrous Second Expedition. Victor and Julia had suffered their minor falls and sprained ankles, but now only in exploration did humans risk climbing around on steep slopes. Much of their work was within safe habitats, tele-operation for exploring and labor. But no machine could deal with the Mat.

"We welcome you to see the unusual activity we have been studying," Liang said, his eyes studying Julia carefully.

Okay, try the truth.

"We haven't seen anything odd," Julia said.

"You see what?—big rushes of liquids, vapor?" Victor leaned forward intently against the rover's sway. "Do those big elephant-ear flaps close behind you, blocking way out?"

"The reverse," Liang said mildly, eyes still wary. "They close us out."

"So you can't get in?"

Liang nodded ruefully. *So they wonder if we can help them get back in...* Julia pondered this and Liang took the moment to unwrap a surprise, some dumplings whose aroma filled the air.

"To give us energy," he said. They all dug in. Liang had fragrant tea in a thermos, too. Years on Mars had taught a central lesson: people crave the flavors and textures of the planet they left behind, the connection to something like home in an alien land.

Entrance Iris

They did a lock and wash at the Chinese base. Thrifty, they had built a big habitat at the entrance to the cave in the steep wall of Gusev crater. Julia and Victor had found the entrance to the vast cave, concealed by a landslide, with some seismic studies. They discovered it in the fifth year of the continuing First Expedition, known Earthside as the Julia & Victor Perpetual Show. Their contract specified regular broadcasts for the entire mission, so when they elected to stay, they had to keep making up staged events to transmit. *Thank God we can finesse this descent*, Julia thought as they walked through the lavish Chinese habitat, *by just not telling them we're doing it. If nothing much happens, no report.*

There was a bit of tea-sipping ceremony in the social room, meeting the descent team members, coordinating comm links and smiling a lot.

"You have experience in opening the elephant flaps?" Liang asked, apparently expecting a firm yes.

Victor said, "Done in early days, yes. Julia more than me."

"Once we learned not to irritate it, no problem," Julia added softly. Too late, she saw this implied the Chinese had screwed up. But Liang kept his face blank. *Better diplomat than I am.*

The roomy habitat's rear exit fed directly onto the cave entrance. The anchored robots who assisted descents stood at the hoist apparatus. Somebody in the habitat made the bots all turn and awkwardly bow as the humans approached. Julia laughed with the others. She had not been here since the new Chinese expedition landed, and noted that their new cable rig was first class. It worked from a single heavy-duty winch, with a differential gear transferring power from one cable to the other depending on which sent a command to the tending robots. It was the same idea as the rear axle in a car, and saved mass.

Sitting warm and snug in the habs, she and Viktor and rotations of crews from China and Europe had robotically tried out dozens of candidate vents. Increasingly, robots did the 3Ds—dull, dirty, dangerous.

In a decade they found that most fissures, especially toward the poles, were duds. No life within the top kilometers, though in some there were fossils testifying to ancient mats' attempted forays. Natural selection—a polite term for Mars drying out and turning cold—had pruned away these ventures. The planet's axial tilt had wandered, bringing warmer eras to the polar zones, then wandering away again. Life had adapted in some vents, but mostly it had died. Or withdrawn inward.

Not this vent, though. It was forty kilometers away from the first vent discovered, with a convenient cave entrance, and the Chinese had made it their major exploration target. They got shelter and access.

The team lowered down twenty meters into it and came to the flat staging area. Unlike the First Expedition, everybody wore white suits—surprisingly spotless, still. Here they picked up the recording and safety gear already delivered by the robots. Bare rock; the robots had cleared away talcum powder-like Mars dust.

Julia knew she would have to report on this so she got Victor to stand still and deliver an opening line, which was, "Now we go down a deep hole to cross examine a life form that looks like carpet."

She laughed despite herself. "Never pass up a chance, do you, weird husband?"

He shrugged, a gesture that in their new slimsuits was visible on camera. Now her pressure suit was supple, moving fluidly over her body as she walked and stooped. The first expedition suits had been the best of their era, but they'd still made you as flexible as a barely oiled Tin Man, as dexterous as a bear in mittens. These had self-cleaning liners and 'freshers and solved the basic problem—most of the older suits' weight hung on the shoulders.

Another descent. She could barely remember the days, decades before, when she had broadcast several times a day, sometimes from this same spot. But then, they had been breaking new ground nearly every day. And betting pools on Earth gave new odds every time they went out in the rover, for whether they'd come back alive. The good ol' days.

"Suit lights off," Victor sent on comm.

They advanced toward the first big iris. A double pressure lock, the microbial mat version of the locks humans used to retain air. As their eyes adjusted, all around them a pale ivory radiance seeped through the dark. Julia knew the enzyme, something like Earth's luciferase, an energy-requiring reaction she had done in a test tube during molecular bio lab, a few thousand years ago. She recalled as a girl watching in awe "glow worms"—fly larvae, really—hanging in long strands in New Zealand caves, luring insect prey. The Marsmat version was similar, though DNA studies had shown that the Mars subsurface ecosphere had parted company with Earthside evolution over three billion years before. These hardy tapestries of dim gray luminosity, able to survive in near vacuum, were fed from below—from beyond the entrance iris.

They stopped at the three-meter-wide gray iris, resembling a crusty elephant ear, and stood in silence. Julia and Viktor knew this moment well, this respectful pause experienced in the company of many other crews. "It closed up yesterday," Liang said, "and nothing we do helps open it."

"Time to use trick," Victor said. He reached around to his hip pack and fished out a square box with two wire leads with alligator clips. He fastened one to the outer edge of the iris and another near the center, where the folds overlapped to seal. He pressed the discharge button at the box center. The iris stirred, jerked—and slip slowly open, driven by the current from the battery.

Liang said, "You never mentioned this method."

"Earthside would accuse us of torturing the mat," Victor said. "Committees, reports, lectures—all from people who have never been here."

"So the mat responds to—"

"High current," Julia said. "I got trapped once, Victor got me out. Turned out I'd done some damage; the mat answered. Victor trumped it, though. The mat uses electrical potentials to muscle its own mass around."

"You did not report this method--"

"Come on through!" Victor urged, leading the way. Warm wreaths of moist gases wrapped around them, frayed away. The Mat kept itself secured from the near-vacuum above with folded sticky layers. This cave iris was classic, grown at the narrow turn. Victor held the iris open with more e-jolts as the crew quickly moved through it. Their head beams stabbed into the murky fog as they went in.

"Think is safe?" Liang asked.

Julie came through last, eyes darting. She would put very little past the strange intelligence that surrounded them now, as they threaded their way through the bowels of a life form that was in many ways still beyond their comprehension. The mat pulsed suddenly, a blue and ivory glow. It knew they were there.

Again Julia felt the churn of somber, slow luminosities stretching into the foggy darkness beyond their lamps' ability to penetrate. There was a sense of silent vitality in the ponderous ferment of vapor and light, a language beyond knowing. As a field biologist she had learned to trust her feel for a place, and this hollow of light far beneath a dry world had an essence she tried to grasp, inside its workings, not with human ideas but by opening herself to the experience itself. To Mars, singing through her bones.

The iris quickly closed behind them as they reached a murky vault that stretched beyond view. Its petals got a seal around their cables, decades-old evidence that the mat learned how to meet challenges. It had done that at the first discovery site, and apparently the knowledge spread—a first sign that the mat was a global intelligence. Or else, had evolved this defense mechanism so long ago—against what? Despite decades of wondering which explanation was right, she did not know.

Snottites gleamed in their handlamps, dangling in moist lances from the ceiling. She steered well clear of the shiny colonies of single-celled extremophilic bacteria--like small stalactites, but with the consistency of mucus. She waved them back. "Those mean the mat is moving a lot of fluid around."

Snottites got their name from how they looked, and their energy from digesting the volcanic sulfur in the warm water dripping down from above. Brush one of those highly acidic rods and their battery acid would cut through suits in moments. A sharp, short *ouch*, quite fatal. The Chinese nodded, backing away. *Good; they've learned some of the many cautions here.*

Meters above in the dim pearly glow she saw mat sheets hanging in a vast cavern. Under their beams this grotto came alive with shimmering luminescence: burnt oranges, dapplings of vermilion, splashes of delicate turquoise. Another silence. Inside the beast.

All around, a complex seethe of radiance. On Earth, mats of bacteria luminesced when they got thick enough--quorum sensing, a technical term. A lot of Earthside biologists thought that explained this phenomenon. But they had never stood in shadowy vaults like this—the thirteenth such large cavern found in over twenty years of exploration. To see the rich, textured ripples of luminosity that slowly worked across the ceiling and down the walls was to dwell in the presence of mystery. Just ahead, thin sheets of mat hung like drapes. Wisps of mist stirred when they passed by. Unlike SCUBA gear, their suits did not vent exhaled gases, so they would not poison this colony of oxygen-haters. In the first explorations she had done just that.

They reached a branching point and elected to go horizontally into the widest opening. Their beams cast moving shadows, deepening the sense of mystery. Within minutes they found orange spires, moist and slick. Beyond that were corkscrew formations of pale white that stuck out into the upwelling gases and captured the richness. More pale, thin membranes, flapping like slow-motion flags. The bigger ones were hinged to spread before the billowing vapor gale. Traceries of vapor showed the flow, probably still driven by their opening the iris diaphragm. One spindly, fleshy growth looked like the fingers of a drowned corpse, drifting lazily in the current. It reminded her that so far, thirteen people had died exploring the mat, all around the planet. There would be more. She always reminded new crews that Mars was always trying to kill them.

But something was wrong. She had been here when the Chinese first arrived, awaiting their major gear to set up the plumy habitat they now had—and the mat then was vibrant, alive. Now big swaths of it were dull, gray.

"Was it like this last time?" she asked.

"Yes, we were here studying the change when the iris lock began closing. We barely escaped."

Julia studied the postures of the Chinese team. Did they seem embarrassed? "Smart. It can respond quickly. Earthside says the samples we sent back in 2025 imply the mat was here about 3.5 billion years back, and we share DNA—so it's been evolving as a single entity since then. It can be quick, but prefers slow. I think it sees us as mayflies."

They looked puzzled, and Ling kept his face blank. "Look—here, pressure is precious. The mat evolved to seal off passages, build up local vapor density. Then it could hoard the water and gases it got from below. But it has to seal breaches fast. It's killed people before; be careful."

The Marsmat kept itself secured from the atmosphere with folded sticky layers. This one was classic, grown at the narrow turn. As nearly as Julia and other biologists had been able to see, these were like Earthly stomates, the plant cells that guard openings in leaves. The iris opened or closed the holes by pumping fluid into the stomate cells, changing their shape. But analogies were tricky because the Marsmat was not a plant or an animal—both Earthly categories—but rather another form of evolved life entirely, another kingdom altogether. Some thought it should be classed with the Earthly biofilms, because some Marsmat DNA closely matched that—but the mat was hugely more advanced.

Yes, the Chinese were both embarrassed and puzzled, judging by their faces. "Take samples of damage," Victor told them. That unfroze them and they spread out, taking small snips.

Liang eyed the entire chamber, "Damage seems worse. It is spreading."

"Glad we could help," Julia said, though not really glad at all. She had killed patches of Marsmat with her oxy vent, in the older suits—but this sickly gray plague was different. "Let's stop pestering it—out!"

Microbial Wisdom

Julia studied their distant Marsmat sites by reviewing past observations, looking for any signs of the gray swaths they had seen. Every time she looked, the intricate Byzantium of the Mars underworld captivated her.

Earthside subterranean life—microbes, mostly—ran many kilometers deep. In total mass it just about equaled the oxygen-loving life above. Underground Mars life had natural advantages over Earthside. Lower gravity meant that cracks and caverns could be larger. The early plate tectonics of Mars had shut down, so the whole planet froze up. Olympus Mons was the largest volcano in the solar system because the lava that built it came up the same chimney, and nothing moved, ever—so the chimney erected a vast shield mountain. On Earth, the same sort of persistent eruption built the Hawaiian island chain, because tectonics kept steadily moving the upper surface, dotting the ocean with new volcanic piles that made islands.

The static Martian crust meant that, once formed, caves and cracks did not get closed up again by the ceaseless movement of rock layers, as they did on Earth. Mars was also cooler, right down to its core. This meant that milder temperatures prevailed further beneath the surface, so the volume of rock available for life to thrive was bigger than the inhabitable surface area of Earth. Even the pores were larger, from the lesser gravity and rock pressure. *Plenty of room to try out fresh patterns*, she thought. *Over four billion years. Over the whole planet. All one big . . . mind?*

They still didn't know how all-embracing was the network of habitable zones available to the Marsmat. Seismic data alone could not tell them what all those open volumes held. To learn that they had to make laborious descents, their reach prolonged by stashed oxygen bottles and supplies—hard, grueling work. Living in a suit for days was not just tiring—it ground down the spirit. The gloom of those chambers, the pervasive atmosphere of strangeness, the creeping claustrophobia—all took their toll through the years. Everywhere they had gone, there was the Marsmat, linked by intricate chemical cues, vapors, fluids.

Julia sat in their very own, original First Expedition habitat—upscaled a lot, but homey—and pondered the 3D cavern maps of the entire nearby area—a Byzantine spaghetti of life zones.

Victor said from his work desk, "Time for dinner."

She said, "In a minute. Vulet over in the main hab is looking through all our old videos for me."

"For the great discoverer, da." Julia's Earthside fame was a running joke between them now for two decades. "Vulet says—here, quote: 'The mat's reaction to repeated violations of its integrity by humans—oxygen exposure from leaks and exhalations from their early suits—never presented the gray swaths seen now in China Cave.' So it's new."

"Chinese at fault?"

"I don't want to provoke them."

"Must poke to know."

###

"Before you get chores done," Victor said a little later, "have interview, we two."

"Gah, this is that 'cultural forum' gig?"

"Da, cannot put off any more."

"Okay, but just half an hour."

While Victor set up the transmission, she reviewed the pre-set questions. He set them to run, bringing up the Face software to represent the interviewer. It could give immediate responses, within a limited conceptual range, of the real person. The 3D photo that ran with this showed a steely-eyed blonde with African skin and a Brit accent, named Nalajna. Fashions on Earth were amusing from a distance, yes. Nalajna's first question was, "How does the Marsmat influence religion?"

"As far as we know," Victor said, "it doesn't have one."

Nalajna's Faceware was smart; her next question came immediately, "Can you be sure? It's some kind of collective mind, true?"

Victor said, "But no way to talk about abstractions."

Again the Nalajna Faceware had anticipated them. "Most people don't think of their religion as a theory. It's a vital part of their lives."

"Wait a sec," Julia said. "You asked how the Marsmat influences religion. I do think it does affect our views."

Victor stopped the interactive system. "Thought you'd brush this off."

"Look, this is an income stream, helps with the little extras we need. Be nice. Plus, I've been thinking ..."

Back online, she said, "Look, we do know the Marsmat explores. It pushes its tendrils—that is, the microbial sensors that can see light and smell stuff—out onto the surface occasionally. It's sniffing, looking, wants to extend its territory. After all, when it was young it lived on the warm, wet surface."

To this, Nalajna's programmed self said, "Can life on Mars mean anything, really?"

A good opener, actually. "It means we're not the only ones seeking to fathom this universe. If there's anything that makes humans special, it's the desire to see beyond the next horizon. The Marsmat can't do that, though it does know just about every horizon on this planet. It keeps trying to learn more--we know that from its responses to our signals."

Nalajna's software self shot back, "Does Mars have anything to say about religion?"

"Look," Julia persisted, "we're the only of the three kinds of chimpanzees—bonobo, ordinary, plus us--that managed to get out of Africa. Now we're on Mars. Modern science is about the expansion of human horizons. So is religion, in a way. The fact that other kinds of life think so too surely means something important."

Victor stopped the software again. "You know I'm atheist. Not going to say so, right?"

She had to laugh. "Nope, that's your faith."

"Not so much I don't believe in god. It's more that I hate him."

She nodded. "Ah, the problem of evil."

"Where going with this?"

"Turn it back on."

He dutifully did. "Here goes. Nalajna, I think that our hunger to explore, and the Marsmat's, comes from the universe itself wanting to know itself. That's why it feels right. That's an emergent property of how the universe was made, how it works. That's my theology." Victor looked at her with surprise. "Never said that before."

"Never thought it through, I guess."

###

Amazing, Julia thought, *how large a month of the hab's shit was!*

The next morning she had showed up for her Task Assignment. The Mars Code was, everybody works. No exceptions. Especially for Earthers—no tourism!

As she passed through the main hab mess hall some of the new Earthside socko music was playing and some were dancing to it. To her it sounded like a rover flange coupling had gotten loose, flapping against the hull, and so the hell with it.

Mars Operations minimized manual labor, but robots couldn't handle everything. Like this. First their team got the plastic bag out from the hab underskirting and onto the hauling deck of a truck that growled like a caged animal, which in a way it was. It doubled as a mobile power source, 100 kilowatts electrical, able to crawl anywhere on hard, carbon fiber treads. She got in the hauler and checked the long-term weather while she waited: a category 4 storm was coming, with winds gusting to 80 km/hr.

She noted that the air lock seal was hissing, so either it had snakes in it or needed a smart patch. She told her helmet to send an alert to Main Hab. To Earthside, equipment failure was alarming; for Julia, it was just "Thursday." Holes? Duct tape. Electro: re-rig it in the shop. Computer? Pull a board, usually, and let the smart 3D printer figure out what needed doing. Mars liked improvisation.

While she worked, the team lugged the goodie bag of brown across the landscape—a big, rich gift to Mars inside a mercifully opaque plastic sack, compacted and frozen solid. The Planetary Protocols demanded that human waste be taken several kilometers from habitats, then buried in perchlorate-rich sands. But not too deep—the site had to be water-poor, unable to let waste trickle down into the volumes where the Mat lived.

Ecology wasn't just some science here, it was life itself. The hab used a toilet that neatly separated solid and liquid waste—nature gave them separate exits, after all—and the urine got recycled, since it held 80% of the useful nutrients in their wastes. Kitchen scraps, of course, went back into the greenhouses. In the early days building the greenhouse, they had used "humdung," the Earthside euphemism, in building the topsoil. Soon enough Earthside had reduced the term to TOTS, Take Out The Shit, an acronym that quickly became a hip shorthand Earthside, for doing drudge work.

The one trick the bio–engineers had not managed was converting most of the solid wastes to anything useful or even non–sickening. Let somebody else "realize existing in situ resources," as the manuals had put it, by composting. Frozen, it would keep.

Yesterday's ground crew had already dug the pit for it, a few klicks away across rocky terrain, using a Rover Boy back–hoe. The perchlorate dust was the bizarre surface chemistry's sole advantage—it plus the constant UV made the risk of contaminating the biosphere below tiny. Perchlorates ate up fragile biological cells in seconds. This surface was the most virulent clean room in the solar system, down to five meters. Any mess that escaped, Mars would kill every single cell within an hour.

As she worked she thought. The Chinese kept their methods secret—that had been only the second time she had been invited into their main hab. So she knew nothing about how thorough they were. Humans were walking litterbugs. They shed human dander, duly vacuumed up and used in the greenhouse for valuable proteins and micro–organisms. Early on, she had set out a sample—"a dish of dander," she had called it in a published Letter to *Nature*—and Mars had killed every single cell within an hour. That kept the Marsmat isolated from both the searing surface and the alien, invading humans.

It took two hours for them to deploy the big waste bag, then more to get the awkward plastic liner pinned up and protocols followed. Mars taught hard lessons. How much Mother Earth did for humans without their noticing, for one. Recycling air, water and food was an intricate dance of chemistry and physics, so they had to tinker with their systems constantly. The greenhouse helped, but the dance of myriad details never ended. Watch the moisture content of the hab's air or they would all get "suit throat"— drying out of the throat until voices rasped. Even then it was hard work in a suit that couldn't get its heating right—cold feet, hot head. She felt drained on the backhoe ride back.

Think Globally

She and Victor sat in the Global Mat Monitoring room, surrounded by screens. There were views from mats in vents and caves all over Mars, most concentrated toward the equator, where the mat density was highest.

Most of her colleagues here were exobiologists, mingled with hardcore mathist types. The mathists tried to invent ways to communicate with the Marsmat, using screens for signaling and occasionally physical models. The mat sometimes responded with figures it slowly shaped from itself. Julia had prompted the first, during the First Expedition's foray into Vent A. The mat had echoed Julia's body shape as a hail.

Now big digital screens stood in dozens of mat sites, trying to build a discourse with the Marsmat. The work went painfully slowly. Drawings of simple rectangles and triangles sometimes got a reply, usually not. The mathists could visualize four-dimensional surfaces in a non-Euclidean geometry, just to make sense of some mat shapes which might be messages. They used terms like "finite state grammars" and talked fast. Apparently, this work took inordinate quantities of caffeine. It further proved that high intelligence did not necessarily guarantee fine table manners. She was happy to leave them to it.

Masoul, a slim Indian woman sitting with them, ran the Monitoring room and kept treating Julia and Victor like minor gods. *If she only knew what job I was doing a few hours ago . . .* Masoul said, "We have seen no major changes far away, but in the Gusev region, 200 kilometers diameter, we see fluid buildup and movement."

"When?" Victor asked.

"For several months now."

"Any progress on talking to the mat?"

Masoul gave them a weary smile. "It is very slow work. We have a vocabulary of shapes and geometries, which the mat echoes. Then it shapes a series of other forms, but we do not know what they mean."

Julia asked, "It shows numerical continuity?—counting in order?"

Masoul said, "Yes, but some of us feel that may involve mimicry. Like dolphins, which are unsurpassed in imitative abilities among animals, the mat may just echo."

"What could select for that?" Victor wasn't a biologist but knew this was always the fallback question: how could the mat be under selective pressure when it was alone on the planet?

"We think the mat, so dispersed, may need to talk to parts of itself. We compared data shape formations and pigmentation changes in distant sites. They differ."

"How many species you now figure in Marsmat?" Victor pressed her.

She gave a small chuckle. "The biologists' mud fight. We think about three thousand different ones, but it's probably more."

"Microbial mats use all of the types of metabolism and feeding strategy that have evolved on Earth, plus some," Julia said. "Our cute Marsmat has gone far beyond that. But we can't talk to it!"

Masoul seemed startled by Julia's irked head-jerk. It shows—here, see, this is new."

Masoul ran a video of a mat responding to a screen that showed another mat, from another site. Fast forward, incremental changes. Within a day it had reshaped itself to resemble the distant mat.

"Um," Julia said. "The same mirror test we use on animals like chimps and dolphins. Good!" The method was simple: put a bit of blood on a chimp's forehead. If it then touched its own forehead in the same place, the chimp realized the reflection is actually him, not another chimp: a crude test of self-consciousness.

Masoul brightened at this approval. "It loves mirrors. At several sites, it reacts with fluid movements when we place a large mirror in a cavern."

"Which means . . . what?" Victor asked.

"Earthside has jumped on the study of mats, so we have a lot of info. In Africa there are big mold-like organisms that can partition its chemical processes, separating out chemicals. It's almost as if the mold were emulating a larger brain piece by piece, saving the results of one module to feed into the next.''

Victor frowned. "So dumb Earthside media are sort of right? I guess we have an intelligent slime mold from outer space.''

"When you have a Ph.D., you call them hypotheses, not guesses," Masoul said.

Indeed, Julia and Victor both had doctorates, based on their papers reporting the First Expedition discoveries. Plus many honorary degrees, some apparently bestowed in hopes they would show up for the ceremony. But the Marsmat was a lot harder to fathom than listening to the whistles and clicks of dolphins.

###

Julia met Liang just beside the sign, made from a crate:

The Garden of ETON (EXTRA-TERRESTRIAL ORGANIC NUTRITION)

"You don't need those," she said, gesturing at Liang's huge, insectile sunglasses. "Not much UV here."

"I see—you have water screen." This was his first visit; the Chinese kept to themselves, worked round the clock. He pointed at the dome where the transparent walls held a meter-thick layer of water, warmed by the big nuke, absorbing UV and solar storms. The walls held nearly a full Earth atmosphere, and subtracted the UV without editing away the middle spectrum needed for plant growth. All so he and Julia could stroll through aisles of luscious leafy crops. The "grass" was really a mixture of mosses, lichens and small tundra species, too, but it felt great to stroll on it. The toughest stuff from Earth made it here—even a baobab, a tall, fat, tubular tree from western Australia, with only a few thin spidery limbs sprouting from its top, like a nearly bald man.

Distraction psychology was everything here, from the new habitat for most of Expeditions 2 through 7, and especially in the ten square-kilometer greenhouse. That meant heating every habitat's water jacket with their nuclear reactor waste therms, so everything was pleasantly warm to the touch. The walls radiated a comfortable reassurance that the stinging, hostile world outside could have no effect here. Still, indoors on Mars was like being in a luxury gulag. The Siberia outside was never far from mind.

She circled them around the constant-cam that fed a view to Earthside, for the market that wanted to have the Martian day as a wall or window in their homes. She knew this view sold especially well in the cramped rooms of China and India. It was a solid but subtle advertisement.

Earthside could see most of the whole base—except in the greenhouse bar. They kept secret from Earthside this little robo-served outdoor restaurant and the distillery it ran. On the patio she could look at the eternal rusty sands through eucalyptus trees—surreal blue-green and brownish pink, the only such sight in the solar system.

The eucalyptus stand towering at the dome's center was her pet project. She had insisted on some blue gum trees from her Australian home, the forests north of Adelaide. Then she had to prepare the soil, in joyful days spent spading in the humus they had processed from their own wastes. The French called it *eau de fumier* or spirit of manure and chronicled every centimeter of blue gum growth—which was fast. But their trunks were spindly, with odd limbs sticking out like awkward elbows—yet more evidence that bringing life to Mars was not going to be easy.

They had drinks in glasses you could have stood umbrellas in—Liang a straight vodka slush, Julia a gin and tonic. Under 0.38 g, there was plenty of time to catch a tipping glass. Not that you needed an umbrella on Mars, for, say, the next a thousand years.

Liang was so tense, she deliberately kicked back in her chair, at an angle much easier in lesser gravity. "Took me years to get Earthside to figure this out and send us the carbon struts." She pushed toward him a bowl of fried, salty mixed insects from the dispenser and they both dug in.

She ducked as a white shape hurtled by, narrowly missing her head. "Chicken alert!" It squawked and flapped, turning like a feathered blimp with wings. "Who would have thought chickens could have so much fun up here, in low grav? Plus we get fresh eggs."

He gave her a chilly smile. She marveled at its mechanical insincerity. "The damage. It still spreads."

"You've made no more descents?"

A nod. "We study it from cameras, just wait."

"The gray—"

"Worse. Older parts, black now."

"You've looked at causes?"

"Of course. Ours is a more advanced site than yours."

"This is a life form we have no intuition about. All these Mears, we've never seen anything—"

"What is 'mears'?"

"A Martian year. Look, from our perspective, it's immortal. It's faced enormous threats as Mars dried out, meteors hammered it, we made our stupid mistakes venting oxy in the Vent A descents decades back—"

"You were crude. We are not."

Liang was stiff about something, but what? Outside, the wind whistled softly around the dome walls. Another reason she enjoyed the big dome—the sighing winds. Sounds didn't carry well in Mars' thin atmosphere, and the habs were so insulated they were cut off from any outdoor noise.

"Um. Meaning?"

"You listen Earthside? The Americans, they used some new weapon to kill all the senior leadership—"

"Of the Peoples' Republic of Korea, yeah. Thermobaric bombs—air ignition of fuel, shock wave, big blast effect. Pretty effective in those Party enclaves all bunched up at the city centers."

A glare, eyes large. "This makes our collaboration impossible."

"We're not a USA expedition! Our stockholders—"

"We cannot work with you."

"Look, Australia isn't the USA. Not nearly! But our science here comes first, right? I think there's some new factor causing the mat diebacks. I dunno what, but—"

He sat back, displaying all the personality of a paper cup. "I came here to serve notice. Do not come to our site again."

She gave him a hard look. "So politics comes first?"

He gave her a hard look, said nothing.

"So we find ourselves, the entire human presence on another world, carrying out the dictates of people on the other side of the solar system," she said.

No response.

She got up and walked away, pretty nearly the hardest thing she had ever done. Time to calm down. She decided to make use of the psychers' classic advice: Take a walk. Breathe deeply. Let the greenhouse calm her. Plus the G&T.

###

Masoul said, "I called you here because things are moving fast. The fluid movement is building. Seismic rumbles, even—between Vent A and the Chinese cave. There are electrical signals in the mat, too, highest level we've ever seen."

Victor said, "What's it mean?"

Masoul frowned. "That gray damage? I tapped into the Chinese feed—they keep it sequestered for days before letting us look, but I hacked their blocks. The gray is growing."

"Forget about working on this problem with them," Julia said. "Latest news feed says this damned war has stalled—nobody wants to be first to use nukes. So they're knocking out each others' satellites."

Victor stood up, agitated. "Go on longer, could cut off our Mars capability. We'll not get resupplied."

"Or go home," Masoul said. "I'm slated to go back next year. I gather North Korea's regime has lost its grip on the country, after the Americans decapitated its Party sites. Who's in the right here?"

Victor grimaced. "Wars don't determine who's right, only who's left."

Marsmat Horizons

Glancing back at their original hab, she was struck by how clunky it looked. A giant tuna can, its lines not improved by the sandbags they'd stacked on the top for radiation protection. Pipes and patches dotted its dusty seams. Still, it had the familiarity of home, and they'd lived in it fairly comfortably for over two decades now, a hab for two.

Compared to Airbus' sleek nuke standing on its tail like a twencen space movie, their gear was now Old School. The Chinese had landed there with a steamy exhaust flourish, then deployed their elegant hab and gear into the cave beyond.

Their rover purred and lurched as Victor took it at max speed toward where this had all started—Vent A. The seismic data showed building pressures all along this region of Gusev crater. The Vent was where Julia and Victor first found the Marsmat, hundreds of meters down.

Three billion years ago, all this had been a vast lake. Now only a desert remained where great breakers had once crashed on a shore. As they passed by a bluff she could see fossil rocks from the early surface life of the Marsmat. These had been noticed far back in 2014, a powerful clue. Plus the mat's methane releases, noted since the 2000s, fed by smoldering heat and moisture. Most of that ancient water still slumbered under the rusted pink-brown sands. Now, some of it was building up below.

They got bulletins from Earthside's war as they lumbered out. More explosions in orbit, space capabilities used like pawns in a brutal global chess game. Nobody wanted a nuclear war in the atmosphere. But space was different. *Mars has a lot of past, and so do we.*

As they reached the vent Phobos rose in the churning ruby sky. "Chinese!" Victor called. There they were, white suits moving in the slow motion skipping dubbed 'Mars gait' by Earthside media.

"They must've felt it in the cave," Julia said. "Step on it!"

They got out and fought against the gathering storm now heading into Gusev, winds howling a hollow moan. She and Victor had first met the Marsmat in a deep descent of Vent A and now, decades later, it fumed with vapor as she had never seen it.

"Liang!" She called on suit com. "What's happening?"

The nearest figure turned. Julia could see from his tormented face that in Liang's mind the frontier between irritation and outright anger had grown thinly guarded, and as his irked mouth twisted she saw that he had crossed the border without slowing down. "Felt quakes, came here. Iris opened, let out liquids, wind. We will deal with this! Go away!"

"We came offering help—hey, this is our vent!"

"Connected to the cave, same fluid surges." Liang's face now showed his jittery alarm. "I found why the gray damage. Our waste disposal, human dung – mat got into it, despite our protocols. Was piping it down, must have –"

"Look out!" Victor called over the moaning winds.

She was used to dust devils on Mars, had seen hundreds—but not this.

It came not from the storm, but from Vent A. The furious vortex was a sulfur-rich yellow stream jetting out of the vent, corkscrewing up. Odd clots danced in it, whirling out and up. The blast of it knocked her down.

She scrambled up and saw the Chinese run, chattering their panic on com. Winds howled with a strange shrill song.

The vortex rumbled now as it twisted high into a ruddy sky. "Blotches!" Victor said. "See?—gray mass. It's ejecting the bad. The shit."

She saw dark masses of it whirring upward in the spreading helix. Something smacked into her helmet. More spattered on her suit and she saw it was the gray, mingled with living parts of the mat itself.

"We did not know—I thought—" Liang was struggling with his confusion, his rage.

"You put your shit *where*?" she shouted over the hammering storm.

"Froze, dried, buried in cave—"

"Not far enough away." *Stupid*, she thought but did not say.

"I had not known—it can expel! Must know its body." Liang's reserve had shattered.

They hunkered down together against the gale. The vortex blow was easing down, wet debris peppering the rusty sands.

She watched it in wonder, thinking hard. "Could be this is a way to transport its genetics, too. Spread it around the planet, looking for new wet spots to populate. Earthside slime molds develop a tree-like fruiting structure, spores--toss them to the winds at the reproductive air-borne stage. The mat must've done that way back, when there was some real atmosphere. Helped build its global mind."

Victor said, "Been here decades, never saw this. Smart. Strange, too."

Julia stood in the strong swirl of the Marsmat's breath and felt an excited joy, a jolt of recognition. *It and we, all coming by this naturally, from the universe itself wanting to know itself.*

"I ..." Liang clung to her, as if he could not stand. "I do not know, such strange place. New ideas ..."

"Look, the mat fixes itself. It's smart that way."

Victor said, "Sharp, the mat is. Blows out its dead, spreads itself, both at once."

Liang peered up into the howling vortex that plowed into the sky. "I... I should... seen this, before."

Julia said, "Nobody sees much ahead. Look at Earthside! We're a funny species—we fall forward, catch ourselves. Two-footed terrors." She could joke him through this, get him straight, maybe.

"And the Korean..." Too much was happening, too fast, for Liang.

Julia said, "If Earthside loses its orbital capability, we'll have to hold out here on our own. That'll take cooperation. We'll be the new Martian race."

"The war, now this—" Liang gazed around at the whipping winds, as if grasping the strangeness of Mars for the first time.

"It's just life finding its way," Julia said.

She could not understand why people feared new ideas. She was frightened by the old ones.

-=-

Gregory Benford, Ph.D., is a Fellow of the American Physical Society, winner of the Lord Prize in science, and the UN Medal in Literature. His fiction and nonfiction has won many awards; he has published 32 novels, over 200 short stories and several hundred scientific papers in several fields.

Come All Ye Faithful

Robert J. Sawyer

First published in Space Inc., *edited by Julie E. Czerneda, DAW Books, New York, July 2003.*

"Damned social engineers," said Boothby, frowning his freckled face. He looked at me, as if expecting an objection to the profanity, and seemed disappointed that I didn't rise to the bait.

"As you said earlier," I replied calmly, "it doesn't make any practical difference."

He tried to get me again: "Damn straight. Whether Jody and I just live together or are legally married shouldn't matter one whit to anyone but us."

I wasn't going to give him the pleasure of telling him it mattered to God; I just let him go on. "Anyway," he said, spreading hands that were also freckled, "since we have to be married before the Company will give us a license to have a baby, Jody's decided she wants the whole shebang: the cake, the fancy reception, the big service."

I nodded. "And that's where I come in."

"That's right, Padre." It seemed to tickle him to call me that. "Only you and Judge Hiromi can perform ceremonies here, and, well ..."

"Her honor's office doesn't have room for a real ceremony, with a lot of attendees," I offered.

"That's it!" crowed Boothby, as if I'd put my finger on a heinous conspiracy. "That's exactly it. So, you see my predicament, Padre."

I nodded. "You're an atheist. You don't hold with any religious mumbo-jumbo. But, to please your bride-to-be, you're willing to have the ceremony here at Saint Teresa's."

"Right. But don't get the wrong idea about Jody. She's not ..."

He trailed off. Anywhere else on Mars, declaring someone wasn't religious, wasn't a practicing Christian or Muslim or Jew, would be perfectly acceptable—indeed, would be the expected thing. Scientists, after all, looked askance at anyone who professed religion; it was as socially unacceptable as farting in an airlock.

But now Boothby was unsure about giving voice to what in all other circumstances would have been an easy disclaimer. He'd stopped in here at Saint Teresa's over his lunch hour to see if I would perform the service, but was afraid now that I'd turn him down if he revealed that I was being asked to unite two nonbelievers in the most holy of institutions.

He didn't understand why I was here—why the Archdiocese of New York had put up the money to bring a priest to Mars, despite the worldwide shortage of Catholic clergy. The Roman Catholic Church would always rather see two people married by clergy than living in sin—and so, since touching down at Utopia Planitia, I'd united putative Protestants, secular Jews, and more. And I'd gladly marry Boothby and his fiancée. "Not to worry," I said. "I'd be honored if you had your ceremony here."

Boothby looked relieved. "Thank you," he replied. "Just, you know, not too many prayers."

I forced a smile. "Only the bare minimum."

###

Boothby wasn't alone. Almost everyone here thought having me on Mars was a waste of oxygen. But the New York Diocese was rich, and they knew that if the church didn't have a presence early on in Bradbury Colony, room would never be made for it.

There had been several priests who had wanted this job, many with much better theological credentials than I had. But two things were in my favor. First, I had low food requirements, doing fine on just 1200 calories a day. And second, I have a Ph.D. in astronomy, and had spent four years with the Vatican observatory.

The stars had been my first love; it was only later that I'd wondered who put them there. Ironically, taking the priest job here on Mars had meant giving up my celestial research, although being an astronomer meant that I could double for one of the "more important" colonists, if he or she happened to get sick. That fact appeased some of those who had tried to prevent my traveling here.

It had been a no-brainer for me: studying space from the ground, or actually going into space. Still, it seemed as though I was the only person on all of Mars who was really happy that I was here.

Hatch 'em, match 'em, and dispatch 'em—that was the usual lot for clergy. Well, we hadn't had any births yet, although we would soon. And no one had died since I'd arrived. That left marriages.

Of course, I did perform mass every Sunday, and people did come out. But it wasn't like a mass on Earth. Oh, we had a choir—but the people who had joined it all made a point of letting each other know that they weren't religious; they simply liked to sing. And, yes, there were some bodies warming the pews, but they seemed just to be looking for something to do; leisure-time activities were mighty scarce on Mars.

Perhaps that's why there were so few troubled consciences: there was nothing to get into mischief with. Certainly, no one had yet come for confession. And when we did communion, people always took the wine—of which there wasn't much available elsewhere—but I usually had a bunch of wafers left at the end.

Ah, well. I would do a bang-up job for Boothby and Jody on the wedding—so good that maybe they'd let me perform a baptism later.

"Father Bailey?" said a voice.

I turned around. Someone else needing me for something, and on a Thursday? Well, well, well ....

"Yes?" I said, looking at the young woman.

"I'm Loni Sinclair," she said. "From the Communications Center."

"What can I do for you, my child?"

"Nothing," she said. "But a message came in from Earth for you—scrambled." She held out her hand, proffering a thin white wafer. I took it, thanked her, and waited for her to depart. Then I slipped it into my computer, typed my access code, and watched in astonishment as the message played.

"Greetings, Father Bailey," said the voice that had identified itself as Cardinal Pirandello of the Vatican's Congregation for the Causes of Saints. "I hope all is well with you. The Holy Father sends his special apostolic blessing." Pirandello paused, as if perhaps reluctant to go on, then: "I know that Earth news gets little play at Bradbury Colony, so perhaps you haven't seen the reports of the supposed miracle at Cydonia."

My heart jumped. Pirandello was right about us mostly ignoring the mother planet: it was supposed to make living permanently on another world easier. But Cydonia—why, that was here, on Mars ...

The Cardinal went on: "A televangelist based in New Zealand has claimed to have seen the Virgin Mary while viewing Cydonia through a telescope. These new ground-based scopes with their adaptive optics have astonishing resolving power, I'm told—but I guess I don't have to tell you that, after all your time at Castel Gandolfo. Anyway, ordinarily, of course, we'd give no credence to such a claim—putative miracles have a way of working themselves out, after all. But the televangelist in question is Jurgen Emat, who was at seminary fifty years ago with the Holy Father, and is watched by hundreds of millions of Roman Catholics. Emat claims that his vision has relevance to the Third Secret of Fatima. As you know, Fatima is much on the Holy Father's mind these days, since he intends to canonize Lucia dos Santos next month. Both the postulator and the reinstated *advocatus diaboli* feel this needs to be clarified before Leo XIV visits Portugal for this ceremony."

I shifted in my chair, trying to absorb it all in.

"It would, of course," continued the recorded voice, "take a minimum of two years for a properly trained cardinal to travel from the Vatican to Mars. We know you have no special expertise in the area of miracles, but, as the highest-ranking Catholic official on Mars, his Holiness requests that you visit Cydonia, and prepare a report. Full details of the putative miracle follow ..."

###

It took some doing—my mere presence was an act of forbearance, I knew—but I managed to finagle the use of one of Bradbury Colony's ground-effect shuttles to go from Utopia Planitia to Cydonia. Of course, I couldn't pilot such a vehicle myself; Elizabeth Chen was at the controls, leaving me most of a day to study.

Rome didn't commit itself easily to miracles, I knew. After all, there were charlatans who faked such things, and there was always the possibility of us getting egg on our collective faces. Also, the dogma was that all revelations required for faith were in the scriptures; there was no need for further miracles.

I looked out the shuttle's windows. The Sun—tiny and dim compared with how it appeared from Earth—was touching the western horizon. I watched it set.

The shuttle sped on, into the darkness.

###

"We speak today of the Third Secret of Fatima," said Jurgen Emat, robust and red of face at almost eighty, as he looked out at his flock. I was watching a playback of his broadcast on my datapad. "The Third Secret, and the miracle I myself have observed.

"As all of those who are pure of heart know, on May 13, 1917, and again every month of that year until October, three little peasant children saw visions of our Blessed Lady. The children were Lucia dos Santos, then aged 10, and her cousins Francisco and Jacinta Marto, ages eight and seven.

"Three prophecies were revealed to the children. The third was known only to a succession of Popes until 2000, when, while beatifying the two younger visionaries, who had died in childhood, John Paul II ordered the Congregation for the Doctrine of Faith to make that secret public, accompanied by what he called 'an appropriate commentary.'

"Well, the secret *is* indeed public, and has been for almost seventy years, but that commentary was anything but appropriate, twisting the events in the prophecy to relate to the 1981 attempt on John Paul II's life by Mehmet Ali Agca. No, that interpretation is incorrect—for I myself have had a vision of the true meaning of Fatima."

Puh-leeze, I thought. But I continued to watch.

"Why did I, alone, see this?" asked Emat. "Because unlike modern astronomers, who don't bother with eyepieces anymore, I looked upon Mars directly through a telescope, rather than on a computer monitor. Holy Visions are revealed only to those who gaze directly upon them."

An odd thing for a televangelist to say, I thought, as the recording played on.

"You have to remember, brethren" said Jurgen, "that the 1917 visions at Fatima were witnessed by children, and that the only one who survived childhood spent her life a cloistered nun—the same woman Pope Leo XIV intends to consecrate in a few weeks' time. Although she didn't write down the Third Secret until 1944, she'd seen little of the world in the intervening years. So, everything she says has to be re-interpreted in light of that. As Vatican Secretary of State Cardinal Angelo Sodano said upon on the occasion of the Third Secret's release, 'The text must be interpreted in a symbolic key.'"

Jurgen turned around briefly, and holographic words floated behind him: *We saw an Angel with a flaming sword in his left hand; flashing, it gave out flames that looked as though they would set the world on fire ...*

"Clearly," said Jurgen, indicating the words with his hand, "this is a rocket launch."

I shook my head in wonder. The words changed: *And we saw in an immense light that is God—something similar to how people appear in a mirror when they pass in front of it—a Bishop dressed in white ...*

Jurgen spread his arms now, appealing for common sense. "Well, how do you recognize a bishop? By his miter—his liturgical headdress. And what sort of headdress do we associate with odd reflections? The visors on space helmets! And what color are spacesuits? White—always white, to reflect the heat of the Sun! Here, the children doubtless saw an astronaut. But where? Where?"

New words replacing old: *... passed through a big city ... half in ruins ...*

"And that," said Jurgen, "is our first clue that the vision was specifically of Mars, of the Cydonia region, where, since the days of *Viking*, mystics have thought they could detect the ruins of a city, just west of the so-called Face on Mars."

Gracious Christ, I thought. Surely the Vatican can't have sent me off to investigate that? The so-called "Face" had, when photographed later, turned out to be nothing but a series of buttes with chasms running through them.

Again, the words floating behind Jurgen changed: *Beneath the two arms of the Cross there were two Angels ...*

"Ah!" said Jurgen, as if he himself were surprised by the revealed text, although doubtless he'd studied it minutely, working up this ridiculous story.

"The famed Northern Cross," continued Jurgen, "part of the constellation of Cygnus, is as clearly visible from Mars' surface as it is from Earth's. And Mars' two moons, Phobos and Deimos, depending on their phases, might appear as two angels beneath the cross ..."

Might, I thought. *And monkeys might fly out of my butt.*

But Jurgen's audience was taking it all in. He was an old-fashioned preacher - flamboyant, mesmerizing, long on rhetoric and short on logic, the kind that, regrettably, had become all too common in Catholicism since Vatican III.

The floating words morphed yet again: *... two Angels each with a crystal aspersorium in his hand ...*

"An aspersorium," said Jurgen, his tone begging indulgence from all those who must already know, "is a vessel for holding holy water. And where, brethren, is water more holy than on desiccated Mars?" He beamed at his flock. I shook my head.

"And what," said Jurgen, "did the angels Phobos and Deimos do with their aspersoria?" More words from the Third Secret appeared behind him in answer: *They gathered up the blood of the Martyrs.*

"Blood?" said Jurgen, raising his bushy white eyebrows in mock surprise. "Ah, but again, we have only blessed Sister Lucia's interpretation. Surely what she saw was simply red liquid—or liquid that *appeared* to be red. And, on

Mars, with its oxide soil and butterscotch sky, *everything* appears to be red, even water!"

Well, he had a point there. The people of Mars dressed in fashions those of Earth would find gaudy in the extreme, just to inject some color other than red into their lives.

"And, when I gazed upon Cydonia, my brethren, on the one hundred and fiftieth anniversary of the first appearance of Our Lady of the Rosary at Fatima, I saw her in all her glory: the Blessed Virgin.

"How did I know to look at Cydonia, you might ask? Because the words of Our Lady had come to me, telling me to turn my telescope onto Mars. I heard the words in my head late one night, and I knew at once they were from blessed Mary. I went to my telescope and looked where she had told me to. And nine minutes later, I saw her, pure and white, a dot of perfection moving about Cydonia. Hear me, my children! Nine minutes later! Our Lady's thoughts had come to me instantaneously, but even her most holy radiance had to travel at the speed of light, and Mars that evening was 160 million kilometers from Earth—nine light-minutes!"

###

I must have dozed off. Elizabeth Chen was standing over me, speaking softly. "Father Bailey? Father Bailey? Time to get up ..."

I opened my eyes. Liz Chen was plenty fine to look at—hey, I'm celibate; not dead!—but I was unnerved to see her standing here, in the passenger cabin, instead of sitting up front at the controls. It was obvious from the panorama flashing by outside my window that we were still speeding along a few meters above the Martian surface. I'll gladly put my faith in God, but autopilots give me the willies.

"Hmm?" I said.

"We're approaching Cydonia. Rise and shine."

And give God the glory, glory ... "All right," I said. I always slept well on Mars—better than I ever did on Earth. Something to do with the 37% gravity, I suppose.

She went back into the cabin. I looked out the window. There, off in the distance, was a side view of the famous Face. From this angle, I never would have given it a second glance if I hadn't known its history among crackpots.

Well, if we were passing the Face, that meant the so-called cityscape was just 20 kilometers southwest of here. We'd already discussed our travel plans: she'd take us in between the "pyramid" and the "fortress," setting down just outside the "city square."

I started suiting up.

###

The original names had stuck: The pyramid, the fortress, the city square. Of course, up close, they seemed not in the least artificial. I was bent over now, looking out a window.

"Kind of sad, isn't it?" said Liz, standing behind me, still in her coveralls. "People are willing to believe the most outlandish things on the scantest of evidence."

There was just a hint of condescension in her tone. Like almost everyone else on Mars, she thought me a fool—and not just for coming out here to Cydonia, but for the things I'd built my whole life around.

I straightened up, faced her. "You're not coming out?"

She shook her head. "You had your nap on the way here. Now it's my turn. Holler if you need anything." She touched a control, and the inner door of the cylindrical airlock chamber rolled aside, like the stone covering Jesus' sepulcher.

###

What, I wondered, would the Mother of our Lord be doing here, on this ancient, desolate world? Of course, apparitions of her were famous for occurring in out-of-the-way places: Lourdes, France; La'Vang, Vietnam; Fatima, Portugal; Guadalupe, Mexico. All of them were off the beaten track.

And yet, people did come to these obscure places in their millions after the fact. It had been a century and a half since the apparitions at Fatima, and that village still attracted five million pilgrims annually.

Annually. I mean *Earth* annually, of course. Only the anal retentive worry about the piddling difference between a terrestrial day and a Martian sol, but the Martian year was twice as long as Earth's. So, Fatima, I guess gets *ten* million visitors per Martian year ...

I felt cold as I looked at the landscape of rusty sand and towering rock faces. It was psychosomatic, I knew: my surface suit—indeed white, as Jurgen Emat had noted—provided perfect temperature control.

The city square was really just an open area, defined by wind-sculpted sandstone mounds. Although in the earliest photos, it had perhaps resembled a piazza, it didn't look special from within it. I walked a few dozen meters then turned around, the lamp from my helmet piercing the darkness.

My footprints stretched out behind me. There were no others. I was hardly the first to visit Cydonia, but, unlike on the Moon, dust storms on Mars made such marks transitory.

I then looked up at the night sky. Earth was easy enough to spot—it was always on the ecliptic, of course, and right now was in ... my goodness, isn't that a coincidence!

It was in Virgo, the constellation of the Virgin, a dazzling blue point, a sapphire outshining even mighty Spica.

Of course, Virgo doesn't depict the Mother of Our Lord; the constellation dates back to ancient times. Most likely, it represents the Assyrian fertility goddess, Ishtar, or the Greek harvest maiden, Persephone.

I found myself smiling. Actually, it doesn't depict anything at all. It's just a random smattering of stars. To see a virgin in it was as much a folly as seeing the ruins of an ancient Martian city in the rocks rising up around me. But I knew the ... well, not the *heavens*, but the night sky ... like the back of my hand. Once you'd learned to see the patterns, it was almost impossible *not* to see them.

And, say, there was Cygnus, and—whaddaya know!—Phobos, and, yes, if I squinted, Deimos too, just beneath it.

But no. Surely the Holy Virgin had not revealed herself to Jurgen Emat. Peasant children, yes; the poor and sick, yes. But a televangelist? A rich broadcast preacher? No, that was ridiculous.

It wasn't explicitly in Cardinal Pirandello message, but I knew enough of Vatican politics to understand what was going on. As he'd said, Jurgen Emat had been at seminary with Viktorio Lazzari—the man who was now known as Leo XIV. Although both were Catholics, they'd ended up going down widely different paths—and they were anything but friends.

I'd only met the Pontiff once, and then late in his life. It was almost impossible to imagine the poised, wise Bishop of Rome as a young man. But Jurgen had known him as such, and—my thoughts were my own; as long as I never gave them voice, I was entitled to think whatever I wished—and to know a person in his youth is to know him before he has developed the mask of guile. Jurgen Emat perhaps felt that Viktorio Lazzari had not deserved to ascend to the Holy See. And now, with this silly announcement of a Martian Marian vision, he was stealing Leo's thunder as the Pope prepared to visit Fatima.

Martian. Marian. Funny I'd never noticed how similar those words were before. The only difference ...

My God.

The only difference is the lowercase t—the *cross*—in the middle of the word pertaining to Mars.

No. No. I shook my head inside the suit's helmet. Ridiculous. A crazy notion. What had I been thinking about? Oh, yes: Emat trying to undermine the Pope. By the time I got back to Utopia Planitia, it would be late Saturday evening. I hadn't thought of a sermon yet, but perhaps that could be the topic. In matters of faith, by definition, the Holy Father was infallible, and those who called themselves Catholics—even celebrities like Jurgen Emat—had to accept that, or leave the faith.

It wouldn't mean much to the ... yes, I thought of them as my *congregation*, even sometimes my flock ... but of course the group that only half-filled the pews at Saint Teresa's each Sunday morn were hardly that. Just the bored, the lonely, those with nothing better to do. Ah, well. At least I wouldn't be preaching to the converted ...

I looked around at the barren landscape, and took a drink of pure water through the tube in my helmet. The wind howled, plaintive, attenuated, barely audible inside the suit.

Of course, I knew I was being unfairly cynical. I *did* believe with all my heart in Our Lady of the Rosary. I knew—knew, as I know my own soul!—that she has in the past shown herself to the faithful, and ...

And *I* was one of the faithful. Yes, pride goeth before destruction, and an haughty spirit before a fall—but I was more faithful than Jurgen Emat. It was true that Buzz Aldrin had taken Holy Communion upon landing on the moon, but I was bringing Jesus' teachings farther than anyone else had, here, in humanity's first baby step out toward the stars ...

So, Mary, where are you? If you're here—if you're with us here on Mars, then show yourself! My heart is pure, and I'd love to see you.

Show yourself, Mother of Jesus! Show yourself, Blessed Virgin! Show yourself!

###

Elizabeth Chen's tone had the same mocking undercurrent as before. "Have a nice walk, Father?"

I nodded.

"See anything?"

I handed her my helmet. "Mars is an interesting place," I said. "There are always things to see."

She smiled, a self-satisfied smirk. "Don't worry, Father," she said, as she put the helmet away in the suit locker. "We'll have you back to Bradbury in plenty of time for Sunday morning."

###

I sat in my office, behind my desk, dressed in cassock and clerical collar, facing the camera eye. I took a deep breath, crossed myself, and told the camera to start recording.

"Cardinal Pirandello," I said, trying to keep my voice from quavering, "as requested, I visited Cydonia. The sands of Mars drifted about me, the invisible hand of the thin wind moving them. I looked and looked and looked. And then, blessed Cardinal, it happened."

I took another deep breath. "I saw *her*, Eminence. I saw the Holy Virgin. She appeared to float in front of me, a meter or more off the ground. And she was surrounded by spectral light, as if a rainbow had been bent to the contours of her venerable form. And she spoke to me, and I heard her voice three times over, and yet with each layer nonetheless clear and easily discernible: one in Aramaic, the language Our Lady spoke in life; a second in Latin, the tongue of our Church; and again in beautiful, cultured English. Her voice was like song, like liquid gold, like pure love, and she said unto me ..."

###

Simply sending a message to Cardinal Pirandello wouldn't be enough. It might conveniently get lost. Even with the reforms of Vatican III, the Church of Rome was still a bureaucracy, and still protected itself.

I took the recording wafer to the Communications Center myself, handing it to Loni Sinclair, the women who had brought Pirandello's original message to me.

"How would you like this sent, Father?"

"It is of some import," I said. "What are my options?"

"Well, I can send it now, although I'll have to bill the ... um, the ..."

"The parish, my child."

She nodded, then looked at the wafer. "And you want it to go to both of these addresses? The Vatican, and CNN?"

"Yes."

She pointed to an illuminated globe of the Earth, half embedded in the wall. "CNN headquarters is in Atlanta. I can send it to the Vatican right now, but the United States is currently on the far side of Earth. It'll be hours before I can transmit it there."

Of course. "No," I said. "No, then wait. There are times when both Italy and the U.S. simultaneously face Mars, right?"

"Not all of the U.S.—but Georgia, yes. A brief period."

"Wait till then, and send the message to both places at the same time."

"Whatever you say, Father."

"God bless you, child."

Loni Sinclair couldn't quite mask her amusement at my words. "You're welcome," she replied.

###

Four years have passed. Leo XIV has passed on, and John Paul III is now pontiff. I have no idea if Jurgen Emat approves of him or not—nor do I care. Dwelling on Earthly matters is frowned upon here, after all.

Five million people a year still come to Fatima. Millions visit Lourdes and Guadalupe and La'Vang.

And then they go home—some feeling they've been touched by the Holy Spirit, some saying they've been healed.

Millions of faithful haven't made it to Mars. Not yet; that will take time. But tens of thousands have come, and, unlike those who visited the other shrines, most of them stay. After traveling for years, the last thing they want to do is turn around and go home, especially since, by the time they'd arrived here, the propitious alignment of Earth and Mars that made their journey out take only two years has changed; it would take much longer to get home if they left shortly after arriving.

And so, they stay, and make their home here, and contribute to our community.

And come to my masses. Not out of boredom. Not out of loneliness. But out of belief. Belief that miracles do still occur, and can happen as easily off-Earth as on it.

I am fulfilled, and Mars, I honestly believe, is now a better place. This *is* a congregation, a flock. I beam out at its members from the pulpit, feeling their warmth, their love.

Now I only have one problem left. To lie to Cardinal Pirandello had been a violation of my oath, of the teachings of my faith. But given that I'm the only priest on all of Mars, to whom will I confess my sin?

-=-

Robert J. Sawyer — called "the dean of Canadian science fiction" by *The Ottawa Citizen* and "just about the best science-fiction writer out there these days" by *The Denver Rocky Mountain News* — is one of only eight writers in history (and the only Canadian) to win all three of the science-fiction field's top honors for best novel of the year: the World Science Fiction Society's Hugo Award, which he won in 2003 for his novel *Hominids*; the Science Fiction and Fantasy Writers of America's Nebula Award, which he won in 1996 for his novel *The Terminal Experiment*; and the John W. Campbell Memorial Award, which he won in 2006 for his novel *Mindscan.* His 23 novels also include *Red Planet Blues*, *Triggers*, *Calculating God*, and the "WWW" trilogy of *Wake*, *Watch*, and *Wonder*, each volume of which separately won the Aurora Award — Canada's top honor in science fiction — for Best Novel of the Year.

Ecce Aqua

James Heiser

There was a tang, followed by a long hiss, and then an indicator flashed green on the upper instrument panel. "Seal secure," Roberts declared, utterly unnecessarily, but entirely according to the regulations. Burnett nodded, then rose from the left seat to go aft and open the crawler's hatch—but not before stealing one more glance out at the view from the front of the crawler. Docked at the north side of Columbia, the crawler faced the canyon walls stretched out in front of them—still breathtaking, even after four years traveling back and forth on this route.

Burnett tapped in his access code for the hatch, then hit "confirm." On the other side of the hatch, one of the station personnel performed the same ritual. A low tone sounded, and then the two hatches swung away from each other. When the hatch swung open, Burnett often imagined that this must be a little like what it felt to be a safecracker, and he wondered if the person on the other side of the hatch felt the same way—not that he would ask, of course. Not given his position.

A drawn face, framed by straight black hair, peered around the edge of the hatch. Dr. Corson. "Greetings, your grace," she intoned, almost suppressing a grin, as she swept out an arm and bowed deeply, "Your flock awaits you."

"Columbia, Columbia, to glory arise/The queen of the earth, and the child of the skies," Burnett answered her, raising his hand, as if to bestow a benediction.

"'...Thy genius commands thee with rapture behold/while ages on ages thy splendor behold.' Timothy Dwight? That seems a little old-fashioned even for you, doesn't it? Ah, well."

"Crawler 7, bound from Kepler to Ares One, reporting at Columbia," Roberts reported flawlessly. It gave Burnett a moment to conceal his frustration; in his now ritual banter of "Columbia" lore, it seemed as if Corson always got the better of him. The woman had a mind made for poetry.

Anita Corson gave Roberts a quick glance from head to toe, then turned back to Burnett. "What happened to Gonzalez? You break another one?" she asked, grinning broadly.

"Reassigned to the 'big leagues,' I'm afraid. He's on the crew of a hopper now, running up to visit Zeus and his friends on Olympus Mons."

"No surprise there. Told you he was A-1 material. If you didn't make a point of irritating Dr. Zules you'd have drawn hopper duty a long time ago."

"Oh, Zeus can keep his model rockets. I like driving a truck."

###

The hoppers formed the link from the landing point on Olympus Mons to the regional centers all over Mars, but the crucial link were the crawlers which carried supplies between all the bases and outposts of a region. As more and more of the necessities—and luxuries—of life were manufactured on Mars, and not imported from Earth, the role of the crawlers continued to grow in importance. There were three crawlers in Valles Marineris now, and they needed two more to properly supply the four bases and fifteen outposts. Things were getting stretched pretty thin. But crawlers were still a heavy lift from Earth, and with six regional settlements divided into fifteen bases and nearly 60 outposts, demand for such heavy equipment was such that it would probably be at least four more years before they would get even one more crawler.

There were 752 souls living in Valles Marineris—a stunning development, since the population had been four when the first outpost was established twenty years before, in 2040. In all, 4,357 men, women and children—37 of whom had been born on Mars—were scattered between all these bases and outposts. And they were supplied by a network of six hoppers and twenty crawlers. Outposts were easy to establish, aside from electronics and certain environmental elements. Besides, they were appealing to the International Board of Governors, who measure progress in settlements, and boots on the ground—not the efficient resupply of mundane elements of daily life, such as food and water. For now, Burnett and the other drivers would simply have to be, in Zules' words, "More efficient."

Corson put on her back-to-work face. "Roberts, feel free to use the visitors quarters to clean up. I know it's a three day ride from Kepler, and I don't need to read the regs to remember that crawler crews are to remain in their suits for the duration of all travel between outposts. Burnett, feel free to join him, but then visit Bill and Alice Chambers. Baby 38 was born yesterday—a girl, by the way—and they will be wanting your services." And with that, she turned and walked down the hallway leading to the commons.

One of the benefits of Burnett's position was that it made it much easier for him to keep in contact with the 114 (soon to be 115) Christians scattered throughout Valles Marineris. He could appreciate the irony that several of his seminary instructors wished he would have been a truck driver—they'd finally gotten their wish, and so had he. Bill and Alice Chambers were two of the fourteen Episcopalians in Valles Marineris. In addition to them, there were 47 Roman Catholics, fifteen Methodists, six Baptists, an Antiochian Orthodox couple, and 30 adherents of his own, Lutheran, confession.

On all of Mars, there were just over 600 members of various Christian denominations—even 15 members of the United Reformed Mennonites living in an (even by Martian standards) Spartan outpost in Chryse Planitia. Even by Burnett's generous estimation, they had seemed the most unlikely of settlers, but they had adapted to their circumstances. They made use of the bare minimum of technological resources (thus freeing up welcome "conveniences" for other outposts), grew flax, and supplied large quantities of grain and cloth to the settlers. The natural fibers produced by the Mennonites had proven a welcome relief from artificial materials, and, surrounded by the harsh desolation of the world around them, became a sort of comforting, living touch to the scattered human settlements. There were already local customs and dyes being developed, and Burnett imagined that in another generation different colonies would have produced something equivalent to local tartans.

Four shepherds served the scattered flocks: in addition to Burnett, who balanced his responsibility as a Lutheran pastor and crawler driver, there was Georg Kuhning, a Jesuit priest and chemist serving at Olympus Mons; William Jacobs, a Baptist lay preacher (and—like Burnett—a driver) at Argyre Planitia; and John Howard, an Episcopalian priest and biologist at Phoenix in Amazonis Planitia. Like every other settler, each one of the four had come to Mars on the basis of their qualifications, not their calling or ordination. In fact, it had taken years for the "Powers That Be" at Olympus Mons to acknowledge what had been their "unofficial" religious responsibilities—before that, it had meant carefully balancing what little leave each one of them received to rotate visits between the growing outposts. Now, although not directly supported by the resources of the Board of Governors, colonists were permitted to pool donated leave time and contribute it to the "worker priests" so that they could more easily perform their ecclesiastical responsibilities. Actually, Burnett figured that the Board of Governors looked at the four of them in pretty much the same way they did the Mennonites' flax cloth: a condescending nod to human frailty, living in a harsh environment. Burnett concluded this—and concluded he didn't care what their motivation was, as long as he could fulfill his calling.

Roberts and Burnett entered the small visitors' quarters, stowed their gear, took their turns in the closed-cycle shower, and put on what Burnett called their "dome duds"—his designation for any item of clothing that could not be pressurized. Then Burnett pulled his folded, white stole from a small pouch in his bag, and with the stole cast over his arm, and his reader in his opposite hand, set off in search of the Chambers.

###

Columbia's primary contribution to life in Valles Marineris was in the realm of fruits and vegetables; every outpost was, of course, responsible for growing a portion of its own food, but the Board of Governors had deemed it more practical to produce certain foodstuffs more centrally within a given region, and then disperse them by means of the crawlers. Bill and Alice were both assigned to "the orchard"—though the designation assigned to bushes and trees all less than a meter and half in height seemed odd. As Burnett entered the orchard, the sight of the dozen or so men and women towering over the trees and bushes seemed ridiculous. Of course, he knew this was just a Terran prejudice; over three dozen children could have no idea what it was like to stand in the shadow of trees which would have dwarfed any structure on Mars.

The Chambers were tending the blueberries, a radically miniaturized variety of the Toro, which average a mature height of a mere half meter, and were thus racked three layers deep. The bottom rack was maturing fruit at the moment, and from Burnett's viewpoint presented a lush blur of rich blue fruit and verdant foliage. Bill was picking the berries—with Alice "supervising," since regulations forbad a new mother from returning to work for seven days. Burnett smiled as he noticed several sealed shipping boxes marked for Ares One. The berries would be at least as welcome at A-1 as the rack of high-grade steel ingots and reader batteries he was hauling from Kepler.

It was Alice who was the first to notice Burnett. "Father Mark!"—the exclamation came out as a squeak, before throwing her arms around the visitor. Then she remembered the blueberries. With a cry, she drew back her hands and wiped them on the smock she wore—too late, of course. "Oh dear, that will leave a stain," she said, inspect the small blue smudges near his shoulder blades, "And this is Mennonite weave, too, isn't it?"

"Alice, don't fret about it. I'll wear it as a remembrance of the seventh Martian I've had the privilege to baptize," Burnett said, grinning.

The new mother wrinkled her nose. "I don't like it when people call them that. Susan is lacking both green skin and antennae, thank you very much." Then she laughed. "And by 'people,' I mean a certain someone," and she nodded at her husband.

Bill snorted. "Hey, if she returns home to Earth someday riding a tripod and firing death rays, don't say I didn't warn you." Then he shook Burnett's hand. "Father Mark, we have the letter from Father John authorizing the baptism, but it's back at our quarters."

Burnett smiled. Episcopalians always seemed to be sticklers for the rules at the strangest of times. "Not a problem, Bill. Everything is just fine." He glanced at his reader. "Dr. Corson gave me the good news as soon as I arrived, but it appears that my reader has already received a copy of Rev. Howard's authorization. He sends his blessings, by the way."

"Thank you, Father." Bill glanced back at the rack. "Father Mark, I know we both want to catch up, but seeing you means we're already behind on getting the berries harvested for shipment to A-1. You leave in the morning, right?" Burnett nodded. "So, we have Dr. Corson's permission to use the mess hall at end of shift a little over an hour from now, for the baptism. Would that be alright?"

Again, Burnett nodded. "Of course! It will give me an opportunity to further annoy Anita."

Alice gave him another hug—berry free, this time. "Did she get the best of you again?" Her eyes had a "the-girls-have-been-talking" twinkle. With a grunt, and theatrical roll of the eyes, Burnett turned and set off in search of Columbia's administrator.

###

Dr. Corson's door was closed, and so Burnett knocked, softly, and announced himself. "Come in, padre!," came the reply, but when he entered, Anita's eyes were flashing back and forth between the screen on the wall, and her reader, and she held up a finger, briefly, forestalling conversation. Finally, with a vaguely disgusted look, she turned to face her visitor. "I'm about ready to join in using your sobriquet for Dr. Zules. 'Zeus' indeed, it would seem. It appears I have been ... instructed... to accompany you and your sidekick, the well-regulated Mr. Roberts, on the slow crawl to A-1. Apparently there has not been a signal from Ecce Aqua for two days, and Zules 'speaks for the Board' that someone with 'administrative authority' must be dispatched to 'assess the situation.' It would seem that I am the nearest such 'authority' and we certainly cannot leave such a weighty matter to truck drivers. Ah, well. It proves the aptness of the poet's words: 'Let no rude foe, with impious hand/Invade the shrine where sacred lies/Of toil and blood the well-earned prize.' It appears I must inspect the safety of the prized H2O, which in yonder outpost lies, while you refill your tanks to the brim to meet the needs of our friends at A-1."

Burnett wrestled for a moment, both with the news, and with the quotation. "First, you would be most welcome. It will give two of us to offend Mr. Roberts' neatly ordered universe. Second, would that be Joseph Warren? And, lastly, when do we leave?"

"Well, perhaps you should get partial credit for 'Joseph,' but it was Joseph Hopkinson, not Warren. Surely you are not confusing 'Free America' and 'Hail, Columbia!,' are you? Ah, well. I suppose Roberts is not going to do any better, is he? I will begin settling matters for several days of absence, and I will see you at the baptism. Zeus' other order was that we depart immediately, but I believe even Zules must yield to One who is truly greater than he."

There were 87 people living at Columbia—three of them born on Mars—and by Burnett's count at least 80 of them were crammed into the small mess hall. He knew that the rest were stationed at critical posts, and that this alone excused their absence. It was not that Columbia was some sort of Christian enclave on the Red Planet; in fact, baby Susan would be the twenty-fourth child of God among their ranks. There were several vocal nonbelievers among the number who called this part of Valles Marineris their home, and Burnett knew that adherents of other religions were certainly among the ranks of Columbia, as well. But regardless of whether or not they agreed with the Chambers' beliefs, everyone member of the tiny community stood together against the cold and near-vacuum of the magnificent desolation outside their walls. It would be an unthinkable insult to ignore such a moment in the life of their community, and the young life of the thirty-eighth native of this once-barren world. Thus Father Mark was not surprised to hear far more than two dozen voices proclaim their "amen" to the words of the Invocation and prayers.

> ...Almighty eternal God, who according to your righteous judgment did condemn the unbelieving world through the flood and in your great mercy did preserve believing Noah and his family, and who did drown hardhearted Pharaoh with all his host in the Red Sea and did

> lead your people Israel through the same sea on dry ground, thereby prefiguring this bath of holy baptism, and who through the baptism of your dear Child, our Lord Jesus Christ, have consecrated and set apart the Jordan and all water as a salutary flood and a rich and full washing away of sins: We pray through your same unbounded mercy that you will graciously behold Susan Gloria Chambers and bless her with true faith in the Spirit so that by means of this saving flood all that has been born in her from Adam and which she herself has added thereto may be drowned in her and engulfed, and that she may be sundered from the number of the unbelieving, preserved dry and secure in the holy ark of your Church, serve your Name at all times fervent in spirit and joyful in hope, so that with all believers she may attain eternal life according to your promise; through Jesus Christ our Lord. Amen.

Even as Father Mark spoke the words of Luther's "flood prayer," they sounded strange to his ears in this tiny, artificial oasis in the midst of a global desert—a desert which would make any Earthly desert seem a veritable paradise. Still, it was also true that this overcrowded outpost was the only environment within several hours travel in which a human being could survive outside a suit or crawler—and if that didn't make one reflect on "believing Noah and his family" then one suffered from a tragic failure of imagination!

Father Mark offered a brief homily on the appointed Gospel from the St. Mark, chapter 10: "Suffer the little children to come unto Me, and forbid them not, for of such is the kingdom of God." The precious character of human life was not a hard point to convey so far from home, he explained, nor was it hard to understand from this vantage point that the Church which is a kingdom, is all the while also a remnant, small in number, and despised by many. He couldn't help but notice Dr. Corson's eyes flash at that remark—she probably thought it was a 'dig' at Dr. Zules' manifest contempt for Father Mark and his 'little flock,' though any such thought was far from his mind before he saw her reaction. In truth, the homily seemed in Burnett's eyes to fall short of the occasion, but he pressed on to the heart of the sacrament. The remnant prayed the Our Father, and answered for Susan in the three-fold renunciation of the devil, and in the recitation of the Creed. Finally, Alice handed Susan to Father Mark, and using a stainless steel bowl taken from kitchen and filled with Martian water from the springs at Ecce Aqua, the new child of God was baptized in the Name of the Father, and of the Son, and of the Holy Spirit. And a few minutes later, Father Mark was once again Mark Burnett, Martian truck driver, getting ready for the run to that station at Ecce Aqua which had fallen strangely silent.

###

"Hatch sealed," came a reedy voice over the radio. "Confirmed," Roberts replied, touching a flashing 'button' on the screen of his reader. "Crawler hatch sealed. Tether disconnected. Confirm GPS beacon." "Confirmed." And without further ado, the crawler, with its two drivers and one passenger, rolled into the darkness of the Martian night.

A night run was far from unheard of, but it was still not common. Roberts, as could be expected, did invoke the regulation which required the two drivers to alternate on 90 minute intervals, and 30 minute communication updates with Columbia were meticulously maintained. None of this bothered Burnett in the slightest; there might be days when Roberts took the rules a bit too seriously, but this was not one of them. It was best to be sharp, especially when one considered why they were making a night run. Ecce Aqua remained silent.

Dawn was less than an hour away when Burnett finished his last shift and awakened Dr. Corson. She blinked a few times, and then looked at Burnett. "I believe that ritual requires me to inquire of you at this point: 'Are we there yet?'" "Not quite yet. And, to anticipate your next question, no, we haven't heard a word from the outpost."

There were only fifteen souls at Ecce Aqua, but the smallness of the outpost belied its importance. Simply put, Ecce Aqua was the "well" from which most of the population of Valles Marineris drew its water. While most efforts to locate easily accessible water in the great valley had been futile, at Ecce Aqua only a few hundred meters of rock stood in the way of an aquifer capable of easily supplying the needs of the hundreds of colonists for decades to come; the exclamation which provided the outpost's name—"Behold, water!"—well summarized its importance. Much of the labor of the fifteen workers at the small outpost was directed toward purifying the water after it was pumped to the surface; they rendered a rather toxic stew into pure drinking water, and stored it in massive tanks for transport by means of the crawlers. Burnett couldn't easily count how many times he had stopped here over the years, and how often he had ferried crews back and forth between A-1 and Ecce Aqua.

Normally, a stint at the outpost was approximately three Earth months in duration, with three teams of five people rotating in and out on a monthly basis. This provided continuity of personnel, while keeping time spent at Ecce Aqua to a bearable duration. It was not, to say the least, the favorite posting, but it was necessary work.

The heart of the Ecce Aqua station remained akin to the early landers. It was cylindrical, with upper and lower decks. The upper deck was devoted to tightly cramped crew living space, while the lower deck was given over to the water processing facility. Four large cylinders ringed roughly 80 percent of the circumference of the habitat; these cylinders were used for storing water which had been processed. The water pumped from the well entered the lower deck on the side opposite the hatch where the crawler would dock; it was then processed and pumped into storage. However, water could also be routed between the four storage cylinders from inside the habitat. The result was a fairly claustrophobic tangle of pipes—even by Martian standards these were cramped quarters. Only the relative brevity of the postings made it possible to keep the station manned.

The problem which worried Burnett was that the rotation schedule which had served so well could prove deadly in a crisis. A crawler had a maximum carrying capacity of ten people—and that was assuming that every last bit of cargo and equipment was stripped out of the main cabin. Quarters felt a little cramped with five passengers, because the crawlers had been built for moving cargo: they were, in the words of Burnett's old partner, Gonzales, "Trucks, not buses." What worried Burnett was the day they would need a bus.

As the pale sunlight broke over the horizon, the tiny outpost came into view, and a few seconds later Burnett's fears were realized. There was not a single light burning in or around the station, and as the crawler drew nearer, it was clear that ice had formed over the windows of the habitat so that it was impossible to look inside. Roberts slowed their approach, and then maneuvered to align the crawler hatch with that of the outpost. Several minutes later, the telltale hiss of atmosphere, and green indicator light indicated a hard seal between the two hatches, but what they did not know was what lay on the other side of the outpost's hatch. All the sensors which should have turned green as the two systems interfaced remained red.

"Well, your grace, what shall we do? Knock?" Of course, Dr. Corson knew that was precisely what Burnett was going to do, even before Roberts could cite the appropriate regulation. They had a "green" seal, so they could open their inner hatch—but only after they took the understandable precaution of donning helmets for the suits they had worn since leaving Columbia.

Roberts pressed the override button, and as the hatch opened, Burnett picked up a length of pipe. "Well, Dr. Corson," he explained, "when the only tool you have is a hammer, everything looks like a nail." Three sharp, ringing tones sounded out as the end of the pipe hit the hatch of the outpost.

For a long minute, all was silence. And then, three faint taps sounded out from the closed hatch. "Thank God," Corson exclaimed, even as Burnett pulled a cable from an access panel just to the left of the crawler's open hatch. " We're set for just such a contingency. We can power their hatch from here, but I didn't want to open it in a vacuum unless we had time to prepare the crawler. Thank God it's not vacuum."

The hatch groaned slightly as it opened; although there was no visual damage, Burnett surmised that there had been a subtle contortion of the hull of the entire outpost. Probably an explosion somewhere on the upper deck.

The door swung open to reveal the haggard face of a man Burnett recognized as "Miles"—he couldn't remember his last name. Behind him, others were huddled in the midst of the pipes around a small, battery powered light.

"A sight for sore eyes—that's the truth of it," Miles declared, grasping Burnett's hand. The others drew nearer to the open hatch, as Miles continued, "Don't suppose you could give us a lift now? We were thinking we'd like to head to A-1 and have us a heart to heart with Dr. Zules about the virtues of upgrading this station to something manufactured during our lifetimes."

"Dreamer," Burnett shot back, with a grin, "But I'd pay good money to listen in on that conversation."

During the banter, Burnett had surveyed the lower deck, counting nine who were still alive, including Miles. "Anyone still upstairs?"

Miles shook his head. "Not that will be needing a lift today."

"Doctor Duncan," Anita asked, "what happened?"

Again, Miles shook his head. "Doctor Corson, my apologies, but I don't know to a certainty, although I have my suspicions. May I?" Miles gestured toward Burnett's vacated seat at the front of the crawler, and then seated himself. At the same time, Roberts, Corson and Burnett removed their helmets, then waited as Duncan pulled up a schematic of the Ecce Aqua outpost.

Gesturing toward a cluster of pipes which entered the upper deck, Miles resumed: "You know that this old station has two power systems. The four water tanks are kept heated by the small nuclear generator that was 'original equipment' when this hab touched down here nearly twenty years ago. It was a lucky thing, having one of the first stations discover so much water near the surface. It would have been an even luckier thing if the bean counters on the Board had bothered to replace a temporary hab with a facility such as you are blessed with at Columbia, or even Kepler.

"Anyway, the nuke keeps the water tanks from freezing, and powers the purification process. It also gives us energy to crack water molecules into hydrogen and oxygen. We also make use of the atmosphere. The end result is an ample supply of hydrogen, methane, and oxygen. You know, the way some of these old habs made all their own fuel to get crews home. We still use the system for our much of our power ... and the oxygen usually comes in handy, too.

"I think a crack developed here"—he pointed to a line running through the center of the upper deck—"where a line passes through the old solar flare shelter. We just use it for storage now. The upper deck was sealed off, according to the usual safety protocol, during the night shift three days ago. I think hydrogen built up in the old shelter, and then something happened to ignite the gas. When it exploded, the whole hab shook like it would come apart, but in the end it apparently cracked the upper hull and vented all the air. Never heard a peep from the six upstairs asleep."

"I say it was Billings," a mousy haired woman chimed in from outside the hatch. "Been crying and carrying on since he got here. He wasn't cut out for working here. Everyone knew it. He could have severed the line, and then ignited the gas."

Miles shot her a look that made it clear to Burnett this was not the first time they had gone over this. "It doesn't matter, does it? All that matters is that they are gone. And this station is off line until a repair crew can come out from A-1."

"That will be a problem," Roberts added. "There are nine of you, and three of us. The limit of ten passengers isn't just a good idea, it's a necessity if you want to keep breathing long enough to get back to Columbia, or press on to Ares One."

For a moment, no one spoke. It all came down to the numbers.

"Can two people survive?" Anita asked.

Miles weighed his answer for a moment. "It's possible. We've been routing water back and forth between the tanks to keep the lower deck heated. We cannot reroute the power from the nuke—and that's dedicated to heating the tanks—but the heat from the lines keeps things from freezing in here on the lower deck, if just barely, at night. Oxygen will be the problem. After the lines were severed, we drained our suit tanks and the backups just keeping breathing."

"We can solve that," Burnett replied, "We've got spares of our own, obviously, and two should be able to hold out much longer on what remains than nine could."

"That only leaves the issue of who will stay behind." At this, Miles became grim. "I, for one, volunteer to stay."

Anita allowed a few seconds to pass, then answered. "Fortunately, that is not your decision. Dr. Zules demanded that I come here so that my 'administrative authority' could weigh in on such a matter. And my decision is that I, for one, will stay behind."

"As will I." This was not a decision for Burnett; it was simply a statement of fact.

"No. You are needed as backup for Roberts," Corson retorted.

"Nonsense. I know that Miles has been trained to drive a crawler"—Dr. Duncan nodded—"And you and I haven't already been stuck here for days. Mr. Roberts is more than capable of ferrying the survivors back to Columbia, and then returning for us. And as I am senior on this crawler, that is my decision."

Roberts shook his head. "It's at least a twenty four hour round trip. A lot can go wrong. We'll spend at least the day returning to Columbia. I can't guarantee we'd even be back tomorrow. With any difficulties, it could easily be the third day before we return. How do you know the hull will hold that long?"

"I thank you for that lovely mental picture," Burnett grimaced, "And I will see that as one more good reason to stay in my suit until you get back. For now, we're just burning oxygen talking about it. Load these people up, help me off load the cargo, and get moving."

###

Within thirty minutes, the crawler pulled away, leaving Anita and Father Mark in the old hab, listening for every creak and groan of the metal. They were surrounded by enough air to last them, if nothing went wrong. And certainly enough food. "I hope you like blueberries," Anita quipped. Certainly water would be no problem.

"Padre, I have another one for you," Dr. Corson smiled.

"Now? Good grief. Well, at least hear Alice Chambers won't hear about my inadequate memory." It was Anita's turn to blush, it would seem. At least that's what Father Mark thought he saw in the dim light.

"Padre, this one is right up your alley. 'Ecce aqua, quid prohibet me baptizari?'"

"Behold, water, what prohibits my being baptized? The Ethiopian's words to St. Philip in Acts 8. Well then, 'Si credis ex toto corde, licet.' If you believe with all your heart, you may."

"Credo Filium Dei esse Iesum Cristum," Anita replied, smiling.

"Anita, I can never really understand you, in English or in Latin. Is this a sincere request, or not?"

"Father Mark, I've always meant every word of it. You're just not very good at listening, are you? Now, are you going to get the water, or not? It looks like we'll have several days for you to explain the faith in exhausting detail, and I'll teach you how to listen."

-=-

The Rt. Rev. James D. Heiser has served since 2006 as Bishop of the Evangelical Lutheran Diocese of North America and since 2005 he has been Dean of Missions of The Augustana Ministerium. He has served as the pastor of Salem Lutheran Church (Malone, Texas) since 1998. Heiser is on the Board of Directors and Steering Committee of the Mars Society, of which he is a founding member. He is the author of three volumes of essays pertaining theology and space exploration and colonization, including *The Myth of Mars—Imagining the Course of Human Destiny.*

The First Seder in Space

Paul Levinson

"The First Seder in Space" is an excerpt from my 2001 novel, Borrowed Tides.

Aaron sat at the head the Seder table. "Everyone knows why we're gathered here this evening," he said, and talked about the meaning of Passover, the Jews were slaves in Egypt, the meaning of the wine and the matzoh...

And Noah, nearly 10-years old, thought about the Stones — the Rolling Stones — one of his favorite groups, and their song "2000 Light Years From Home." Well, they weren't that far — Earth was just 2 light years away now — but what were a few more decimals among family and friends?

Around this table sat everyone in Noah's world — everyone he'd ever known in this universe. Aaron with his plush felt yarmulke on his bushy white head, Jack with the little frown that was really the smile that Noah knew was always there, and Noah's biological dad, Roger, who still couldn't talk to him with words. . . . And Uncle Hiro and Uncle Bo and Auntie Viva and Auntie Nikki — "auhntie not antie, Noah — even an honorary aunt doesn't want to be called an ant" . . . And of course his mother. And oh yeah, his little sister, Alicia, too.

"... and the charoses symbolizes the mortar that the Jewish people used to build the pyramids when they were slaves in Egypt," Aaron said, and passed the stuff around the table. It was a mixture of apples, cinnamon, nuts, and wine -delicious, a lot better tasting than the ancient mortar must have been. Everyone smiled and nodded their appreciation to Hiro.

Alicia was asking the four questions. "Why is this night different from all other nights?" she asked.

"Because we're still way out in deep space, traveling backward in time?" Bo asked.

Aaron laughed. "That's as good an answer as any," he said.

Of course, for Alicia and Noah, space wasn't different — it was the same. Planet life would be different. And as far as traveling backward in time — that's all Alicia had ever known. And even Noah had no real memory of what the ship was like when the fuel and food stocks and everything else got less and less as they were used, not more and more.

"Noah, would you like to take over the reading now?" Aaron asked.

"Sure," he said. And Noah read aloud about the four sons — the Wise Son, the Wicked Son, the Stupid Son, and the Son with No Capacity to Inquire.

The Wise Son already understood the reason for the Seder, so the Seder was not necessary for him. The Wicked Son with his arrogance that none of this was true put himself outside of the group, so the Seder wasn't for him either. (Noah always felt like him, because he didn't really believe the ancient stories, and sometimes these Seders went on way too long.) The Stupid Son's questions could be answered very quickly and simply, so no whole convoluted Seder was needed for him. But the son who had not the capacity to inquire — he posed a problem because no one could know what was on his mind. So he was the reason for the Seder, and the telling again and again of the Passover story...

Noah knew what everyone was thinking when he talked about the son with no capacity to inquire. They were thinking about his real father, about Roger. Noah took Roger's hand under the table and squeezed it. It's ok, Dad, he thought.

He could tell Roger the story of their voyage, like the story of Passover. How Aaron had half-tricked the government to get this voyage going. How Uncle Bo had almost mutinied half way out but Aaron talked Auntie Nikki into overriding Bo. How the crew lost someone they loved — her name was Sarah. He could talk about the hulk, about their rollback voyage home. But Noah was sure that Roger already knew all of that, and more—

"Let's eat," Aaron finally said, and passed a plate of Hiro's chicken soup that Aaron swore was better than his grandmother's. She must've been one great cook.

###

Nikki and Bo and Viva and Hiro were gone by eleven. Roger too. Alicia was sleeping on the couch. Aaron and Jack and Kathy were talking around the table, aware that Noah was there but talking as if he wasn't, a scene he had been part of so many times.

"You're worried because you can't do anything," Jack said to Aaron. "Worried not so much because there's a clear-cut problem, but more because you couldn't do anything if there were. We've been over this before."

"That's right," Aaron answered. "We have no effect on the universe around us now — anything we do hasn't happened the very next moment, so every cause is robbed of its effect."

"Has a nice ring to it," Kathy said, dreamily. She finished off a glass of sweet red wine.

"May have a nice ring," Aaron said, "but it means we've lost our power, utterly, to influence anything beyond this ship other than in the infinitesimally immediate term. Even here, inside the Light Through, there are lots of things we can't do. We just all go along with the reverse flow. And yes, that always worries me."

"We didn't have all that much effect on the universe going out to Alpha Centauri in the first place," Jack said.

"There's always some loss of control when you're going into the unknown," Aaron replied. "But that was a different situation entirely."

Jack shook his head. "You express a culture that puts itself above the flow — that thinks it can reorder events to suit its purpose—"

I can do things," Noah blurted out. "I can make events have consequences. I plant seeds and they grow."

That was a mistake, Noah realized. He should learn to keep his mouth shut. That way he learned a lot more. This way, he attracted everyone's attention.

Sure enough, Kathy started to say it's his bedtime—

Fortunately, Aaron broke in. "You're right," he said softly and reached over and rubbed Noah's back. "You do have some power to make new things happen, because you weren't part of the time we're rolling back on. But so far, as best as we can tell, your power — and Alicia's — is strictly local."

"And seeds are living systems," Kathy said.

"I know," Noah replied. "We can do things with living systems. All of us. And I can make other things happen here too, inside the ship, but anything that I try to do outside the ship — like sending out a test marker — is gone the next minute too."

"Right," Aaron said, "because those markers are subject to the ship's backward displacement in time."

"I know," Noah repeated, "I understand. But here's what I was thinking about: I could go out in one of our shuttles. Since I wasn't part of your trip out here — we're past the part of space where I was born, right? — don't you think I could control some more things from that shuttle? Because I wouldn't be part of our ship's backward, ahm..."

"Space-time field," Jack said.

"Yeah," Noah said.

"Out of the question," Kathy said.

"You might have more control out there," Aaron said, "and then again, you might just disappear. Because that's not your time. Here, the ship's internal temporal field — comprised in part of our own living processes — seems to protect you. I know, it's complicated — and we don't fully understand all of it yet either. But that's what your mother — and all of us — would be worried about if you left this ship."

"And also," Jack said, "why would you even want to try that? Our rollback is going fine just as it is — we're right on course back to Earth, to the instant we first left on our voyage."

"I don't know," Noah said. "I guess I want to find out what I could do out there — free of this ship. TheLight Through the only place I've ever known — I really have no idea what's going to happen to us when we return."

Aaron said: "You're right about that. I think we all feel that way."

"Out of the question," Kathy said again.

###

They finally agreed to a limited shuttle jaunt from the ship, with Hiro as well as Noah aboard. The shuttle went about 100,000 miles, then suddenly bounced back to the ship — "like a rubber band contracting," Hiro kept saying — though he was pumping the shuttle in the opposite direction.

"The ship's space-time field is too strong," Aaron said to Jack and Kathy, when they thought Noah was asleep in the next room. "The shuttle couldn't overcome our reverse momentum. Could be Hiro's connection to the past is stronger than Noah's freedom from reverse, or maybe Noah's power just doesn't extend beyond this ship."

The ship had an area, a field — both inside it and a certain unknown distance around it — that was traveling back with it to the past, Aaron reasoned. Everything in that field was part of the time rollback. But it was even more complicated, because in addition to the ship's field, Aaron thought people on the ship had their own reverse-flowing fields around them too. Everyone except Noah partially and Alicia completely — because Noah wasn't around for half of the trip out, and Alicia wasn't at all. Except now Noah's was probably completely gone too, because the ship was way past the point in deep space where he was born. So: Noah goes with Hiro on a shuttle in a direction away from the ship, trying to break loose of the ship's reverse pull if they can. They go a fair distance, and then: pop, they snap right back to the ship. Probably because the combination of the ship's backward pull along with Hiro's outweighed Noah's.

"Inconclusive," Jack agreed.

"How's this gonna end?" Aaron asked. "I feel like we're prisoners of this process. We get back to Mars Vestibule, the instant that we left. The 16 years that have just passed for us traveling at half the speed of light, out to Alpha Centauri and back, haven't happened yet for anyone else, haven't happened for the non-living systems on this ship. And then what? Every message that we've sent, every bit of evidence on this ship, is gone? I just can't fathom our situation when this voyage ends."

"We've been over this already," Jack said. "Recorded scientific evidence isn't the only kind of evidence."

"We have Noah and Alicia," Kathy said.

"Naomi can say we smuggled them on the ship," Aaron said.

"That woman can say anything she wants," Jack said. "But Noah and Alicia are indeed the key. We've got to look to them for our answers."

"I'd feel happier about that if we had some indication of the kids' survivability off this ship, on their own, without someone like Hiro connected to the past, protected by it," Aaron said...

"Don't even think about it," Kathy said. "We're not sending Noah or Alicia out on any shuttle without an adult on board."

"Once we get back to Sol," Aaron continued, "Noah and Alicia will have to live off this ship, in a time in which they never existed."

"You'll frighten him if he hears you say that," Kathy said.

###

Getting past Bo and Nikki's security rigs three nights later was child's play for Noah, even though he couldn't remember ever feeling like a child. He had the shuttle fueled and coursed and ready to go within an hour. The false readings he'd programmed into the central system would tell anyone who scanned his quarters that he was sound asleep in bed. And the shuttle's readings would say it was in stasis.

But he intended take this shuttle just beyond where Hiro and he had been, and keep it there for two days. That would prove to Aaron and everyone that Noah had real freedom from this ship. He knew that would make Aaron happy. Aaron was worried that the kids wouldn't survive this voyage, but Noah would prove to him that they could.

Noah initiated the final computer check and launch sequence. He took a sip of orange juice. The computer purred in his ear that everything was all right, then –

A screech nearly punctured his eardrum. It was some kind of alarm. He called up visual explains — someone else was in the shuttle bay!

Noah jabbed a key to stop the launch, got out of his seat, and opened the shuttle hatch. He'd been so careful to make sure no one had followed him.

He walked slowly out the door, ready with an explanation. There'd be hell to pay for this with his mother—

"Mommy's gonna be *very* angry at you," a voice said.

"Alicia, get out of here," Noah said. "It's way past your bedtime. You should be sleeping."

"You should be too," Alicia said.

Ok, he had to be calm about this. No point in screaming at a five-year old. "Look, I have something really important I have to do here tonight. And it's important that Mom doesn't know about it. Can I count on you to keep this secret? Please?"

"Mommy says you'll *die* if you go out there," Alicia said, breathlessly.

Noah laughed. "That's ridiculous. You know Mom — she overreacts about everything."

"What's 'over carrots'?" Alicia asked.

"'Over reacts' — you know — she always says things will be worse than they really are. Like when she says you'll get high blood pressure when you're older if you don't eat lots of carrots now."

Alicia smiled. "Or when she yells that your brain will rot away from playing too much virtel?"

"Right," Noah said. "So you shouldn't really listen to her when she says this is dangerous." He pointed to the shuttle, its door open and inviting. "It's nice and safe in there."

A big mistake.

Alicia's eyes seemed to open even wider. She looked at the shuttle and the viewscreen beyond for a long time.

"Can I come too?" she asked.

"No!" Noah said. "I mean, it's perfectly safe and everything, but you're only five years old."

"So?"

"So that means Mom needs you here on the ship..." But Noah realized what he was saying wasn't very convincing. Maybe he should take Alicia along after all.... That would keep this a secret long enough to let them leave. And if what Aaron was saying was right, having Alicia on the shuttle would give it another person who wasn't tied to the past. She was a pain lots of the time, but she came from even less of the rolled-back time than Noah. Maybe her field, or whatever it was, could be just what they needed to break away...

But he still didn't want to take her. And it wasn't just because he was afraid she'd get some of the glory... Noah had to admit that maybe it was because deep inside he believed there was a tiny little chance that maybe the shuttle would never return from this hop. Or return with its passengers dead...

He didn't want to die. He didn't want his little sister to die...

Noah opened the outside panel on the shuttle and poked in the seal-up and return-to-stasis sequence. The lights went off inside.

"What are we gonna do now?" Alicia asked.

"We're going back to bed." And he took Alicia's hand and they walked out the door and quickly down the halls. . .

Noah slid under the covers and closed his eyes, and remembered what he'd heard Aaron say about this ship.

It was like a never-ending Seder. It was like Planet Earth. It didn't want you to leave.

Epiphany

Arlan Andrews, Sr.

A version of this story first appeared in Analog Science Fiction and Fact Magazine, *September 1987.*

Brother Henry Crook watched intently as the huge alien strode down the dusty road in front of his church. Dogs barked, a couple of barefoot boys in overalls stood in awe, peeking from behind an old oak as the tall humanoid walked in measured paces—six feet at a step—and slowly moved its gigantic head this way, then that, as if searching for something. Brother Henry was reminded of Beanstalk Jack's antagonist and wondered if the boys considered their bones might be ingredients of alien bread. He smiled and wiped away sweat from his brow and his lip. The fierce July sun in Arkansas made the humidity unbearable, and as preacher, Brother Crook didn't like to use the air conditioner until Sunday morning.

Outside, the lazy summer was suddenly quiet, silent as space. Brother Crook looked up from his pulpit to see alien duck through the open church doors, barely clearing the seven-foot openings. The being looked around the empty church in mild surprise then caught the preacher's eye, and started up the aisle toward the front of the church.

The man from the stars was a light-skinned, clean shaven humanoid, like himself, but where Brother Crook was five eight and one hundred sixty pounds, the visitor was wide-shouldered, broad-chested, six hundred pounds; at least eight feet tall, maybe nine. A giant. And handsome as an angel, the preacher thought, in its—his, he corrected—his multicolored covering that shimmers as might the surface of a star.

Brother Crook kept his gaze on the stranger's eyes as the distance between them diminished. Dark, those eyes, and weary, set deeply back under a powerful brow. How strange such contradiction from so awesome and commanding a figure. A lost soul? Brother Henry wondered. Does it—he—have a soul?

Face to face they stood, eye to eye, with the preacher's position behind the raised pulpit making up the height difference. So close, Brother Crook could see the depths of infinite space from whence the alien had come to this small church in rural Arkansas. So close, the large sad eyes bespoke mysteries witnessed, unimaginable forces contested and tamed.

The alien spoke.

"Why do you call yourself 'Brother'?" it demanded, the diction and accent reminiscent of a popular aristocratic British television personality. "And," a giant arm seemed to envelop the volume of the small church, "why do you stand in an empty space? Alone?" The giant's stare returned to plumb the soul of the small human. The alien grunted and backed up to deposit its large mass on a squeakingly protesting front row pew.

Brother Crook's gaze followed the alien and he forced a smile. "Brother from the stars, I welcome you to the Crystal Valley Missionary Baptist Church. I am plain Mr. Henry Crook, the called preacher for this congregation. I don't call myself 'Brother.' They do.

"And we are all brothers and sisters in Jesus Christ, our Savior." He held up the old Bible that he was using to plan his sermon. "I am here alone today, Brother, because I wanted to practice my sermon."

The giant crinkled his cheeks in a sardonic grin. "You know about us, the Gnarthi, human?" Ignoring the preacher's friendly demeanor and slight nod, the alien continued. "We alone amongst the millions of intelligent species have spanned the entire Galaxy." With great arms appealing to the tattered acoustic tile ceiling, almost touching it from a sitting position, the Gnarthi cried out in a booming voice. "In my twelve thousand years of existence, human, I have visited a hundred thousand worlds. This Earth of yours is only a mote, less than nothing!"

Halfway between pleading and threatening, the alien stood again, fists clenched and trembling, and looked toward the tiny human who stood with open mouth and pounding heart. "In all this vast Universe we have never found another culture like yours. Preacher, tell me why you believe!"

###

The Gnarthi lightships had arrived some weeks before, an instantaneous and simultaneous materialization in the capitals of all 203 countries of the Earth. They appeared to be mostly traders and scholars, not invaders. After the initial shock of knowing that "We Are Not Alone" wore off –something a world saturated with space opera movies and television had always suspected—only human traders and scholars cared much. Nice-looking but secretive giants who otherwise seemed human and spoke all languages were not all that interesting, after all, compared to the odd people on reality TV shows.

In the United States, they were seen mostly on talk shows. The odd Gnarthi scholar might be found in the Library of Congress or at a computer terminal in a university or library. They were not showy; the technology they offered in trade was not all that advanced, and their interstellar travel tech was off-limits. Poverty and war on Earth? None of their business. Disease? A little help with druzhba and mutAids. Nothing else, though. No rides for humans to other stars, no visits to the Milky Way. The aliens had vaguely hinted that a Galactic moral or legal code kept them from interfering with normal development of a newly contacted race. Most everyone wondered why they had even bothered to come to Earth at all, a question the Gnarthi had never answered.

###

"Why do I believe, Brother Gnarth?" the preacher replied, knowing well that the aliens all used the same appellation and apparently did not comprehend the humans' use of individual names. He lovingly lifted the Holy Bible and spread it open for the Gnarth to see. From television he knew that the giant's amazing eyesight could easily allow him to read the text from fifteen feet away. "This book, I believe, is the Word of God. And it tells me what to believe. And how to believe."

The giant sat unmoved, not responding.

"Brother from the Stars, this ancient Word tells me that God sent Jesus Christ, His only begotten Son, to die that we mortal sinners might have eternal life."

The alien interleaved his enormous fingers. Flexing his hands, the knuckles cracked like a machine gun. The Gnarthi approached the pulpit, shallow breaths a wheezing gale.

Face to face once more, Gnarthi spoke to human. Slowly, evenly, the alien spoke, gargantuan energies barely repressed, overweening intelligence glaring from sad eyes. "Brother Crook—I call you by your title only, no kinship conferred—the Galaxy is twenty thousand light years thick at the Lens, and one hundred ten thousand across. If a lightyear of distance were scaled down to one foot of length, the Galaxy would be the size of this whole county of yours!

"In this enormous volume are four hundred billion suns, a hundred million intelligent races. And in all of this—'Creation' you call it—not one other race dares to think themselves favored of a God, a Creator of All, a Caring Intelligence. Give me evidence. Convince me!"

A cur dog sniffed at the church door, positioned itself, relieved its bladder in a loud puddling noise. The preacher shouted past the alien, "Get out, Butch! Bad dog! You know better!" The Gnarthi turned its massive head and studied first the dog, then the human. The eyes are mirrors of the soul, but I see nothing reflected, the human thought. Brother Crook wondered if the alien was comparing the behavior and the relative intelligence of the two Earth life forms. Though he would never know, his supposition was correct.

"My belief comes from this Book," the human began. "God's Word says—"

"—Not proof! Circular reasoning!" boomed the Gnarthi from the doorway where he was shushing away the confused canine and closing the doors. "Objective proof, human!

"Tell me, Brother. How did your Creator Create this Galaxy we Gnarthi stride through at will?"

"In Genesis, God says that He created Heaven and Earth in six days and rested on the seventh."

"And you believe such nonsense?"

Brother Crook glared back with a fierceness that took the alien aback. "Of course I do! It's in the Bible!"

As the morning wore on, they hashed and rehashed Evolution, Free Will, Sin and Original Sin, theological arguments old hat to Brother Crook, but apparently totally novel to the Gnarthi. Finally, exasperated, the alien picked up the Bible and asked softly, "Brother Crook, tell me how you, an educated, intelligent and well-read human being, can believe these legends, myths, rumors, half-truths that you know are not true?

"How can you use this book as a basis for evaluating your interface with the Universe when you can be certain that it is flawed?"

By this time, the preacher was weary of body and amenable to relaxation of the soul. "You know, Star Brother," he said with a crooked grin, "You're the very first person to challenge me with that precise question." He stood and paced in front of the pulpit, in the prayer row, taking his Bible from the giant's hands. He stroked the worn cover as a mother might caress her firstborn. "Since you are not really a human, by Earth standards, if I have your word not to repeat any of this, I will tell you what I have told no other man." The giant nodded slowly. "I love this Book, Brother Gnarth. As a young man, I accepted its words as literal. Then in seminary I learned how it had been collected, translated, reinterpreted. Undoubtedly it does not read the same now as it did two thousand years ago. No doubt it is incomplete and imperfect." He turned to the Gnarthi and smiled. "And that forms the basis of my belief, now, Brother Gnarth."

The alien jerked his head back, puzzled. Brother Crook held up his hand for silence. "In a minute, Brother. Just let me finish. This Bible is flawed, but so are humans. The stories change from translation to translation, from scholar to scholar, but so do human stories. The morality, the ethics, all vary from culture to culture. The interpretations vary with time. Truth is relative.

"What Jehovah required from a primitive nomadic tribe had to be different from what Jesus expects of a civilized nation." Alien and Man locked eyes. "Or what He expects of a civilized race. In the New Testament, God even goes so far as to reorder the priorities, giving us a personal Savior, a way into heaven.

"I know you find this hard to, ah, believe," he stumbled over the word as the Gnarthi frowned, "but I have no difficulty reconciling this old collection of myths and legends and morality plays with biology, evolution, quantum mechanics, psychology—even star travelers like yourselves!"

The alien could stand it no further. "Why, human? Why, in the face of all knowledge and experience do you still believe?"

Brother Crook came over to the Gnarthi and put his own steady hand over the giant's trembling one, and both on the Bible. "Because, Brother, God recognized human limitations. Why would He a perfect record for imperfect beings? What would be accomplished by a precise revelation of universal truth to irrational, approximate minds? It would be only a source of constant irritation, unrealizable goals. Properly understood, though, and properly utilized, this Bible is a compass that leads Mankind, however inefficiently, to God.

"Mutual love, understanding, cooperation we find in the Bible. A strong race must have those, true, but they are not enough."

"Necessary but not sufficient," the Gnarthi murmured. "A mathematical tenet."

"True," answered the preacher. "And now, the final one—faith."

"And why that?"

"I interpret the Bible's insistence on faith—in God, in Jesus—to imply that imperfect, irrational humans cannot understand the totality of laws that operate the Universe. We are implored to seek Truth to make ourselves free, but beyond that, to surrender to the overwhelming mystery of the Universe and feel it flow through us.

"That is Faith, Brother: the power that lies beyond Reason, the binding force of all Creation, fleshing out the interstices of SpaceTime; the ethical Ether, the philosophical touchstone upon which the very quanta and quarks play out their eternal games of light and dark."

The alien stared, surprised. He said, "Human. Brother. An emptiness suffuses our race. Wars and tragedies abound in the Galaxy and great despair is a permanent condition, everywhere else but Earth. To be sure, your race has seen, still endures, wars, poverty, misery, but somehow a core of – hope, you call it? -- remains; a seed that blossoms when conditions are propitious. An ember that billows when the wind of hope blows once more.

"And in your rationalization of your acceptance of acknowledged myths as a basis of interpreting the role of intelligence in the Universe, you have exercised 'fuzzy logic,' a form of reasoning that provides useful answers from imprecise algorithms. Acceptable conclusions from flawed theorems. A very useful survival trait from a most primitive society.

"You have given me, our race, perhaps the Galaxy, a most precious gift."

"Faith, Brother?"

"And hope, Brother. Hope." Gracefully the alien bowed and gently clasped the human's free hand. In silent understanding, Brother Crook passed over the ragged book of ancient knowledge to his alien visitor. The Gnarthi said, "I shall carry your message across the Galaxy."

"Will they believe?" Brother Crook asked. "An irrational message from this small insignificant place?"

The alien smiled for the first time. "This book tells of a man from a tiny primitive village who used advanced knowledge of human psychology to spread a message to billions of humans. Do you think the Gnarthi less capable? There is a way." He walked down the hallway, ducked clear, then paused on the steps, turning toward the human. With the evening sun at the giant's back, Brother Crook saw him only in silhouette, but he could have sworn the oversized eyes radiated an infinite weariness.

"Brother Crook, I will carry the message personally," the alien said. Then, a sudden great sadness in his voice, he continued, "In my culture, you see, I am a lowly craftsman, a manipulator of atoms, an artisan. You humans might me a carpenter."

Through the open doors Brother Crook watched silently as the alien walked slowly down the empty road and into the darkness.

-=-

Arlan Andrews, Sr. DSc, PE, is founder of SIGMA, a think tank of science fiction authors, and is a Registered Professional Engineer. Andrews is a former ASME White House Fellow in OSTP (White House Science Office). He also served as Manager of the Advanced Manufacturing Initiatives Department at Sandia National Laboratories in Albuquerque, New Mexico. He cofounded several high-tech companies, including Muse Technologies, Inc. (NASDAQ: MUZE, 1998 – 2001) and Kinetic Biosystems, Inc. He held positions at AT&T Bell Labs and White Sands Missile Range, New Mexico, and is presently an Environmental Program Manager for the U.S. Navy at Corpus Christi, Texas. He has published more than 400 fiction stories (many in *Analog Magazine*), fact articles, computer books, and opinion pieces in 90 venues worldwide, including the first White House endorsement of nanotechnology in 1993. He holds six patents.

The Right of Interference

Marianne J. Dyson

The sweeping arms and eyestalks of the unusually tall horan pointed toward the perimeter of the orange tent. "Brothers and sisters, we are gathered here today, in this House of God, to worship together, to pray together, and to bear witness to the true power of the Living God that will raise us up from destruction."

Near the edge of the crowd, a horan whose large snout and great height compared only with the speaker's, leaned over to an older companion with a scowl as deep as the ragged gash which sealed one of his ear holes. "Sweldron, did you hear that? Do you think he knows of our plan?"

"Rahstov, you starting to believe in this bunk? Only the Family knows what the Family plans. And we're sending that sweet-talking angel to heaven where he belongs." Sweldron emphasized his remark by spitting obaco into the sandy soil and stomping it with a boot. He turned watery eye stalks to Rahstov and crinkled his snout, patting the puffy sleeve of his black dress blouse where the syringe of poison was hidden.

Rahstov nervously glanced at the podium, then back to Sweldron. "Do you have to kill him? Couldn't you just hide him or something?"

"Shut up, Rahstov. The Stalk himself gave me the contract. You know what happens if you break contract."

Rahstov's eyestalks scanned the ragged scar on his right wrist where the physico had reattached his severed hand. He knew all right. He had refused to inject that innocent female with a shot of obaco six months ago, and . . . His mouth dropped open in surprise as he saw the very female, blue eyestalks swaying just arm lengths away.

He clutched his dark cape around him, suddenly chilled in the hot tent. It was obvious someone else had done the job on her. Her eyes were so cloudy she wasn't likely to recognize him. But the sight of her made him feel the guilt that had been growing in him ever since he started studying the teachings of the horan he was to impersonate. How he wished the words were true: that there was a power greater than the Family: a force strong enough to overcome the addiction of obaco.

The intensity of the preacher's voice vibrated through the volume of the tent as light reflected from his white suit. "Let us ask for divine inspiration as we read from the Word." Lowering his eyestalks, the horan flipped open a black-covered book to a place marked with a fringed tassel. A blanket of silence descended upon the crowd gathered to hear the great speaker as he momentarily closed his lids and contracted his snout. "Remember the words spoken before you, how that they told you there should be mockers in the last time, who should walk after their own ungodly lusts..."

Rhastov's tongue almost bled as he gnawed it, bowing his eyestalks in prayer before whispering to his brother, "I still don't like it. What if I get my stalks crossed or snort my lines?"

Sweldron waved his stalks side to side. "Don't worry, you could be his brother instead of mine. And in that outfit we stole, even his own momma would think you was him."

"If he has a momma," Rahstov mumbled, feeling like the devil in an angel's white suit. It still bothered him that the Family, known for its underworld connections, had been unable to trace this guy who dressed in white suits and called himself John. In only six moon cycles he had stirred thousands of horans to quit selling and using obaco. The Family "business" was in jeopardy. All Rahstov had to do was play John for a week or so while they collected donations and forged his will. Then Rahstov/John would mysteriously disappear, leaving his holdings firmly in control of the Family. Rahstov's reward was that he and his brother would continue living. He exhaled, extending his snout to full length. He planned to do some good for a few weeks anyway.

The horan at the podium continued in a loud, commanding voice, "Behold, He cometh with clouds; and every eyestalk shall see Him . . ." Rahstov closed his lids and licked his snout. What does he mean? Does he know we're coming to get him and is warning us that everyone will know I'm not him?

###

"Captain, braking maneuver initiated, expected arrival in planetary orbit in seven minutes."

"Affirmative, Astrogator." The captain nervously fluffed his wings and rubbed his white bearded face. He punched a yellow button on the arm of his command chair. "Lawyer Prewnoa, please report to the Bridge."

A few moments later, a door slid to the side to reveal Lawyer Prewnoa, his horns nearly scraping the top of the door as he stepped onto the bridge like he owned it. But he dipped his head in acknowledgement of the captain. "At your ssservice, Captain," he hissed through his forked tongue.

Even though he respected their ancient standing in the United Galactic Federation, Captain Meertee swore he would never get used to the devilish appearance of the Beelzee race, especially the barbed tails which bobbed in the low gravity of the spinning ship.

"Lawyer Prewnoa, we have come to this system at your representative's request. I understand we are to beam aboard a humanoid who is wanted for illegally influencing local development. For the record, would you please enter the charges against this person?"

"Sssertainly, Captain," the Beelzee lisped as he approached the captain's chair. The captain could feel the heat rising off the Beelzee who was fresh from his sauna-like quarters. "The accused, who calls himself John, takes on many disguises and easily ssspeaks every known language. He has been reported to use these talents and medical and psssionic technology not available to non-spacefaring sssitizens to heal their sssick, sssolve their ssshychological problems, and initiate development of sssertain key sssocial ssstructures that sssustain belief in a universal God."

The astrogator, a young officer on his first patrol, quipped, "So what's the harm in that?"

"Please mind your station, young man," the captain stated quickly. "Our job is not to question the law, but to enforce it."

"Your officer's question is not trivial, Captain," the Beelzee began, turning to scrutinize the young officer, still downy under his wings. The captain smiled. His crewman was going to find out the hard way why it wasn't wise to ask questions of a Lawyer.

"The Sssupreme Galactic Court has determined that it is illegal for any race to interfere with the natural development of another race, benign as it may ssseem in sssome cases." The Lawyer splayed his fingers, his long red-painted nails arrayed like a handful of knives. "First," he began, holding up one nail...

The captain noted the young man was looking to him for rescue already. He winked at the astrogator and diverted the Lawyer from the list of cases that was as sure to follow as debris after an explosion. "Do I understand correctly, Lawyer, that this man has refused to come before the Court and explain himself?"

The Beelzee swung around to face the captain. "Not exactly, Captain. We have never been able to catch him or his companions, called apostles. They have a ssstardrive whose power sssystem is a complete mystery to our best ssscientists. They sssense our ssships' approach and are gone before we can question them. That is why our representative asked for help from the Patrol. Perhaps you can take them by sssurprise?"

The captain let out a sigh. This close to retirement, about the only thing he wanted to take by surprise was one of his grandkids. "Perhaps," he answered.

"Computer, show us the accused," the captain ordered. A full-sized, 3-D image of a tall, snout-nosed member of the horan race, complete with eyestalks and white suit appeared in the air in front of the captain's chair. The deep look in the eyestalks was enough to ruffle the captain's feathers. It reminded him of an ancient painting from his own world, but of course this John could be no relation to that one. "Lawyer, how will we locate this horan on the surface?"

"Ssscan for a sssun-colored ssstructure sssuch as this," he replied. An image of a tent appeared on the Lawyer's briefcase computer screen.

"Computer," the captain ordered. "Load image and estimate scan time."

"Scan may require one planetary revolution," the computer replied.

"Execute." The captain looked at the Lawyer who seemed to have steam rising from his red skin. "We should have him within seventy minutes, Lawyer Prewnoa. I will have him beamed aboard, so you may question him."

The Lawyer bowed deeply and quietly exited the Bridge, his tail swaying behind him. The young astrogator continued staring at the door that slid closed on the Beelzee. "You see a vision or something?" the captain said. "Get back to work."

"Yes sir. I mean no sir. I was just wondering if you believe in God, sir?"

The captain tugged at his long beard, remembering how his wife once pointed out the uncanny similarities in religions of races spread throughout the galaxy, most including a prophet like John. Was this proof there was a God, or of a shared need of pre-spacefaring races not to feel alone? The captain smiled the way he did when he answered her, "Of course I do."

The astrogator's eyes widened. "Do you suppose this guy is for real working for God?"

The captain thought of the Lawyer unsuccessfully trying to stop this John from doing good throughout eternity. "Never hurts to hope."

###

Rahstov shifted from foot to foot, caught in the rhythmic swaying of the crowd. He sang with enthusiasm, "Oh when the Lord, appears above, oh when the Lord appears above . . ." His brother placed a heavy hand on his shoulder.

"It's almost time," he whispered.

Rahstov swallowed as Sweldron urged him closer to the front.

The Reverend John shouted over the din, one hand raised to heaven, the other clutching his microphone. "And the Spirit and the Bride say, Come. And let him who heareth say, Come. And let him that is athirst come. And whosoever will, let him take the water of life freely!"

Horans pressed forward to kneel on the platform where the Reverend could lay his large hands on them. Rahstov wondered how John could claim to heal anyone by simply laying his hands on them? It didn't make sense. But if he really could, it seemed to Ranstov that the Family should recruit him, not kill him.

Rahstov watched as the Reverend, eyestalks to heaven, tears streaming down them, asked God to heal yet another horan. The old female fainted and was carried from the tent by others.

Sweldron urged Rahstov to go forward, to get close enough to distract John while he injected the poison. "Isn't that the blue-stalk female that almost cost you your hand?" Sweldron asked, nodding his head toward the drugged female Rahstov had noticed earlier.

"Yes," Rahstov admitted.

"Come on then," his brother said. "Serve her right to be used to help get you back into favored status with the Family. Follow me."

Sweldron worked his way over to her, grabbing her by the arm. "Hey bumba, let's go forward and get delivered!" She was so out of it, she didn't resist as he pulled her along with him and ungraciously plopped them both at the Reverend's feet, the syringe ready for the right moment.

"God will deliver you from obaco," John said to the female, taking her limp hand. "Will you ask Him into your life?"

"Yes," the female said weakly, her lids drooping like day-old flowers. Sweldron stood near as if to catch her if she fainted. Rahstov shuffled beside him and froze, wishing he could somehow stop his brother from becoming an assassin.

The singing slapped at Rahstov's earholes like storm stones. It seemed the tent swelled like a waterbag and would explode any minute from the vibrations of the drums, strings, and shakers played with frenzied emotion.

The Reverend sank to his knees praying, the female slipping to the ground beside him. The worshippers followed the Reverend's cue and fell to their knees also, lids closing over eyestalks. "Surely He comes quickly!" he shouted.

Sweldron held up his left hand to signal Rahstov to be ready to drop his cape. His brother grabbed the Reverend's ankle and plunged the needle in deep.

As Rahstov watched, the air around the Reverend rippled like a reflection in a pool, and then he disappeared.

Rahstov stared in shock at the empty space where the Reverend had just been. His brother, who had thrown a cloak over John with plans to carry him out while Rahstov took over, snatched Rahstov's cloak from his shoulders. "Go!" Sweldron urged.

"But where is..." Rahstov blurted while Sweldrom pushed him toward the podium.

In the dense crowd where most of the horans had their lids tightly shut, no one seemed to notice the switch. Rahstov made his way stiffly to the podium in his white suit, a perfect lookalike for the Reverend himself.

Gradually lids opened and followers quieted as Rahstov waved his arms to quiet the crowd. Rahstov bowed his eyestalks in prayer and the worshippers did also.

Even though he'd practiced the lines, Rahstov now heard the words of the prophet as his own condemnation. "And behold, I come quickly; and my reward is with me, to give every horan according to his work." All lids were open now, and fixed on him. Then suddenly, the scene shimmered, faded, and disappeared.

###

Rahstov stood in a swirling spray that stung his eyestalks. Then he was hit with a hot wind that seemed to pelt him with sand. When this unnatural storm subsided, he opened his eyestalks. He was alone, and no longer in the tent. What had happened to him? Had someone poisoned him? Was he dead?

His eyestalks soon expanded to absorb more light from his semi-dark surroundings. He was in a small strange room, not much bigger than a humpback stall, with a 5-sided figure glowing on the floor under his feet. His snout warned him of an enemy approach. He turned quickly and gasped, backing up against a sticky, hot wall. He swallowed the spit of fear, and waited for the two-horned beast before him to begin his torture in Hell.

"SSSo," the beast said, "I finally have you!"

There was no doubt in Rahstov's mind that he deserved to suffer for eternity. He had studied the words of God's prophet and then knowingly betrayed him to the Family. Rahstov lowered his eyestalks. He had let his brother kill the one horan who offered hope of a life without obaco: hope of a life worth living. He extended his snout in regret. Had he really believed his plan to siphon off some of the funds to orphans would redeem him for his heinous crime?

The beast, which Rahstov assumed was the Devil or one of his minions, continued speaking. "I have the authority to ssspeak for the SSSupreme Council," it said. "You are accused of being in violation of Galactic Law Code 666 paragraph alpha one revision omega which ssstates that it is a crime to willingly interfere, alter, or redirect the development of a pre-ssspacefaring race."

Rahstov opened his lids, blinking. He expected double-talk from the Devil, but this pronouncement made no sense to him whatsoever. "Excuse me?" he managed to say.

If it were possible, the beast looked angrier than before. "SSSo! You deny plans to change the natural course of events?"

Rahstov lowered his eyestalks again. "No," he admitted. The large head of the beast loomed closer, its eyes full of blood, the horns on its head threatening to sever Rahstov's eyestalks.

"Well, then," it said, tail twitching, "I am prepared to offer you a deal." On black hoofs, it clopped over to a small podium and clapped its hands together, while hissing some command. To Rahstov's surprise, a window appeared in front of him. The view was one of heaven except the stars didn't twinkle. One moved swiftly, then glowed blue and disappeared. The Devil pointed to that place. "Give me the sssecret of your ssstar drive's power, and I will sssee you receive mercy from the Judge."

Rahstov pulled in his snout, sweat dripping. Was the devil trying to trick him? He wanted to know what power drives the stars in heaven? Echoing words he'd learned from studying John, he said slowly, "All power comes from God."

With knife-sharp fingernails, the Devil nabbed Rahstov by his already scared wrist and hoisted him into the air. Searing pain shot up Rahstov's arm as the fingernails pierced his flesh. He then threw him to the floor like a sack of feed.

"You bleed," it shouted, pointing to Rahstov's wrist.

Rhastov bowed his eyestalks and squeezed his lids shut. Blood soaked into his white suit. The Devil must have thought he was the real John! But the real John could heal himself. "I cannot lie to Satan, the father of lies," he said standing up slowly, clutching his bleeding wrist to his side. "I am not John. I am Rahstov."

While Rhastov watched, the Devil stomped through a magic portal that sealed behind him. Rahstov fell to the floor, prepared to suffer for eternity for what he and his brother had done.

###

"What do you mean he's the wrong man?" the captain said over the comm to Lawyer Prewnoa who was pacing in his red-hot quarters.

"The lie detector is never wrong! He said he is not John. And he called me SSSatan!"

The captain smiled in spite of himself. Perhaps there was hope for this poor race of horans after all. "Lawyer Prewnoa, do you want me to beam him back?"

"Yesss! The law ssstates we cannot hold a being without charges filed before the SSSupreme Galactic Court."

The young astrogator turned to the captain. "Excuse me, sir, but a ship just, well, it just appeared in orbit! One minute not there, then the next it was! It must have been cloaked."

The captain nodded. "We see a ship in orbit now. That explains what happened to the real John, right?"

On the screen, the captain saw the Lawyer nod his large head. "Yesss. They sssensed our approach again, and snatched their man away. I was hoping we could get the plans for that ssstar drive."

"We'll collect as much data as possible," the captain replied. "Anything else?"

The Lawyer snarled, his sharp fangs showing. "You will need to use the restorer beam of the transport. The prisoner was more delicate than I thought, and he has ssstained his clothing."

The captain winced. He knew lawyers sometimes resorted to violence to get confessions, but he didn't approve. At least the transporter beam could be used to heal superficial wounds and remove stains from clothing by restoring the proper atoms to the sequence stored earlier.

"He is also rather upset. It would not be appropriate to return him in sssuch a ssstate. Sssince he is obviously frightened by my appearance, and the law does allow captains to interrogate prisoners, which of course he is until he is returned . . ."

"I'll go see him, Lawyer," the captain interrupted.

"No, Captain! He could be dangerous. In accordance with article 4382 concerning wounded prisoners ..."

"Okay, okay. I'll use a projection," the captain said, smiling at the young astrogator who suddenly pretended to be busy.

The captain switched the screen from the Lawyer to the prisoner who was kneeling in the transporter/decontamination chamber. He had his hands over his eyestalks, praying. Poor guy, probably scared to death. The captain initiated the projection, put on his best grandfatherly smile, and waited for the horan to look up at the image before him.

The horan was visibly trembling, and the front of his suit was stained dark purple. The captain adjusted the brightness of his image. "Don't be afraid, son. You will be healed."

The male prostrated himself before the image. The captain rose from his chair and placed a virtual hand on the horan's head. "Rise up, son. I'm a friend."

The horan rose on long, wobbly legs, but kept his stalks bowed. The resemblance to the image of John was amazing. The captain shivered. Was he in the presence of one of God's truly chosen or a primitive over influenced by an interstellar missionary who just happened to be his twin?

The captain ruffled his feathers uncomfortably. How to explain legal proceedings to a primitive? He decided to be straightforward. "You're being sent back to your world."

"What about the Reverend John, the real one?" the horan asked softly. "Is he being healed and sent back, too?"

The captain hesitated. Should he tell him he didn't know? Better to get more information. "Where do you think he went?"

The horan didn't hesitate. "To heaven!"

Orbit would be heaven to a primitive. But what about its religious significance? "Why did he go there?"

"Because he died when my brother and I poisoned him!" The horan fell to his knees again, sobbing.

The captain realized now why they had beamed up the wrong man. John must have had a vital signs indicator that activated his ship's transporter when the poison stopped his heart. It was standard equipment for visitors to primitive worlds. That also explained why that ship had suddenly appeared: probably shut off its cloaking device while the transporter recharged. But the apostles weren't likely to send John back to the planet. They wouldn't want him picked up by the Lawyer.

"So, you believe that John died and went to heaven. And what happened to you?"

"I was supposed to take his place, so I went to the podium. But then everything went all fuzzy and I ended up here. So someone must have poisoned me, too, and I was sent to hell."

The captain suppressed his desire to laugh. This primitive had no idea how many people equaled dealing with Lawyers to being in hell. But his job was only to get the horan calmed and reintegrated into his society. The best thing to do was to let him create his own rationalization of what had happened that was consistent with the facts.

"John did indeed go to heaven, but he is not dead. He might return to your world someday, but that decision belongs to a higher power." The horan would assume he meant God, and considering the almost unlimited power of the courts if they ever did catch up with the apostles, it hardly mattered.

The horan's eyestalks wiggled excitedly. "It's a miracle!"

The captain nodded, thinking many a client would consider rescue from the likes of Lawyer Prewnoa a miracle. Yet this horan wasn't blameless. He admitted he intended to kill John. He deserved some kind of punishment, and obviously thought he had gone to hell. "Why do you think we are sending you back?"

"To continue the good work of John," the horan said. "And I promise I will! I won't let the Family steal his donations. But... how will I heal the sick?"

"How did John do it?" the captain asked.

"He asked them to believe, and then he laid hands on them and prayed."

The captain considered that the Lawyer would have fumigated the prisoner before making physical contact. So this horan was now degermed and loaded up with micromeds that would keep him disease free for years. He could easily spread those helpful microbes to others through physical contact, ridding the population of many common illnesses. “It will work the same way for you,” the captain said.

“But how will I know what to do? How to behave?” the horan asked.

The captain smiled. This was one question he knew how to answer. It was, after all, the basis for all of galactic civilization. “Always do unto others what you’d have them do to you. Now, it is time. Go with God,” he said sincerely as he activated the transporter.

“He’s gone,” the captain said, still seeing the intensity of the horan’s look as he faded from view. He envied him, living in a time when belief could change lives, a time before everything was explainable by science, and morality dictated by law.

“Captain, the apostle ship just moved in inclination with no energy released!” the astrogator reported.

“That’s physically impossible, Astrogator,” the captain said. “No wonder the Lawyer wants that drive. Just collect as much data as you can.” He smiled. Maybe not everything was explainable after all.

###

When the angel said, “Go with God,” the five-sided symbol under Rhastov’s feet glowed. He felt that disembodied feeling again as the room faded and then his old world reappeared. Rahstov stood unsteadily, head bowed, staring at his hands, running them over his suit which was no longer stained. Not only were the deep cuts on his wrist gone, so was the old scar. A miracle! He took a deep breath and looked up to see the astonished faces of the crowd. He was back on the platform, his brother Sweldron standing there holding the cloak he’d thrown off, what seemed like an eternity ago.

Rahstov could tell that his brother was trying to discover if he were the real John or not. If he were going to fulfill his promise to God to carry on John’s work, Rahstov would have to convince the Family he was the original John. Rahstov must remain dead.

He reached for the microphone, still lying on the platform.

His voice was soft, almost timid, “An attempt was made to kill me tonight,” he said. “But God knew of this plan,” he said more forcefully, “and used it to demonstrate His power!” The crowd cheered. Rahstov saw his brother’s eyes go wide. This was not the script he was expecting. Sweldron stepped backwards and bumped into the blue-stalked woman behind him. Ranstov noted that her eyes were clear! She’d been healed.

Rahstov continued. “He pulled me from your midst, healed me, and sent me back as a witness to his healing power.” The crowd clapped, bounced, and roared like the sea during a quake.

"Come pray with me and let God deliver you!" he said, feeling their joy wash over him. They began to sing the "Rapture" song. "Glory, glory, when that trumpet sounds, and all the saints of God are leaving town. The horans will look and the horans will stare, but glory to God we'll be with Him in the air." Sweldron used to joke they all had air in their heads. He didn't look like he thought that now.

When the meeting was dismissed with the final amen, Rahstov found Sweldron waiting by the private coach used by the Reverend. Sweldron grabbed him by the right hand, rubbing the place where Rahstov's scar had been. Sweldron let go of the arm like it were a burning ember.

Rahstov wanted his brother to know the truth, the real miracle that had happened to him. He leaned over and whispered, "Rahstov has gone to another world, Sweldron Hasiblok."

Sweldron jerked back. Rahstov had spoken a name only the two of them knew. He studied the familiar face as the snout wrinkled. "It is you!" Sweldron shouted, embracing his brother, but Rahstov pushed him away.

"No, I am God's servant, John. You must understand that."

Sweldron winked one eyestalk. "I understood you are pretending to be God's chosen, with more power than the Family in the eyes of the people. But where can I find, um, Rahstov?"

He meant the body of John. How could he explain the miracle of what had really happened? "I am not pretending. I am John now. I told you, Rahstov has gone to another world. He is alive, but he will not be back."

Sweldron wrinkled his snout. "Did my brother rat me out and make a deal with you? He didn't want me to kill you. So you hypnotized us all and spirited him away?" He shook his snout side to side. "The Family won't give up you know. They'll just send another assassin."

"You don't understand. Killing me will not stop God from raising up another. His message of hope and healing will continue."

Sweldron laughed. "You put on a good show, Reverend, but no one is more powerful than the Family."

Rahstov took his brother's hand. "My brother, there is no power greater than God's. Let Him heal you. All you have to do is bend your head." Sweldron rolled his eyestalks but acquiesced. Rahstov laid his hands over the ragged wound across Sweldron's earhole that had been slashed by the Family after he'd failed his last assignment. Rahstov felt warmth pulse through his hands. He prayed for God's healing to come to his brother. "There. It is done."

Sweldron blinked his eyestalks open and gingerly touched the top of his head where the scabs had been. "It's smooth!" His eyestalks expanded in wonder.

Rahstov nodded his eyestalks. "God has power over all things, even the stars." He pointed to the sky where a new star shone brightly.

###

John sipped a hot liquid to help his body regain strength after Paul's prayer had neutralized the deadly poison. "Did you drop the cloaking device to let the Devil know we are here?"

"Yes, indeed," Paul remarked. "While you rested, God moved us around, too. I'm sure it was a humbling experience for the Devil's crew." His white hair made a halo around his head against the backdrop of stars out the dome of their celestial chariot.

"Did the Devil send our chosen one back with micromeds?" asked John. He secured a warmed cloth wet with holy water over his face. It felt good to get his eyes back in his skull, though he had to admit that eyestalks had been fun to wave around.

"Of course," Paul said. "Though we know that faith was all he really needed."

John chuckled. "It is ironic that the Devil has now interfered with the natural selection of God's people, making them even more likely to survive and thrive." John ran the cloth over his head, restoring his ears to their default size again.

"Yes, it is ironic," Paul agreed, "but just like God to let even those with bad intentions do good." He pushed off the wall and caught his bare feet under a strap. He studied a star map displayed there. "God has chosen another race for us to influence in the right direction," he said.

"A water world?" John asked. When he ran the cloth over his toes, they had tingled, and he felt webs growing between them.

"Yes. The chosen ones are in the Dorathi sector," Paul stated. He turned and slid into a seat facing John's. The two apostles joined hands in prayer. "Though the path be difficult, we are ready to serve, Lord. Let Your power take us where we are needed. Amen."

###

On a computer screen elsewhere in orbit, a blue flash flared and a ship miraculously disappeared.

THE BEGINNING

-=-

Marianne Dyson has a degree in physics and was one of NASA's first female flight controllers, the subject of her Space Shuttle memoir, *A Passion for Space.* She is best known for her children's books about space that have won the Golden Kite and the American Institute of Physics Science Writing awards. She recently coauthored *Welcome to Mars* with Apollo 11's Buzz Aldrin for *National Geographic.* Dyson is a member of Clear Lake Presbyterian Church in Houston. To invite her to speak, please visit: www.mdyson.com.

Birth of a Pantheon

Kyle Aisteach

There is no god of aerobraking. By the time people hit on the concept of using a planet's atmosphere to slow down a spaceship, the peoples of the world had stopped naming new deities. It was too bad, Nuwan Muswazi mused, because it would be nice if there were some divine force he could entreat as he barreled toward the toxic clouds of Venus without power.

In the dim light from the emergency lamp, Nuwan checked his pencil-on-paper math once more, struggling to keep himself from floating away from the work surface. A sextant he had rigged up from a cannibalized starfinder gave their position relative to the planet, but with a larger margin for error than he liked. The fuel explosion two weeks ago had not only cost them two course-correction burns, but it had also knocked them off their original course. The other colony ship's generators had limped them through the evacuation, but even that power was gone now that the tether had been released.

As best Nuwan could measure from the command deck, they were at least close to the right course. "All right," he said into the portable radio, "lock it down now."

Almost immediately a piece of metal came down in front of the command deck window, and then another. The improvised heat shield was being built out of the anchor cables and surface-operations equipment from both ships. The gear was designed to operate at 1000 Kelvin. The aerobraking would generate heat more than eight times that amount.

Candace Elder floated up onto the command deck, her sun-bleached hair splayed out in every direction. She looked a little green. "How are we doing?" she asked.

"I'm not confident the course is what it should be," Nuwan said, "but there is a chance."

"Ok," Dr. Elder said. "If there's any doubt, any at all, I want you to come with me over to the other ship. We can replace the ship. We can't replace you."

Nuwan shook his head. Even Candace Elder, with all her money, couldn't get a replacement ship to Venus in time. "That would be fine if we want to terraform but not eat."

The pair of ships -- designed to be tethered together and spun to create artificial gravity while in transit -- were anything but identical. Without this one, this particular ship, there would be no way to produce enough food once they got to Venus.

Candace Elder placed a hand on Nuwan's shoulder. "Good luck."

"Thank you," Nuwan said. "Now I want you to exit via airlock 2, and take the pressure in the airlock down to 34% before opening the exterior hatch. Open it on the 'go' signal, not before."

"Thirty-four percent," Dr. Elder acknowledged. Those little blasts of air out of the ship would constitute the last-minute course corrections that could make all the difference. Candace Elder disappeared belowdecks again.

"We're done out here," came a report over the radio.

Nuwan looked at the window. Sure enough, the makeshift patchwork of rover parts now completely obscured it. "All right," he responded. "Good luck, and remember your jump-off points. Do not power up your personal thrusters until you are at least 30 seconds away from the ship."

"Acknowledged."

There was nothing more Nuwan could do on the command deck. He switched off the emergency lamp and groped in the blackness until he found the hatch in the floor.

Nuwan knew every inch of this ship, but he knew it walking. Floating, weightless, in total darkness, pulling himself along by the handgrips... that was an experience he had not yet gotten used to. A faint pop and hiss in the otherwise silent corridor told him that Candace Elder had opened the airlock. He hoped she remembered to take the portable timer in there with her when she left. Any equipment left behind on this ship was equipment that might not be available to the survivors should he fail.

The number 1 airlock led out onto an enormous platform at the rear of the ship, where the anchor cables had been stored. As he neared it, shafts of sunlight began to appear in the corridor. The improvised heat shield only protected the front of the ship. The rest would have to function with the built-in heat shield, designed for a much slower atmospheric entry. Some of the aft window coverings had been cannibalized. Some had shot off into space with shards of fuel tank embedded in them.

The environment suit proved challenging to get into alone and in microgravity. Nuwan hurried into the airlock without doing the pre-EVA check.

As the airlock door swung open, he couldn't help but gasp. They were approaching Venus on the night side, of course, but the Sun was beside them, not behind them. As a result, the deck glinted and reflected in an intense sidelight. He could still discern stars, stretched out across the infinity beyond. Earth wouldn't be visible, but the constellations of the ecliptic quickly resolved.

The other ship -- officially called Colony Ship A because Candace Elder refused to let it be named after herself -- glinted in the sunlight. A faint cloud formed around it as it executed a braking maneuver. Its wings were already shifting into the shuttlecock position that would keep it stable during its belly-first, low-speed entry into the atmosphere -- exactly what Nuwan wished his ship was still capable of doing.

Nuwan's sextant tried to float away, but its tie line restrained it. Nuwan flattened his nose against his faceplate. The ergonomics of using a sextant inside an environment suit was another factor nobody had really weighed. But, to do the final course check, he needed the exact positions of the stars.

Those vast stars. It was easy to imagine ancient people across Earth's various cultures staring into the infinity and dreaming up gods. Historically, his own people were monotheists, of course, and their god played very little role in their everyday lives. Probably because the everyday lives of the Swazi people required very little divine intervention. The people Nuwan grew up with all believed there was nothing they couldn't accomplish if they set their minds to it.

But crossing the vast nothingness between planets wasn't an everyday activity. Extraordinary circumstances require extraordinary divinities. That was probably why so many monotheistic religions also had saints or spirits with specific concerns. And right now, he didn't just need a patron spirit of aerobraking. He needed a god of spacefaring.

Because he was off course.

Nuwan had initially hoped he was just getting distortions off the curved visor. But, no, Alpha Arietis and Aldebaran were both almost a quarter of a degree off from where they should be. Not much, but enough to destroy his safety margin. On his current course, Nuwan wouldn't be aerobraking; he'd be plunging to the surface in a fireball.

Perhaps this close to the Sun the ship was acting like a solar sail, spinning like a weathervane. Perhaps his math and measurements had been off all along, since the navigation computers hadn't worked in two weeks and the other ship's computers could only estimate. But he didn't have time to speculate. He dragged himself back into the airlock.

His best bet would be to send a controlled blast of air out of the number 2 airlock, four decks below. The theory of using blasts of atmosphere to change course was as old as space travel. In practice, however, it rarely worked as planned.

Number 2 was the largest airlock, built as a launching point for surface rovers. The ship itself would never reach the surface of Venus. Once in the atmosphere, it would convert into a dirigible, operating 55km above the surface where the temperatures and pressures were not unlike equatorial Earth.

Nuwan emerged into the bottom deck by the seed storage bay, which no one had dared open since it had depressurized in the explosion. One solid push sent him sailing across the cavernous room, the ship's ribs scrolling past in shades of darkness. The number 2 airlock stood sealed in the next chamber. A quick glance through the window confirmed that Candace Elder had left the exterior door open.

It also revealed that she had forgotten the timer.

Whatever the god of spacefaring was named, he had just smiled on Nuwan. With the timer still there, he could work out the course correction without removing his environment suit to work his watch. Nuwan fumbled to grab the pencil and clipboard floating on an aircraft cable by the airlock and frantically calculated.

Goddess. The deity in charge of spacefaring would have to be a goddess, not a god. A protector deity, maternal in the way it shields something as cosmically insignificant as a spaceship or a human being.

The course correction, this soon before entering the Venusian thermosphere, would take most of the air in the ship.

Nuwan turned the manual release wheel on the airlock and pulled. All he succeeded in doing was jerking his own body around. The door stubbornly refused to open. Large door, designed for equipment, not people, Nuwan reminded himself. Its surface area meant a great deal of air pressure pushing back on the door as he tried to move it, and he had no leverage.

In weightlessness, there is no "up." Nuwan spun himself around and used the wall as the floor. He planted both feet firmly beside the airlock door, and squatted. Gripping the release wheel with both hands, he lifted.

The door budged. Then it hissed. Then it opened a quarter of a meter and roared. Even through the environment suit, he felt the force of the air whipping around his legs.

Nuwan's feet went out from under him.

The airlock door slammed down onto Nuwan's thighs. Pain roared through his entire body. If his legs weren't broken, they'd certainly be damaged to the point of uselessness.

Nuwan forced his eyes to focus on the timer still attached to the wall in the airlock. Another small favor from the nameless goddess of spacefaring -- it hadn't blown out into space. Ten more seconds. It would take him at least that long to extricate himself.

Nuwan used his whole body to lift the door again. He grabbed the clipboard. The line holding it to the wall stretched at the connector joint. Nuwan felt himself praying to that unnamed goddess as he dragged himself back inside.

The force of the escaping atmosphere grew steadily weaker. Nuwan swung his feet out of the way and allowed the remaining air pressure to slam the airlock shut.

Sunlight streamed through the unprotected windows at a different angle now. The blast of air had certainly done something.

Nuwan's head throbbed. A flicker of orange tinted the sunlight. The plasma shock. He was already in the upper atmosphere. And his legs were useless.

There is nothing that cannot be done if you put your mind to it, he reminded himself. He quickly sealed the airlock and pushed off with his arms.

The corridor leading to the command deck seemed even darker than before. As he turned to head toward the front of the ship, the walls started to move by entirely too fast.

The ship was decelerating. And he was hurtling forward like a loose object in a car crash.

Nuwan twisted.

The corridor ended abruptly. Nuwan's legs hit first, both bending in a place legs aren't supposed to bend, slightly above the knees. As he crumpled, screaming, into the forward bulkhead, he felt the G-forces. He should have already been safely buckled in on the command deck. Now he wasn't sure he was going to be able to get up there. It felt like the ship was trying to shake itself apart.

The goddess of starfaring would need to have a name that was both beautiful and ubiquitous. She was, after all, everywhere and nowhere at once. A common name, yet appropriate. Suranjika. Suranjika was the most popular name a few generations before, and had since become a female generic. Somehow that felt right. Even as Nuwan's head spun, that felt right.

The shuddering subsided. Nuwan realized that he was beginning to drift away from the bulkhead again. The first aerobraking pass should have taken almost half an hour. Had he lost consciousness? His vision didn't seem to be adjusting to the darkness as it should. He pushed off with his left hand, feeling out with his right for the hatch to the command deck. Now he wished he had left the emergency lamp on. Add that to the list of things they hadn't trained for.

His hand found the ceiling first. His left fingertips found the hatch. He pulled himself through it, and groped until he found the emergency lamp. He couldn't feel the switch through the gloves, so he raked his fingers numbly across it until the folds in the fabric caught something and it switched on.

Several items had rattled loose and now floated like debris caught in an aquarium. The paper he had been doing calculations on drifted free of its clipboard along with two pencils, several empty food packets, and what looked like a rubber duck. He'd have to remember to ask about that if he survived this.

The portable communicator suddenly lit up as it acknowledged a transmission within range. Nuwan switched his suit communicator over to the same frequency.

"Are you there, Dr. Muswazi?" Candace Elder's voice asked.

"I am. I think I've injured myself, but so far I am alive."

"I'm glad." She sounded sincere about that. "Listen, it doesn't look like the heat shield is going to take a second orbit. You hit the atmosphere cocked and burned the port side disproportionately."

"What do you recommend?"

There was a pause before Candace Elder answered. "The dominant winds are going to be tail winds as you come in again. We think that you should deploy the wings and go shuttlecock while you're in the thermosphere."

The wings weren't designed to give any lift -- except, of course, that they would become the support structure for the gas bladders that would support the ship in its dirigible mode. Rather, the wings, once deployed, reached upwards like arms exalting an unseen deity in order to make the ship aerodynamically resemble a badminton birdie. "I'm nowhere close to sub-orbital speeds. The ship wasn't designed to enter this fast."

"We know," Candace Elder responded. "I'm chatting with the engineers here. The built-in heat shield has a 20:1 safety factor. If we're right about how fast the winds are blowing, you're only going to exceed its rated capacity by a factor of 23."

Which, Nuwan understood, meant that if it was overbuilt as well as overengineered there was a slim chance the heat shield could take it. "Very good," he said. "I don't suppose there's any possibility that you might still have radio contact with me when it's time to do that?"

"No," Candace Elder's voice answered. "I'm afraid you'll have to wing it."

Nuwan knew "wing it" was Dr. Elder's attempt at humor. "In that case," he said, "I shall attempt it when it feels like I'm slowly shaking apart instead of quickly shaking apart. I don't want you docking my paycheck to replace the ship, after all."

If Dr. Elder laughed, she didn't open her mic for it. Instead, a moment later, she said simply, "Good luck."

Nuwan was already going through the motions to lock himself in to the manual wing controls -- purely on muscle memory -- when he remembered that his legs wouldn't support his weight any more. The engineers who built the ship had, in fact, anticipated the possibility of power loss during atmospheric entry. Most everything had a manual-control backup. But most of them used foot straps to create the leverage needed to use them without gravity.

The environment suit's air had developed an odd, salty flavor. Blood. He was bleeding into the suit.

Nuwan pushed off with his right arm and grabbed the nearest foot strap with his left hand. He clipped the tether line from his sextant to it, and then clipped his safety line to the other foot strap. Not the same as having legs, but at least as he turned the crank he wouldn't simply yank himself around in a circle.

And Nuwan waited. He had never believed in any god or spirit. But there was no harm in asking. "Suranjika, goddess of starfaring, please help me with this."

Candace Elder's voice answered, garbled with dropped data. "I didn't know there was a goddess of starfaring."

"I just invented her," Nuwan said. How had he forgotten that the suit microphones are voice activated? "Now don't be denying my deity."

There was only a short pause. "We're praying to her over here, too."

The lights on the portable communicator across the room switched back off as the other ship fell out of range. Nuwan held on.

The ship began to shudder again. The G-forces increased, pulling Nuwan forward against the tethers.

Nuwan pressed his brain to remember his basic physics. Why was it so hard to think?

The force on the heat shield would be greatest at the closest point to the planet, but it would continue to heat even as the ship decelerated around the other side of the planet. His velocity would be slowest just before exiting the atmosphere, but he would not be in an atmospheric-entry trajectory at that point. When was the right time to deploy the wings?

A new source of light cast an orange glow across the command deck. Outside the command deck window, the makeshift heat shield began to show a spiderweb of molten metal.

That was Nuwan's sign. He pushed with every muscle he had on the crank. It grudgingly began to turn.

Each turn on the crank strained the tethers. But with each turn the next turn became successively easier, until finally the crank broke free from his grip and spun the rest of the way on its own.

Nuwan settled into a seated position on the floor by the foot straps. The G-forces now pulled him down toward the floor instead of forward. He disconnected his tethers and dragged himself across the floor.

Somehow he had to reach the ceiling to activate the manual controls to deploy the helium bladders -- easy if he could stand on the floor. Without usable legs, Nuwan lay staring helplessly up at the final levers he needed to pull in order to survive.

"All right, Suranjika," Nuwan said aloud. "Now is the time. If you are there, please help me now."

As if on cue, weightlessness came back. Nuwan began to drift upwards off the floor.

They were through atmospheric entry, and the ship was now free-falling.

The manual deployment levers for the forward and port gas bladders found their way into Nuwan's left and right hand. Bracing his shoulder against the ceiling, he pulled.

Nuwan couldn't hear anything, but the command deck began to lean. He switched his hands to the aft and starboard levers, then pulled them, too.

Gently, as if set down by a guiding hand, Nuwan came to rest on the floor again. The gravity on Venus is about the same as Earth's, and now that the ship had converted to a dirigible, everything settled back to a normal -- if messy -- attitude on the command deck. Nuwan's broken legs were folded under him, but he no longer felt the pain. He straightened them out as he slid himself over to the emergency air canisters.

The other ship needed to slow down on orbit before making its powered entry, and would then need to either fight the winds or accelerate faster than him in order to rendezvous. The wind speeds in the upper atmosphere of Venus are comparable to orbital speeds for some of the smaller bodies in the solar system. It would take time.

But Nuwan Muswazi wasn't worried. He had saved the ship. There would be food for the colonists as they started the terraforming process.

And he knew, after all, that Suranjika, Goddess of Starfaring, was watching out for them.

-=-

Kyle Aisteach lives with his husband in Fresno, California, where stepping outside in the summer feels a lot like atmospheric re-entry. He teaches college writing at three different schools and sings with various ensembles, including his church choir. His first short story collection, *Little Dystopias*, was released in 2015.

Kayanoga's Decision

Dave Creek

Why does that mass of stars seem to be reaching out to me? Kayonga Tedesco wondered as he floated within the clear viewing bubble of the starcraft *Belyanka.* With the lights out and giant Jupiter on the opposite side of the ship, the full glory of the stars shone before him, and one particularly large grouping of those points of fire appeared to him as misshapen arms advancing toward him. *My own personal constellation*, he thought.

Kayonga knew this was an illusion borne of a restless mind searching for patterns as he waited for the priest to arrive. All the same, he accepted the image as a comfort, something he'd found in short supply in recent days.

The viewing bubble's door slid aside and the priest floated in, pushing off against the edge of the doorway with a practiced ease. He landed next to Kayonga and offered his hand to shake. "Father Dominic Clarkson."

"Kayonga Tedesco."

Father Dominic indicated the starfield beyond the clear walls. "Beautiful, isn't it?"

Kayonga decided not to share his impression of the stars reaching out for him. "Almost beyond Human understanding, I'd say."

"I believe it takes us back to our most primitive days. When all the stars were above us, not all around."

"Uh ... how do I go about this?"

"Typically, a Catholic says, 'Forgive me, Father, for I have sinned. And you tell me how long it's been since your last confession."

"I'm not Catholic."

"Oh. Well, as ship's chaplain, I can do any number of flavors."

"I've described myself as a sect of one. And we were just looking at its scripture."

"I think I understand," Father Dominic said. "Then let me just ask how I can help you."

"I'm scheduled to leave on this ship, to become an explorer. But I'm uncertain as to whether I should."

"What's caused that uncertainty?"

"Haven't you heard of my actions, Father? Don't you know why I come to you so ashamed?"

"Never mind what I've heard. I want to hear your story as you need to tell it."

"Very well, Father."

###

It involved a rescue attempt gone awry deep in Jupiter's atmosphere (Kayonga told Father Dominic), and it threatened to become a double disaster. And I found myself the only person in a position to bring help in time.

It meant running to the only shuttle on Callisto Base that could get fired up and ready to go in time, and even then bypassing a dozen safety protocols and pre-flight procedures. Not to mention leaving without a co-pilot, which was strictly against protocol. But I had to lift as quickly as possible from that moon's dark, pock-marked surface.

Once I had the gravitic drive straining to erase the distance between Callisto and Jupiter, I got on the comm to my friend Michael Shannon, and found myself fighting to keep my voice steady and professional, not letting the fear I felt for him leak through: "What's your shuttle's status?"

Michael's response came back through a background of static: "Drive's out. We're sinking slowly so far, but sinking all the same. We've got no chance of making it on our own."

Michael and his co-pilot, Donna Gage, had launched earlier on a mission to help five Jupiter whales, three of them seriously injured.

Humans from Callisto Base had been communicating with the whales for several years, and Michael and Donna responded immediately to their call for help, only to find themselves traveling through a series of thunderheads nearly fifty kilometers tall that was generating lightning far stronger than any storms on Earth.

They took the risk.

And a bolt ten times as hot as the surface of the Sun struck their shuttle, knocking out most of its systems. The craft immediately began to sink into the depths of Jupiter's atmosphere. Soon the pressure there would crush the shuttle. It was slim consolation that it would only take a fraction of a second, too short a time for the Human nervous system to perceive it or feel any pain.

"What about the whales?" I asked as Jupiter loomed ahead, with some of its yellow, red, and brown bands of clouds as wide as six hundred kilometers. I was guiding the craft to an area of the giant planet several hundred kilometers north of the Great Red Spot, which was a storm as wide as Earth itself.

Michael said, "They're having a tough time of it. Two of them trying to lift three others — they're all getting pretty tired."

Adult Jupiter whales could grow to be half an kilometer long. Their bodies were filled with helium and heavier gases, allowing them to glide within the depths of the gas giant's atmosphere.

Three of them had flown down into calmer skies where they fed on much smaller lifeforms. One of them, however, a youngster, strayed from the calm and wandered into an area where winds topped out at just over 360 kilometers an hour. The young whale's body couldn't take the buffeting, and two of the adults also ventured into the high wind area to rescue him. They were injured, in turn, and two more adults also risked their lives extracting all three of the stricken whales.

Now the two uninjured Jupiter whales were trying to bring the three injured ones up to calmer climes. They'd hoped Michael's shuttle could use its enticement beams to help lift them, but now that craft needed rescue, as well.

"How much time do you have left?" I asked.

Michael's voice was unsteady as he said, "About eight minutes until enough systems break down that we're crushed."

I measured his speed against the distance he had to cover. "I can just make it."

Another voice came over the datalink: "This is the Human Kayonga Tedesco?"

One of the Jupiter whales, I realized. "Yes, it is."

"This is Entai, the mother of my pod. We are all weakening. We will fall into the world before your shuttle does. I fear all of us will die."

Another quick check of speed and distance, and I said, "I can't bring you up and the Human craft as well."

"I am looking out for my pod. I will sacrifice myself if you can save the other four of us, then the Humans."

I shook my head. "I still wouldn't be able to save both them and the Human shuttle. Michael, are you sure of that timeline?"

"Just seven minutes now," Michael said. "Are you headed this way?"

A chill went through my body. "I...gotta decide!"

"*Decide?* Com'on, man, your mom's like an extra parent to me. What would she say?"

I realized exactly what she would say, as memories welled up:

My mother letting me decide, at age seven, whether to "tell" on another boy who'd stolen a ring from one of her friends. I told, even though I knew some of my friends would shun me.

Age fourteen, taking on a 17-year-old who'd knocked a young boy to the ground. I took a pounding, but the 17-year-old left the younger boy alone after that.

Michael's voice was back in my ear: "Kayonga, we're friends! Donna's got sisters, nieces back home! You can't be considering — "

"That's a whole family of whales — there's ... there's ..."

"Just two of us? I don't like putting it like this, but — Donna and I, we're, you know."

Human, I thought.

Entai's voice broke in again. "As someone who is a different species from you, I understand if you save the Humans. But as a mother, I ask you to save my youngest, Itrak, and my other children Lilyn, Therach, and Serild."

I made my decision. I set the shuttle on a new course. "Michael — Donna — I'm sorry."

"Goddam it, Kayonga! How can you do this? I — I loved you!"

As I neared the Jupiter whales and activated the shuttle's enticement beam, all I could say was, "You had it right. About what my mother would say."

I remembered my mother praising me, hugging me after I revealed the identity of the thieving child, remembered her telling me how proud of me she was as she treated my cuts and bruises from the bully's beating.

And as Kayonga's shuttle approached the whales and its enticement beam drew them upwards toward safety, as I wished I could press my hands against my ears to shut out Michael's final, screaming protests, I remembered just what she told me each time: "You can usually tell the right choice to make," she said. "It's the one that hurts the most."

###

As he finished his story, Kayonga floated with his eyes tightly closed against the brilliance of the stars. Father Dominic said, "Do you really believe that?"

Kayonga looked at the priest. "I don't know what to believe, Father. In the last few days I've been called a murderer. A traitor to my own race. Why would God test me in such a way?"

"The eternal question. All religions must try to answer it at some point. I'm partial to one of the Psalms -- 'Your word is a lamp to my feet and a light to my path.'"

Kayonga rubbed his eyes. "That doesn't seem to provide an answer, Father. Just comfort. And I'm not a Christian."

"All right, then. Other flavors. The Quran says, 'No calamity befalls on the Earth or in yourselves but is inscribed in the Book of Decrees before We bring it into existence.'"

"So the pen writes, and we're helpless before it? That's not even a comfort."

"All right. The Buddha taught that we suffer because we desire something."

"Is desiring not to be thought of as a murderer so wrong?"

"I'm running out of flavors, Kayonga. One of my dearest friends is an atheist. Sometimes I think he sums it up perfectly."

"How's that?"

"Shit happens."

Kayonga smiled. "If only it were that simple. Maybe I should take heart from an explorer from several decades ago. Alexander Barron -- you know the name?"

"Of course. Made his name out here in Jupiter space. Flew the first missions into its atmosphere."

"He once said, 'I've never believed in God; but I believe in Creation.'" Kayonga aimed his gaze toward the stars again. "I believe I understand what he meant. The very idea of God mystifies me now."

Father Dominic said, "But you see His works before you."

"And that guides my decision," Kayonga said. "I'll become an explorer. I'll head out among the stars." He pressed his hand against the surface of the bubble, as if he could touch that mass of light that appeared to be reaching toward him. "They, at least, are willing to reveal themselves to me."

-=-

Dave Creek is the author of a novel, *Some Distant Shore*, and the short story collections *A Glimpse of Splendor* and *The Human Equations.* He has also published a series of novellas, including "The Silent Sentinels" and "A Crowd of Stars," with "The Fallen Sun" forthcoming. His short stories have appeared in *Analog Science Fiction and Fact* magazine along with the anthologies *Far Orbit Apogee* and the forthcoming *Dystopian Express.* Find out more about Dave's work at www.davecreek.net, on Facebook at Fans of Dave Creek, and on Twitter, @DaveCreek. In the "real world," he is a retired television news producer, and lives in Louisville, Kentucky with his wife, son, and cats.

The Miracle on Tau Prime

Alex Shvartsman

The investigators arrived in the morning. Father Laughlin and Father Sauer trudged through the dense, chilly fog from their shuttle to the spaceport terminal just as the twin suns of the Tau system began to paint the eastern horizon in yellow hues.

"Thank Christ you're finally here," said Abbot Fierni, who was waiting for them in the relative warmth of the terminal. "I've been bombarding the Vatican with messages for weeks. He's on to The First Epistle of John by now and should be finished within days. I fervently prayed that you would arrive in time to witness the miracle firsthand."

Both priests shook his hand and made no comment on the timing of their arrival. The Abbot was outrageously lucky; the Vatican's typical response to a miracle claim this far out on the edge of occupied space was measured in years rather than weeks. The fact that they were nearby, looking into a stigmata report on a planet only ten light years away, was a minor miracle in its own right. But informing the Abbot, so certain of the urgency of his case, would've been unkind.

###

"Here he is." The Abbot made a show of opening the thin wooden door into one of the monastery's living spaces. Inside the small room was a bipedal insectoid alien, its five foot tall chitinous frame hunched over a workbench. It was writing in an enormous book.

The alien's pincer held a thin bone stick that looked like a featherless quill. With rapid, fluid motions it dipped the stick into a glass inkwell and applied it to a half-empty page. It wrote neat lines of symbols so precise they could be mistaken for having been printed. There was not an ink stain or a careless mark in sight.

"That's Koine Greek, all right," Father Laughlin whispered, not wanting to distract the alien.

"It is," nodded the Abbot. "He started with Genesis and made his way through all of the Old Testament in a month or so, as best as I can tell. Wrote down the whole blessed thing in Hebrew and Aramaic, he did. I can't read those languages but I've been comparing the symbols to an original and it looks to be an exact match. Then he moved right along to the Gospels and switched to Greek."

Sauer cringed at the Abbot's loud voice reverberating through the room, and the man's insistence at calling the alien a 'he'.

"You can speak at full volume," Fierni added. "Xitzl has been in some sort of a trance since he began transcribing the holy texts."

Abbot Fierni riffled through a thick stack of completed pages, lifting them only a few inches off the left side of the tome so as not to disturb the page Xitzl was currently writing on.

Father Laughlin took a step forward and leaned in for a better look. Unperturbed, the alien continued to fill the page with line after line of Greek script. Laughlin crossed himself and retreated toward the door.

###

"This isn't a miracle," Father Sauer raged in the privacy of a study the two investigators commandeered at the monastery. "It's a travesty. Or maybe some sort of a scam. Or some alien idea of a joke. Who knows what this critter is capable of—perhaps its species can memorize pages of text at a single glance."

"Don't rush to judgment," cautioned Father Laughlin. "According to the Abbot, this Xitzl creature expressed interest in our faith long before the miracle business. That in itself is extremely rare."

"Little good would it do it," grumbled Sauer. "The oversized cockroach has no soul, and so it can't be saved."

"It's archaic attitudes like this that prevent more of our intergalactic brothers from joining in Christ's love. Why should they, if they're told that his love is reserved only for the descendants of Adam?"

"Careful," said Sauer. "Last I checked this 'archaic attitude' is still the official position of the Vatican."

"I pray that His Holiness may one day reconsider," said Laughlin. "Anyway, I anticipated the eidetic memory argument. So I sent a recording of the completed pages to the experts at the Holy See. Their findings were surprising, to say the least."

"Oh?" Sauer looked up sharply. "What have they discovered?"

"The Bible our alien friend is writing down isn't just accurate—it's overly complete. In addition to the standard texts, Xitzl appears to have added in all the apocrypha. And I mean all of it—including texts not available outside of the Vatican vaults for over two millennia."

Sauer stared at his fellow investigator, head tilted.

"There are passages in there so obscure it took the labor of some of our best scholars just to verify their authenticity. But verify it they did. Xitzl didn't simply copy a Bible he found in some hotel room. We may have finally discovered a genuine miracle. This is the real deal."

"So what are we supposed to do with that?" Sauer got up and began to pace across the study. "Invite this alien into the College of Cardinals? Beatify it after it dies? Make it Saint Bug of Who-Knows-Where? I'm not comfortable with this."

"For now, we do what we always do. Observe and wait. Xitzl made it to the middle of Revelation already. Perhaps it can shed some light on the mystery directly, when the book is finished."

###

Father Laughlin burst into the study. He was disheveled, his clothes cut in several places, stains of fetid orange discharge covering the front of his shirt. He clutched the large handwritten volume to his side.

"Come," he told Sauer. "There's no time to explain. I must leave this place now. Please," he pleaded, "hurry."

Reluctantly, Father Sauer joined his associate. Laughlin revealed nothing on the ride to the spaceport. He shivered, clutched the book to his chest, and prayed intently, his lips voicelessly sounding out the supplications. It wasn't until their shuttle was racing away from Tau Prime that Sauer coaxed a few words from the perturbed priest.

"I didn't mean to do it," Laughlin kept saying. "I didn't know it was so fragile, so brittle. All I wanted to do was to make it stop writing."

"Calm yourself, Father," said Sauer sternly, "and explain."

"I watched the alien finish writing down the Book of Revelation," said Laughlin. "I stood there and watched, eager to know what would happen next, after it ceased writing." Laughlin stared past Sauer at the shuttle wall as he recounted the event. "Only it didn't stop, didn't even pause. It kept going. It just kept going..."

Laughlin focused on Sauer now, his eyes full of pain.

"I didn't mean to hurt it. I tried to take away the book, or the writing tool; anything to make it stop, but it wouldn't comply. We fought." Laughlin pointed at the stains on his clothes. "I ... broke it. Crushed its body with a few careless blows. Killed it." Laughlin's last sentence was barely audible.

"What did..." Sauer began to ask but stopped himself and reached out a hand instead. Wordlessly, Laughlin handed over the book.

Sauer flipped through the pages to find the last one filled with text. There were twenty verses in the last chapter of Revelation, just as there should have been. But it didn't end there. The next book of the Bible was started on the following page, a text written in a language Sauer had never seen before, a language not of Earth.

The two priests sat in silence for a long time. Finally Sauer took hold of the last page and tore it from the tome. He methodically ripped at it, shredding it into smaller and smaller pieces, until nothing discernible remained.

"Even the Holy See isn't prepared for certain truths," he told Laughlin. The other priest nodded slowly.

Sauer disposed of the destroyed page and began preparing a eulogy. He decided that someone should pray for Xitzl's soul after all.

-=-

Alex Shvartsman is a writer, translator and game designer from Brooklyn, NY. Over 80 of his short stories have appeared in *Nature*, *Galaxy's Edge*, *Inter-Galactic Medicine Show*, and many other magazines and anthologies. He won the 2014 WSFA Small Press Award for Short Fiction and was a finalist for the 2015 Canopus Award for Excellence in Interstellar Fiction. He is the editor of the *Unidentified Funny Objects* annual anthology series of humorous science fiction/fantasy. His collection, *Explaining Cthulhu to Grandma and Other Stories* and his steampunk humor novella *H. G. Wells, Secret Agent* were both published in 2015. His website is www.alexshvartsman.com

The Universe Emerges from Information: 10^{-43} Seconds in the State of Awareness of an Exo-Designer, 2055

Tom Klinkowstein

Just as 10^{-43} seconds or, the Planck epoch, is considered to be the earliest period of time in the history of the universe – a moment poised between instability and the inauguration of a period of unification – so is the mental landscape of this designer, as her ideational activity is poised between wants and pragmatism.

Her thoughts reflect an external world where bodily integrity has no particular value and the boundary between the present and the future is blurred by an ability for the non-material self to reach out and interact with lives in the future (the "exo" in exo-designer).

Refuge, Enticement, and Prospect are metaphorical mental spaces:

- Refuge is a place of comfort.
- Enticement offers assurance that the unknown can be handled by experiencing it as a source of pleasure.
- Prospect seeks resources and the extraordinary.

Balance (Ego)

This week I perceive myself and my future differently than (probably) next week. I have enough insight in my inner self and my states to know that it is just the state I am in this week. When circumstances change (in or outside of me), my state could also change. To know that it is temporary makes it easy to cope with the state (feelings, thoughts, emotions) I am in right now.

Desire (Id)

The experiment's aim is nothing less than determining what an individual could do on behalf of all sentient beings, and to understand the biggest arch of the narrative of humanity and its extensions so that we can more wisely choose what to aim for.

Virtue (Super-Ego)

Design is a symbol of a confident society, fulfilling a deep need for something to believe in, something vast and powerful yet rational and contemporary.

The dominance of form as the constitutive fabric that regulates meaning has to be augmented by time and prediction in the creation of meaning, moving towards a future that is hedged-upon, sacrificing natural behavior in order to more gracefully come closer to a techno-social epiphany.

Working hard now so that my descendants may travel the stars in social-chic.

In fewer than 10 years:
Use media extensions to create a worldview of engagement.

In fewer than 20 years:
Bounce a signal off an exoplanet.

In fewer than 30 years:
Prove other Earths exist.

In fewer than 40 years:
Achieve communication via quantum entanglement, necessary for outer-planetary and inter-stellar projects.

In fewer than 50 years:
Generation of life from computer code, without cellular systems.

In fewer than 60 years:
Sink carbon faster than it is being created for the purpose of terraforming other planets or moons.

In fewer than 70 years:
Non-propellant satellite to Oort Cloud.

In fewer than 80 years:
Robotic landing on a star.

In fewer than 90 years:
A trip to a star that includes a form of portable human consciousness able to survive a multi-decade trip.

In fewer than 100 years:

The digital self reaches out to touch lives in the future.

This story is based upon my three-meter long artwork of the same name, created with Patrick Gibson, with quotations and inspiration from Constance Adams, Nicole Barth, Dr. Emy van Dueuzen, Grant Hildebrand, Dr. Derrick de Kerckhove, Dr. Renate Geuzinge, Jeff Greenwald, and the 100-Year Starship Study (NASA, DARPA). - TK

-=-

Tom Klinkowstein is President of Media A, LLC, a design and consulting group with clients such as IBM, NASA and Reuters. He has spoken to over 250 arts, business, political, and academic audiences, including the United Nations Conference on the Information Society. Klinkowstein is also a Professor at Hofstra University on Long Island, NY, and an Adjunct Professor at Pratt Institute of Art and Design in New York City. His 10-meter long digital artwork, *A Networked Designer's Critical Path: 1990-2090,* was shown at the Fifth Avenue (New York City) Gallery of the American Institute of Graphic Design. The Museum of Modern Art in New York recently acquired work designed by Tom Klinkowstein for the artist Laurie Anderson to be part of its permanent collection.

Jumping the Road

Jack Dann

This story first appeared in Isaac Asimov's Science Fiction Magazine, *October 1992.*

It really isn't right that I should give you my name. True enough that this is history; and history, if it is to be kept alive, must be recorded for posterity. But the name of Isaac ibn Chabib of Philadelphia need not be mentioned.

However, does not the *Pirkei Avos*, the *Ethics of the Fathers*, demand that we repeat a saying in the name of the one who said it?

I will admit to being Isaac ibn Chabib, fool, hypocrite, rabbi, and unregenerate disbeliever in miracles.

So for posterity, for all those who will listen, here is my story.

###

First of all, I should tell you that I didn't want to go to Tobias.

Tobias is not even the real name of the planet. The Jews who live there call it Bharees, or Covenant, because the remnants of one of its moons form a ring of dust and stones that appear as a gauzy rainbow in the night sky. It is, I will admit, a beautiful sight; and as if that's not enough, the comets rain across the heavens and sheets of aurorae shimmer like tinted crystal.

Everyone else calls the place *Ulim*, which means world. We named it Tobias, after Martin Tobias, President of the United States of Canada. But I'm getting away from the point. The point is that all Jews — any Jews on any planet — must trace their cultural heritage back to Earth. There can be only one Sinai, one Torah, one Adonoi.

If Jews have scaly skin like alligators and yellow eyes and seven fingers on each hand, that's fine. Good for them; they're converts. The Torah doesn't discriminate. At some time, some adventurous Jews colonized Covenant and converted the natives. Or the natives listened in on our radio transmissions — not that Jews have so many programs on the air — and decided to become Jewish. (Which just goes to prove that you don't need to be human to be a masochist.) That's the only logical explanation why the Good Will Traders discovered Jews on Covenant.

That was my argument, but the xeno-historians and cultural anthropologists had written an *Encyclopedia Galactica* detailing that the "*Ulim* Jews" were as indigenous to the planet as the electric cats and the flimflams that soared in the sky like birds and burrowed into the earth like worms. It seemed that Judaism had actually, impossibly, evolved *independently* on a different planet. Oh, there were plenty of theories about how such a thing could happen, but they were as wild and esoteric as anything Leibniz or the Lurianic Kabbalists could have imagined: ghostly quantum worlds splitting into imperfect copies of themselves (not so different from the mystic's worlds of angels and demons), the Copenhagen collapse, mirror universes, splitting universes, the Everett Wheeler Graham metatheorem, the turbulent effects of chaos, the great fractal chain, and who knows what else.

So now we are to believe in two Sinai's, two Torahs, and four Talmuds, for like us, the *Ulim* Jews had two versions of Talmud, which, in case you might not know, are chronicles of Jewish culture, law, and myth. They even spoke Hebrew . . . well, they spoke something like Hebrew.

###

Why didn't I want to go to Tobias — to Covenant, to *Ulim*, if you like? Why wouldn't I want to verify a miracle and renew my faith?

The truth?

I was afraid. I had come to terms with history. Faith could not supplant reason. The evidence was incontrovertible.

Had been incontrovertible . . .

###

The shuttle landed in the country of *Chakk*, which had once been the Mesopotamia of this planet. Although it was in a northern latitude, it was quite temperate. The landing field was huge, for this was a major spaceport; but it was, in effect, a crater in the center of a coral green city of bole and root and leaf the size of New Boston. I waited in the airlock, alone, staring out the bolted plastocene door, as if I was a pariah; the crew and other passengers had debouched earlier. As this was my first visit, I had to wait in isolation. It seemed like days, but it was only hours. By exposing me to enough radiation to make me glow like a tropical fish, they would certainly make me kosher. I guess they didn't trust anyone's infection control procedures but their own. So what could be lost but a little time? I'm ninety-seven years old. I've got a slow metabolism. A little radiation won't kill me, and if it does, that wouldn't be such a loss.

The *Tzaddik* — the "Good Jew who makes miracles and talks with God," the grand rabbi, my boss — would just have to send someone younger and less cynical to discover the nature of God.

So I stood before the lock and stared out into the landing field. It would soon be time, for an alien stood on the field below and waited for me. He didn't wave, nor did he move around or shift his weight from foot to foot. He stood still as stone, his yellowish eyes fixed on me. He wore a blue yarmulke that fitted tightly to his bald, blue-grey head — the kind of yarmulkes handed out at bar mitzvahs on Long Island, and a black-striped prayer-shawl was draped over his shoulders. Suddenly a crowd of Ulimites gathered before the shuttle, but they stayed well away from the one dressed as a Jew. Those that came too close to him, moved away quickly with nervous grins on their faces. Except for the Jew, they all seemed agitated. The Ulimites were dressed in fine linens that billowed and ballooned, multi-hued gowns and coats and breeches that were meant to create new shapes rather than accentuate or improve nature. It reminded me of sixteenth century English fashion, the kind of clothes worn during the reign of Henry VIII.

A human delegation arrived, all in evening clothes; so I was to be formally received.

I would have preferred to go off quietly with the alien in the *tallis*.

Then the ship wished me farewell, the lock sighed open, and I walked down the enclosed gangway. The mossy smells of forest and grass, which were carried on gentle breezes, were overwhelming. I shook hands with the ambassador from the Canadian States and his officers from the foreign office, and was introduced to the alien ambassador and other dignitaries who extended their seven-fingered hands to greet me. Their skin was surprisingly hot, and leathery as the case of an old book. It took a moment to get used to looking at the aliens and listening to the translator, who was a young woman with a hard, shiny face and a deep voice.

Two men clutched my elbows as if I were a fugitive and gently propelled me toward what looked to be a slidewalk the size of a thoroughfare. They were going to ghost me away before the alien in the *tallis* could introduce himself. "Excuse me," I said to the man on my right (after all, I'm right-handed), "but what about my friend there?" I waved to the alien in the yarmulke, who stood alone away from the crowd. He frowned, which for an Ulimite is the same thing as a smile. (I had had the whole voyage in the starship to study, so I knew a *few* things.)

"*Shalom*," he said in a voice that carried over the noise of the others. The intonation was odd: he pronounced the word as if it were divided into three distinct syllables, and he glottalized the "al" and "om".

I asked him who he was: "*Mee Ahtaw*?"

He spoke quickly, as if the group surrounding me would stop him any second, but it was as if he didn't exist: his brethren either didn't notice him or were purposely ignoring him. Although he used words I had never heard, I understood most of what he said. His name was Tahlmeade, which meant student, at least in Terran Hebrew.

A member of the Ulimite delegation stepped right in front of me, even as I was speaking to Tahlmeade. I though it very rude, and odd; but Tahlmeade simply moved around the periphery of the nervous crowd and re-established eye-contact with me. As he moved about, like a child playing peekaboo, I could not help but smile. All the Ulimites were short — about four and a half feet tall — and their flattened features, serious expressions, and roundish heads made them seem . . . cute. But even to think about them that way was condescending. No, more than that. Was it not just another form of prejudice? Of racism? Indeed, the human dignitaries might well think that an old man with a long beard and earlocks was *cute*, especially one wearing a fur-brimmed hat, and a black caftan with a silk cord knotted around his waist to separate the Godly parts — the mind, the soul, and the heart — from the lower parts.

And who knows what the Ulimites thought of *humans*? Most likely, they didn't perceive us as cute. Perhaps they considered us smelly, sweaty, brutelike, fleshy as mushrooms, and most likely crazy: *meshuggener*.

The uniformed young man beside me motioned to Tahlmeade. He was with the consulate mission and held onto my elbow as if I was on my last leg and about to fall face-flat on the ground. "Don't worry, Rabbi, he knows his way around. He'll catch up with us later."

"I should *hope* he knows his way around, but where are we going?"

"To the consulate. A party has been prepared in your honor." The young bureaucrat was quite handsome: dark hair, a good sharp nose that you could see, a strong chin, and dark eyes that would make women talk.

"Please, let's bring the alien in the prayer-shawl along with us. It's obvious that —"

"I'm afraid that would not do, Rabbi."

"Would not *do*?"

The young men pulled me along, and I, of course, did not resist; I just walked slowly — after all, I'm an old man.

"After the briefing, you'll understand."

"Ah, now it's a briefing!" and after a step or two, I asked, "So if Jews are not allowed at this party, what am *I* going to do there?"

"With all due respect, Rabbi, you're jumping to conclusions," said the ambassador, who walked beside us; he was tall and grey, and wore a thin moustache that was black as a pencil mark. Then he frowned at the aliens and smiled at me. The Ulimites frowned happily back at us, indicating that all was well with their world.

As I was whisked across the spaceport, I looked over my shoulder. But Tahlmeade and the ship had disappeared, replaced by an architectural chaos of brown and green. The city of Khârig, the largest and most fabulous city on Ulim, was a sculpted garden, and I was passing through it at a hundred miles an hour. Arches, stadiums, peristyle courts, statues as large as skyscrapers, castles, rotundas, pavilions, halls, lodges, offices, governmental complexes vaulted over razor-cut avenues; they grew out of the ground complete with flying buttresses, towers, domes, and cupolas; their architectural styles were as exotic as the Hagia Sophia or the Cetian monoliths. I imagined that I could see the façades of San Carlo, the Doric porticos of Hagley Park, the Romanesque and gothic pinnacles of the Milan Cathedral, and the glass skyscraper needles of Van der Rohe. The Ulim had planted a city, had shaped trees and shrub and mirrored leaves into habitation: into civilization. I felt dizzy, overwhelmed, enraptured. I felt swallowed by the silvery green *alienness* of it all.

So this was culture shock.

If such a thing could turn an old man with earlocks into a poet, imagine what it might do to someone who still had some *juice* left inside him?

###

The cocktail party was endless, the talk small, and although the ambassador took special pains to provide me with some ninety-proof Slivovitz whiskey (which he thought all Jews drank), I left all the *schnapps* alone; neither did I take any narcodrines or enhancers; neither did I attend any of the Virtual parties that were also being held in my honor. I am a simple man. I drink in private. I am too old for sex. (I could still perform, I suppose; but, I've courted peace and privacy for far too long to give them up for a wife.) I like to read, go to bed early, eat like a glutton at the *Tzaddik*'s court, argue *pilpul* and philosophy with the other rabbis, smoke the flat, foul-smelling cigarettes from Turkey, and wake up with the cock (not what you think!) to begin another — and perhaps final — day.

Yet I felt like the alien here, and not because I was carrying on conversations with creatures with yellow eyes and blue-grey skin the texture of alligators (albeit through my interpreter, who indicated that she would be willing to warm me up during the night, and then gave me a blank look when I told her that I was no Ghandi — she probably thought "Ghandi" was a Jewish perversion); no, I felt just now like the hypocrite I was. You see, Jewish guilt is indeed a fact. I was a fraud, and these people, both alien and human, thought they were talking to a real *Chassid* master *rebbeh*, a living anachronism, a mystic who believed in kabbalah and amulets, who had his own *derekh*, his own special channel to communicate with God, and who knew His secret name: the *Tetragrammaton.* Indeed, they thought they had found a human who would understand and could explain the mystery of the Jews of this planet. The "Jewish Mystery" seemed to be a major philosophical problem for the intelligentsia of *Ulim*, both human and alien. It was as if they had to go to secondary sources to find out about these Jews . . . as if it never occurred to anyone just to go and ask a blue-skinned Jew.

So they asked me, a human hypocrite who remained a *Chassid* and a rabbi only because that was all I knew. I was too old and frightened, too corrupt, to leave the *Tzaddik*'s court and die alone among strangers. I needed respect, and wasn't willing to give up my few servants and my small congregation. I could tell you that I lost my faith because of Auschwitz, but who remembers Auschwitz? Not my *Tzaddik* who believed himself to be the *melits yoysher*, the one who pleads for the Jews who violate any one of the six hundred and thirteen positive and negative commandments, who believes that all *tsores*, all the troubles visited upon the Jews, are punishment for collective and individual sin. So six million Jews die because they sinned . . .

Oh, I argued with the *Tzaddik*. I told him that only a madman could believe in prayer after the Holocaust. If there was a God, He was no longer in the world; He was not the God of history. He could not be propitiated. After all, what terrible crime had we committed? The Torah says, "for our sins we are punished," but who was punished, who was murdered? The poorest, the faithful, the most pious. This, then, was the revelation, the holocaust was the modern Sinai — if one could call an event that happened two hundred years ago *modern.*

So what did my *Tzaddik* do? He told his three thousand followers that *I* had had a revelation, that God had revealed himself to me alone, that *I* was now a *Tzaddik.*

And *that's* why he sent me to Tobias instead of going himself.

###

I told the story of my *Tzaddik* to my hosts, and everyone frowned and shook my hands; until I actually almost began to feel like a *Tzaddik* who could do no wrong. I told them funny stories, and they especially liked Rabbi Nachman of Bratslav's story of the wise but skeptical man who had been sent a message from his king, but refused to open it because the messenger couldn't prove to the wise man that the king existed; nor could anyone else.

"'Now do you see?' the skeptical wise man said to the messenger. 'People are foolish and naïve and believe what they wish. They live a lie because they fear the truth.'"

Everyone agreed with Rabbi Nachman, who probably would have gotten a kick out of knowing his story was being told by a poor Jew to *goyim* who lived in the heavens.

Against all my good judgment, I began to enjoy myself a little; and just when I was about to indulge in a finger of Slivovitz (even if it tastes like rubbing alcohol, why break tradition?), the ambassador's aide relieved me of my newfound admirers and took me down narrow, labyrinthine corridors to an inner sanctum for the threatened briefing. I have to say, though, that these people were poets; they knew a good metaphor when they saw one. Although the striated walls of this grand salon seemed to be made of wood, they looked like meat. Whether it was sap or water, I don't know; but the very walls seemed to be sweating.

And there were no windows in here. A perfect place for an interrogation.

"Well?" I asked the ambassador, who was sitting opposite me with his staff beside him. We sat at a conference table made of the same stuff as the walls, but I didn't touch the table or anything on it. There was a setting before me: blue monochrome Delft china, heavy silverware and crystal; and within easy reach were sandwiches on painted porcelain plates, and liquor, juice, and wine in clear Bristol goblets. A pear-shaped silver coffee pot took up an entire corner of the table, which seemed to be sweating profusely under the feet of the pot. The slightly acrid aroma of coffee was delicious.

"It's all kosher," he said, gesturing at the food and drink. "I noticed you neither ate nor drank at the party. Surely you must be hungry . . ."

"Why all this fuss over a rabbi from Brooklyn who's not even published?"

"Because it seems that you're the key to the mystery."

"Ah, yes, the mystery of the Jews," I said. "Why are these blue people asking me to tell them about their own Jews."

"Ulimites," the ambassador said, correcting me; yet there was no condescension in his voice.

"Ulimites." Then after a beat, I said, "They had a Jew right at the shuttle port. Why didn't they ask *him*? And why wasn't he allowed to come along?"

"That's just the problem. They can't even see him. They have some kind of proprioceptive sense that he's there, but that's all."

"That's crazy!"

The ambassador shrugged. "The Ulimites can't see Jews. Why? We don't know. Yet they're absolutely obsessed with finding out all they can about the Jews."

"Well, they certainly seem to be able to see me," I said. "So either I'm not a Jew or —"

"They have no trouble seeing humans whether they're Jewish or not," the ambassador said, humoring me. After all, what else could he do?

"So before you came to colonize —"

"Not to colonize, Rabbi. We do not colonize planets that —"

"Excuse me for my ignorance, Ambassador, but before you came here to visit —"

"— To establish diplomatic relations."

"— How could they be obsessed with finding out about Jews *before* you arrived, if they couldn't see Jews or ask anyone else who *could*?"

"It was like an itch they couldn't scratch," one of the aides said; the one with the handsome face and good nose.

The ambassador glanced at the aide, who reddened slightly, and then said to me, "They discovered various Jewish texts that had not been destroyed. "

"Destroyed?"

Again he shrugged. "We know very little about what happened. We expect, or hope, that you can answer those questions for us. But the Ulimite Jews here seem to be the only religious group on the planet. None of the other Ulimites have any sense of the spiritual at all. It's as if part of their psyche has been entirely wiped away, lost."

"They lost their ability to hear their God, or gods," said the aide who had spoken before. "That's what they've told us, anyway."

"And what about the . . . encyclopedia your historians and anthropologists wrote about the Jews?"

"All correct, as far as we know."

"Then they interviewed the Jews?"

"No," the ambassador said. "All the information is gleaned from secondhand sources. Although we know where the Jews live — or think we do — we have not been able to initiate any direct contact, except with their intermediaries."

"Ah, the *shtadlans*," I said. "The fixers. So Tahlmeade is a fixer . . . But why *should* he help you? You treated him as if he were *dreck*. A nothing."

"He had planned to see you, Rabbi. He understood that it would be impossible for him to join us."

"Why? If no one can see him, what's the difference?"

"They sense him and become very nervous. Believe me, it would be a mistake; but you'll see for yourself soon enough."

I waited for him to tell me what I would see soon enough, and when he didn't, I let it alone; I would find out due time. "How can one believe anything when it's all secondhand and censored, when nothing is mentioned about your claim that the Jews are . . . invisible?" I asked. "Why wasn't that in your reports?"

"This is a very sensitive and . . . explosive issue," the ambassador said. "We considered what to do very carefully, and finally decided to keep the mystery confidential until we've resolved it. All the reports and monographs, although true, are smoke-screens." He paused, as if to study my expression, but I have what's called a poker-face, which I understand has something to do with an ancient game of chance. "There are too many implications for Jews at home," he continued.

"Implications?"

"Something terrible has happened here. We do not wish to give extremists an excuse to kill any more Jews, not after what happened in Savannah."

I didn't retreat from his stare. History repeats itself in different guises. What had once been America was now like ancient Poland.

"You know," I said, "I'm going to ask you something every Jew asks himself: Why *me*?"

The ambassador pushed his chair back, and an aide stood up to help him, although I saw no reason why he needed help. The ambassador was a relatively young man. "Because the Jewish government here, if indeed there is a government, *asked* for you."

"Asked for *me*?"

"Over a month ago, Earth time. The one you call Tahlmeade made the request."

"He asked for *me*?" I was sounding like an echo, but I couldn't help it.

"Yes. He specifically asked for you, by name."

"How could he have known my name?" I asked.

The ambassador stood up and looked at me until I felt uncomfortable. "That's exactly what *we'd* like to know, Rabbi."

###

Tahlmeade came to the consulate to pick me up. He had come right into the suite where the party was being held in my honor, and was standing in the doorway waiting for me. His prayer shawl was wrapped around himself as if for protection, but it didn't seem to be Tahlmeade who needed protection. The other aliens in the room seemed somehow dislocated, lost; they moved aimlessly about the room, every one in a sudden state of agitation. I could not help but imagine that they were in some kind of psychic pain, yet — if I didn't know better — I would have thought them happy. They were all grinning at each other, at me, at the tables and walls and ceiling.

But their grins were frozen.

And I knew that on Ulim, a smile was not a smile.

Tahlmeade and I left quickly. We rode an elevator though the center of the building, which was a tree, or a forest that had grown into one solid mass. We stepped outside; and for a few moments we were in the streets, streets that smelled like thyme and roses, that were as clean as my wife's (may she rest in peace) table. But the street crowds were agitated, too; people dashed past us and eddied around us, giving us a wide berth.

We were the quiet eye of the storm.

Then Tahlmeade led me below ground, into what seemed to be another city. We waited on a transparent platform that seemed to be situated on the edge of an abyss. Above and below were contrasts of light and dark; but below were huge organic stalactites and stalagmites worked with glastex and metal: trees as large and high as skyscrapers, their flesh smooth and irised. People lived in these illuminated boles, which were connected by communication grids and transportation tubes. I looked down into the descending levels of habitation. I might have been looking at jewels, at strings of light set upon velvet; I might as well have been looking into the eternity of space.

Just looking down made me dizzy, made me a little *meshuggener.*

Made me, God forbid, want to leap into the darkness. But such things I ignore; even when I was young, I had a fear of heights.

A transpod rushed into the station and hushed to a stop. The pod cracked open and we climbed in. Tahlmeade punched in the coordinates, and it suddenly seemed as if we were falling. Yet there was no definite sense of motion, just the buildings rushing past us as we sped forward through tubes that choked through the city like transparent vines.

"If you would close the windows," I said in Hebrew, forgetting that that was slang for "opaque the walls". "I'm getting dizzy." But Tahlmeade seemed to comprehend what I meant immediately, for in an instant, grey walls surrounded us. Graffitoed images glowed redly over the grey: some smart youngster must have figured out how to change the light patterns.

My dizziness passed and I asked, "Why can't they see you?" Only after I spoke the words did I realize how blunt I had been.

Tahlmeade frowned at me and said, "Perhaps for the same reason that they are able to see you."

I was going to ask him what he meant, yet somehow I knew . . . I knew what he meant.

They could not see Tahlmeade because he was a Jew.

But they *could* see me.

And what did they see?

A fraud, a fool, a counterfeit. A phony.

###

We hurtled forward at three hundred miles an hour, a slight rhythmic vibration and the digital read-outs on the control console the only indications of movement. I tried to communicate with Tahlmeade, but he was preoccupied. One thing was certain: to him I was not a *Tzaddik.* He stared at the control console intently as if the apocalyptic words of the Torah were flaming across the screen, and tented his fingers. I interrupted his thoughts a few times, but he simply frowned and then turned back to the console. He was, of course, shutting me out. My questions would have to wait . . . at least, until he awakened.

For he gave himself away when he began to snore.

So our species were not so different, after all.

It took five hours to reach our destination: *Michborah.*

Which meant graveyard.

###

This was mountain country: cold, rugged, inhospitable, and beautiful. The mountains — white and bald and worn, except for foothill sheathing of bright green scrub — seemed to reach into the hazy expanse of red sky like the towers of a completed Babel, and huge cumulous cloud formations scudded past above, carried on storm-winds. The sky was in constant movement: continents formed and reformed, arms and ships and towers swirled into being, and then dissolved; phantoms and spirits roiled and sailed in pursuit, one after another, chasing themselves into the ominous blackness of a storm, which suddenly erupted, dropping torrents and covering the world in a caftan of fog. The sun was smeary, and low; and night, which came fast on this planet, was but footsteps away.

But night would be like twilight, and the sky like the inside of a dance hall.

I pulled my threadbare coat tightly around me for protection from the rain, which splashed from the wide brim of my hat, and I followed Tahlmeade down the winding road that cut into the side of a mountain; the road was paved with sharp, jagged, and slippery stones. As would be our luck, we were walking along the side of the mountain that offered us no protection from the pounding rain.

Lightning snaked across the sky ahead of us, lighting up cliffs, gorges, and the grotesque rock cones in the valley ahead. I shivered and remembered the blessings: the blessing upon seeing lighting and — I waited a few seconds for the crashing boom of thunder — the blessing upon hearing thunder. A Jew must pronounce a minimum of a hundred blessings every day: a blessing when he gets up, when he eats, prays, goes to bed, puts on clothes, eliminates, sees a rainbow, a scholar, a beautiful or strange-looking person, or hears bad news, or good news. Breathing itself is a prayer, yet breathe as I might, I had been silent for years. Only in public would prayers pass through my mouth as naturally as greetings and commands. Yet just now I remembered my *tata*, my father, teaching me the prayer over lightning as we both stood in just such a rain as this one.

"*Borouch ahtaw Hashem Eloheinu melech ha'olam . . .*"

"Well?" Tahlmeade asked. "Are you going to say the blessings, or not?"

Startled, I glanced to the side, as if I would see my father standing there, my father who had been dead for over thirty years: Tahlmeade had asked the question exactly as my father used to, with the same intonation, the same voice, the same accent. In fact, it was as if my father had just spoken to me from heaven, where there is no distance.

Of course, I didn't believe that for a moment, but nevertheless . . .

"Did you read my thoughts?" I asked him.

"The blessing . . .?"

I said it: "Blessed are You, *Hashem*, our God, King of the Universe, who makes the work of Creation."

Together, we said the blessing for thunder: "Blessed are You, *Hashem*, our God, King of the Universe, for His strength and His power fill the universe."

" . . . *v-g'vuraso mahlay olam . . .*"

The rain became drizzle as day gave way to twilight.

"Well," I asked again as we walked. "*Did* you read my thoughts?"

"Yes, but not the way you think."

"Then how?"

"You'll see, I assure you, Reb Isaac." It was kind of Tahlmeade to address me by the title of teacher, but perhaps that was an Ulimite form of sarcasm. Who could know?

"Nevertheless, I *don't* see."

"You will," Tahlmeade insisted, yet I had the very strong feeling that he was speaking by rote, as a good salesman often does when making a sale, although his thoughts might be entirely elsewhere.

I suddenly smelled something acrid, like smoke, and tar, and as I looked around to discover the source, Tahlmeade said, "Do you smell the volcano, Rebbe? It's old and quiet now, but it was quite an artist in its day, and still wakes up to cough and fart." The road turned and then abruptly ended in a sheer drop. Ahead was a chasm, and below and beyond were canyons within canyons, ravines, and a huge dry lake. Steps cut into the rock led down to a high plateau that was filled with conical fairy chimneys, which were over fifty feet high and capped with hard stone: natural sculptures created by millennia of wind, rain, and snow. But the chimneys were dwarfed by stone chimeras that stood hundreds of feet high and were evenly spaced along terraced cliff walls that had been carved and sculpted and hollowed into a city. The chimeras had heads like cats, or tigers, and the bodies of eagles — that's what they looked like to me anyway. Yet as I looked down at them, I felt a terrible emptiness, as if somehow gravity itself was leaching away the stuff of my soul, as if I were falling, falling into a grave; and I could only think of Auschwitz, of death and the choking, second-by-second eternity of gasping pain that ended in the chest-still darkness of the ovens.

I felt as if I was looking straight into hell, and I felt soiled and frightened, for it was horrifyingly, terrifyingly beautiful, in the same way that a cat must appear to the bird caught in its claws.

"Thought is like an atmosphere, like clouds," Tahlmeade said, although I must admit I was still caught by this place, by its dead immensities, and I heard Tahlmeade's voice as if it was my own thoughts, my own internal voice. "Usually you can make out vague shapes, and sometimes you can see with absolute clarity, but not as often as we'd like. So you're making out shapes now, am I correct? And what do you see, Rebbe? What do you see?"

I was fixed on the chimeras and the city carved out of the cliff behind them; the city was like a bas-relief of rust-red arches, columns, cupolas, pavilions, spires, and balustrades, all fluted, the arches and horizontal planes covered with chimeras, smaller versions of those that stood guard, blindly waiting through the centuries. The storm had blown itself away, leaving the sky pink and still; spirals of clouds seemed to cling to *Me'al'lim*, one of *Ulim*'s two moons, which was now a pale crescent.

"I don't know," I said, replying to his question.

"Yes, you do, Rebbe. Reveal yourself."

"I fear I am already revealed."

Tahlmeade was silent.

"I feel empty in this place, as if something terrible has happened here. It reminds me of death, of what Jews on Earth refer to as the Holocaust."

"It reminds you of Auschwitz."

"So you know of our history," I said.

"Yes, Rebbe. We know each other's histories."

"What do you mean?" I asked, but Tahlmeade led the way down the steps into the valley, and I followed him.

Into hell.

The emptiness seemed to take everything from me, especially my questions; it was as if I could feel gravity pulling harder on me with every step. I clung to the side of this stairwell chipped out of the mountainside, afraid that I would become too heavy and fall. Water pooled in the hollows of the steps, and I was careful, for the stone was slippery. I was soaked, and my clothes smelled musty. Once at the bottom, we walked toward the chimeras. The sandy ground was muddy from the rain. As we walked, the sun set, shadows deepened and lengthened, and the shattered remains of *Ulim*'s third moon appeared as pale fire overhead: a celestial rainbow. Now there were two moons in the sky, one vague, the other as sharp and distinct as Earth's; and the stationary fireworks above provided enough light to read by.

I saw movement ahead of me in the distance, and at first imagined that smaller versions of the chimeras were alive and prowling about. They glowed like ocean algae and fluoresced with every movement.

"*N'már.*"

I turned to Tahlmeade, happy to hear a sound in this desolation . . . and then I realized that he had not *said* anything. I thought he had said "tigers".

"This is their mating season," Tahlmeade said; and this time he *was* speaking. "They come here to mate, and to die. Ancient peoples worshipped them, for they believed the animals had souls, which were what they saw glowing." Tahlmeade's skin, which was scored, as if made up of thousands of shale pebbles, glistened, and his wet tallis clung to his shoulders like a mantle. "But don't worry, Rebbe, voracious as they can be, they can't see us . . . or smell us. We are like ghosts, even here — *especially* here."

I felt suddenly weary, exhausted; every step was a trial. I could only concentrate on getting out of here, of putting the great stylized, stone chimeras behind us, souls or no souls, ghosts or no ghosts.

"Now you have no questions," Tahlmeade said. Or perhaps it was a question; I could not be sure. After a beat, he said, "You see, Rebbe, you *are* a *Tzaddik*."

"What do you mean?"

"Because you can see, and feel, and hear."

"So can all men."

"No, not all men . . . nor all of us."

Although we had turned away from the chimeras and the glowing tigers and had cut across to the southern edge of the field, which was close to us, I felt the place pulling at me, pulling me back as if into a vortex, pulling me to its center, which I imagined was as deep and lifeless as the pits in Poland. Mass graves . . .

"It is," Tahlmeade said.

"What?" I asked, still shocked at the soft explosion of his thoughts touching my mind.

"It is a mass grave, all of it a cemetery. As are the cliffs, the cities in the cliffs: a necropolis. On Earth you have nothing like this, Rebbe. You ask where the Jews are." He swept his hand in the air, as if he were throwing sand. "They are *here*, all twelve million of them. We walk on bones, on lives, on ashes."

"How did this happen?" I asked, but for an instant I could see engines of death working in the labyrinths behind the carved façades in the cliffs. I could smell the charnel house. Here was where Ulimite technology had reached its perfection.

"It happened as it happened on your world. Those who killed us, if they were alive to talk, would say their gods told them to do it. *Those* Gods, the *N'már* that guard the ground."

"But you are alive," I said, and there was desperation in my voice. "*We* are alive."

"Do you feel alive . . . here?" Tahlmeade asked, and I felt rooted to the ground, as if their gods had buried me where I stood. For an instant I panicked; but I could indeed still move my arms, my legs.

"Is it because of what happened here that your brethren can't see you?" I asked.

Tahlmeade did not answer my question, but said, "The statues are almost as old as the cliffs. This place is known as the Valley of Creation." He frowned, as if savoring the irony, and then led the way to a corner of the cliff wall and into an arched entrance flanked by fluted columns, all carved into the stone.

I followed him through pitch-dark catacombs.

I was blind, but I could feel the weight of the dead all around me, as heavy as the crushing darkness itself.

I was breathing it, dissolving in it.

I could hear Tahlmeade's voice. Or his thoughts.

And then I saw light, a dim flicker at the end of a long tunnel. I felt relief, as if I had escaped the death that permeated the very air of the Valley of Creation; death was like a thought, and thought like a vapor, or perhaps an odor, a perfume that could be breathed, inhaled and exhaled, passing from one person to another. Thus could I feel the heaviness of the martyrs buried in the valley . . . thus could I hear Tahlmeade even when he didn't speak.

We walked out of the catacomb into the bright night, and my mood suddenly lightened, as if the mass of the mountain we had passed through was acting like a psychic shield.

"Good *Shabbos*," Tahlmeade said. He frowned at me and nodded his head; his mood, too, had changed.

So on *Ulim* it was Friday, *Erev Shabbos*: Sabbath eve.

"I apologize that we had to pass through *Gehennà* to greet the Queen Bride of the Sabbath, but I assure you, she is here."

The Sabbath was a Queen to be made welcome, for she was the foretaste of heaven, God's great gift to those who obeyed his Torah. But for me, for years, *Shabbos* was not a gift, not a freedom, but a prison of rules and regulations. It was, of course, not enough merely to obey the Law. You had to *believe* in it, take joy from it, give yourself up to it.

I was bursting with questions, but *Shabbos* would not allow sadness or bitterness: I would have to wait.

A *Shabbos* calmness came over me, such as I hadn't felt in years.

"Good *Shabbos*," I whispered.

###

We came to a sheer cliff that looked unscalable. Tahlmeade guided me through a concealed opening in the rock, and we took a lifter deep inside the mountain.

It was cold and bitter atop the mountain plateau, yet this place was verdant: trees were thick, if stunted, and we took a winding road through forest. Past the edge of the forest with its sharp tang of wood and sap, we came to fields covered with flowers that appeared translucent in the night light; and the ring glittered above, a metallic rainbow of color that appeared and reappeared as cloud masses scudded across it. The haze of aurorae was purple and pink, sheets of gauze that seemed to shimmer in the sky like illuminated silk curtains.

"It's beautiful," I said. "But how can anything grow in this cold?" I pulled my coat around me.

"The ground is warm, Rebbe. You see, your feet aren't cold. The mountain is alive, it breathes, and one day, it will explode." He frowned. I was beginning to understand his humor.

Children were shouting ahead; they stood on the edge of the field and were bundled in shiny black caftans and caps. Behind him was the village, which seemed ethereal in the colored veils of night. The town seemed to be cut out of the mountain itself, but it was an incongruous, yet charming marriage of wood and stone: elongated domes sat upon thick towers, buildings were tent shaped, and had galleries with open sides to give shelter; and everything was glimmerous and multi-hued, as if the village was mimicking the heavens.

"Rebbe Tahlmeade," they shouted and waved their arms. "Good *Shabbos*."

Tahlmeade motioned to them, and then stopped walking. He looked up at the sky, at the ring — at *Ulim*'s night rainbow — and made a prayer. He gazed at me steadily and said, "The rainbow is our covenant, just as it is yours."

He continued to stare at me, making me uncomfortable. I was beginning to realize that Tahlmeade was not merely a fixer, an intermediary, as the ambasador mistakenly thought, but that he must be the *Tzaddik* himself.

"Have you nothing to say to that?" he asked.

"The children, if they are children, are waiting for you."

"Waiting will not hurt them. And, yes, Rebbe, of course they are children."

"What do you wish me to say, Rebbe." I had to smile, for I had not called him a rabbi before. Then I caught myself, for I remembered that a smile did not signal pleasure to a Ulimite.

"I wish you to say the truth. That you believe the Covenant has been broken."

"Can it be otherwise?" I asked. "You have been nearly destroyed. Did God hear your prayers? And do *nothing*?" I recited the words of the Prophets, one of the Thirteen Articles of Faith, "'I believe with perfect faith that the Creator, blessed be His name, rewards those who keep His commandments and punishes those who transgress them.' Is that not the pact between God and the Jewish people? But if Jews are to remain Jews, they must suspend that; they must suspend all traditional doctrine and remove God from history, for it would be sacrilege even to *contemplate* that God would allow millions of innocent children to die as punishment for the sins of other Jews!" After I said that, I asked, out of respect, "But do you wish to speak of such things on the Sabbath?"

"One can always question, Rebbe, especially on the Sabbath, for that is the time when God is most visible."

"Let me ask you then, if you *knew* that the Holocaust would come to the next generation, would you raise your children Jewish? If Jews are responsible to each other, you to me, me to you, and both of us to all of them" — I motioned toward the children, who were waiting impatiently — "then those who died in the Holocaust did *not* die because they failed to keep the Covenant. They died because their grandparents and parents kept it. So, Rebbe, I suppose I answered my own question. They did die because of the sins of others . . . the sin of their parents for remaining faithful to the Covenant!"

"So God has abandoned us?" Tahlmeade said.

"Unless you wish to believe our respective Holocausts were the means by which God tested his people, as he did Job. But I cannot imagine such a cruel conclusion."

"Then what *do* you imagine, Rebbe?"

"Emptiness," I said. The cold worked itself over my face until I felt I was wearing a mask.

"Better Job." Tahlmeade frowned and then made a coughing noise, which I understood as a laugh — but I could not tell if it was good-natured or derisive. He opened his arms and walked toward the children, who ran to meet us. Their small, pebbled faces seemed very grey; perhaps it was the light of the night, or the cold.

"Perhaps you'll feel differently when you jump the road."

"What?" I asked, surprised. "Jumping the Road" was an old superstition, like the "evil eye".

"We'll talk tomorrow, Rebbe, after you've —" The children distracted him with questions.

But I learned what he meant that night.

In the middle of the night, as light poured like mercury though the small high windows of my little room in the highest part of Tahlmeade's house, I listened to the voices downstairs and dreamed.

I felt myself being hurled into the darkness. Yet who could imagine speed without the reference of light or the pressure of gravity? Perhaps I flew. Perhaps I fell.

To Earth. Into the heart of Philadelphia. Into the *Tzaddik*'s court.

Into the *Tzaddik*'s dream.

"So, have you renewed your faith?" he asked. "We sat on stone steps in the ruins of a synagogue; after all, it was my *Tzaddik*'s dream.

"I'm asleep," I said.

"As am I, but certainly you'll remember this when you wake up."

"Remember what?"

"That you jumped the road and spoke with your *Tzaddik*." He smiled at me, and then looked down at his age-freckled hands, which rested on his lap. He was several years younger than me, yet I always thought of him as much older. (Of course, how much older than me could anyone *be* and still be alive?) His beard was mottled white and grey, which gave it a yellowish cast.

"I told Tahlmeade that you were a *Tzaddik*," he continued. "I told him that you had the '*kuk*', that you could 'see'. But I told him you didn't know any of these things."

When I didn't reply, he said, "Of course, Tahlmeade helped you jump, just to get you started."

To "jump the road" was to see into other places without being there. It was the miraculous means by which *Tzaddiks* could help and protect other Jews who were in trouble.

It was pure, unadulterated, medieval, Jewish superstition.

"If it's superstition, then what are you doing here?" the *Tzaddik* asked. "You came to me."

"I am not here," I said.

"Well, as long as you aren't here, do you wish to ask me a question?"

"Ah, so you'll give me proof that I've jumped the road."

"Tahlmeade told you that you would do so. Doesn't that tell you anything?

"It tells me that I'm suggestible."

"Ask him how Jews came to be on two planets," the Tzaddik said. "And tell Ruchel that I send my felicitations."

Ruchel was Tahlmeade's wife. But *I* knew that, and it was *my* dream.

I awakened with a start and stared up at the ceiling, which, like the walls, seemed to be constructed out of one solid piece of wood the color of mahogany. I wiped my eyes, for the ceiling seemed to be moving, undulating ever so slightly, but that had to be an effect of the light drifting in.

I heard something, whisperings that seemed to be right here in the room. A voice that could not be denied, for I could not help but think that God was speaking directly to me.

Giving me a history lesson.

###

The children woke me up with an aromatic glass of sweetened tea. It was barely dawn, and the light made everything in the room seem soft and gauzy. My back ached from sleeping on the mattress on the floor, for I was too large to fit on the bed, sumptuous as it might be. I sat up and thanked these two tiny versions of Tahlmeade, dressed in their Sabbath best. They fell over each other to get out of the room and made loud chirping noises as they ran down the hallway; I assumed they were feigning terror, for I understood their chirps to be laughter. Last night at *Shabbos* dinner, they stared at me throughout the meal, except when Tahlmeade made them sing the *z'miros*, the traditional songs of praise.

As I dressed, I remembered that I had dreamed of my *Tzaddik*, and that he had told me — no, a voice whispered to me, whispered the answer to my questions . . . but I couldn't remember. It frustrated me for a moment, and then I shrugged it off and went downstairs. Dreams were always like that. They make sense only to the sleeper.

By the time I came downstairs, the house was already filled with people, male Ulimites wearing shiny hats and large black-and-white prayer shawls the size of blankets. Like Tahlmeade, they dressed in black caftans that were tied around the waist with cords to separate the lofty parts from the profane. There must have been sixty Ulimites in the living room and more crowded in doorways, all here for the privilege of accompanying Tahlmeade to synagogue. Tahlmeade's home, I should mention, was huge, more an inn than a house for a single family. It was all rather plainly furnished, except for the dining room, where the candelabra and kiddish cups were kept. Tahlmeade's table could comfortably seat twenty-five, and at the head was his golden chair: a throne. The table was filled for every meal, for many of his followers had sacrificed to come to his court; in return, he gave advice and relief and expounded the word of God — who better to do so, for was he not a direct conduit to the Creator?

We went to the *shul*, to the synagogue, like a conquering army returning home. It was a parade, and everyone was in uniform, as I was. I was dressed no differently than the Ulimites — in black caftan and prayer shawl — and as I entered the *shul* with the crowd, as I was seated near the eastern wall — a place of honor — I remembered that I had jumped the road last night. I remembered my dream, talking to my *Tzaddik.* There was more to the dream, though, but I could not recall what it might have been.

Tahlmeade sat in a plushly upholstered high-backed chair beside the red curtained Ark where the Holy Scrolls reposed; he looked out upon his congregation, as if each person was a book that he could read in a trice. The *shul* was packed, every seat accounted for, both upstairs and downstairs (for the women, dressed in their drab finery, sat together in the balcony, separated from the men by tradition, if not choice); and in the rear, around a study table, stood the *prosteh yidden*, those without learning.

"Better an educated bastard than an ignorant rabbi."

That's from the Talmud, which has something to say about everything.

A cantor led the morning *Shacharis* service, and I *davened*, which is how Jews pray — we rock back and forth, as if shaking out the prayers from a salt-shaker. Like shaking oneself into a trance. Well, that's how the Ulimites in the *shul* prayed, every one of them; their yarmulkes were pulled over their hairless heads, their pebbly faces expressionless. I must confess to becoming caught up in the mood, caught up in the familiarity of the surroundings, the chanting, the prayers and blessings, the readings from the Torah that was resplendent upon the *bimah* platform, which was itself crowded with honored "guests of the Holy Scrolls". It was true: a Jew can go anywhere among Jews and be at home. So did I feel at home on this faraway world, with aliens whose faces were like blue leather with bumps. I felt sleepy, as I always did in *shul* on *Shabbos*, for it was a day to rest. One could not light a fire or switch on a light, for today God was in control. He was the maker and shaker. Not us.

But could I *believe*, as I sat and rested with strangers who looked like nothing I had ever seen?

Let's just say that I was comfortable. That was enough; and I could lose myself in the moment, in the prayers that were said standing up with feet together, as if at attention. I was called up to the *bimah* to read from the Scrolls. I bowed and shook everyone's hand when I was finished. I returned to my seat. It was *pro forma*, familiar. Like sleeping in your own bed. As I prayed, I thought about my dream, and remembered. "Ask him how Jews came to be on two planets," my *Tzaddik* had said. And what would Tahlmeade tell me? That Jews have been jumping the road for centuries, for millennia?

That would explain how these Jews came to be.

Or perhaps it would explain how Jews on *Earth* came to be . . .

But it was superstition. I could more easily believe that worlds and universes were splitting into 10^{100+} imperfect copies of themselves: the Isaac ibn Chabib quantum theory of creating Jews.

###

"He who pays attention to dreams should have his head examined."

That's from Isaac ibn Chabib, not the Talmud.

###

Thus the service went on, from the morning into the afternoon, sleeping hours dissolving into an aromatic Jewish stew of routine and memory. As we prayed, I suddenly realized that, indeed, the world around me was dissolving. Praying was a dream, and the congregation dreamed.

They dreamed Tahlmeade's dream . . .

And I found myself alone. In the Valley of Creation.

The Jews who had died, their twelve million souls massing like clouds in the sky, whispered to me, telling me their myriad stories. They were safe, beyond pain and chance and care.

But the *other* Jews — those who were alive and singing and chanting and praying with me in the synagogue — had disappeared.

For their dream was death and oblivion. It was protection. It was a river: Lethe, the drowning river of forgetfulness.

A river that covered the world.

###

So this was a dream . . . and it wasn't a dream. If I were religious in the sense that I had set out to be when I entered the rabbinate, I would call it a revelation. I had entered what the sages called *Pardes*, which means orchard, or Paradise. Ah, irony of ironies, that revelation would come to me on the mountain of graves. The Talmud tells the story of the four rabbis who entered *Pardes*: Ben Azzai, Ben Zoma, Ben Abuyah, and the great Rabbi Akiba. (Of course, it's not the Talmud that tells the story. But for Jews the Talmud is like a person; when we read the sages in this tractate or that, it is as if the Talmud itself is talking.) They all entered *Pardes* through their dreams, which took the form of fiery chariots. Akiba said to the other travellers, "Don't be distracted, lest you lose yourselves," but Ben Azzai looked about and lost his soul, Ben Zoma lost his way, and Ben Abuyah became an apostate. Only Rabbi Akiba entered in peace and departed with his life.

I'm certainly no Akiba, or Ben Zoma — perhaps a Ben Abuyah, God forbid — but here I was in the dream that was not a dream. Like them I had, indeed, jumped the road; and this time without Tahlmeade's help. If Tahlmeade was worth his robes, he would be searching for me frantically right now. But I had learned a few more things, and I wouldn't let him in.

Here I sat in the Valley of Creation beside a fairy chimney the color of chalk, facing the stone chimeras and the city of death hollowed out of the cliffs. The chimeras rose above me like Incan cenotaphs, huge and stylized and not yet worn smooth by the turbulent elements. The sky was clear, washed of clouds, and the cliffs stood sharply against it. It was cold, but I felt nothing of the physical senses: wind was an idea, sight a shadow, voice an abstraction.

And as I sat facing death, listening to the instructions of dead martyrs, the collective unconscious of the Ulimite Jewish race, I watched the glowing tigers, the N'már, padding around me, sniffing the air. They were frustrated, for although they could see me, they couldn't detect my essence.

You see, Tahlmeade hadn't told me that the tigers could not be seen by most people. That was their defence mechanism. But through the eons there were those who had learned to see them . . . who saw them as souls glowing in the light. Who worshipped them and learned to use them as familiars.

Just so had Tahlmeade, who had inherited the second sight and the mantle of the *Tzaddik*, learned to use them to protect those in his charge: all the Jews. He had learned from *his* father, who had learned from his father.

Thus, Jews had become like the *N'már*.

Invisible.

Invulnerable . . . for how can you kill what you can't see?

A tiger stood before me, gazing at me, as I gazed at him. The creature seemed to draw my essence through its burning eyes, and I had to anchor myself to my own reality — to my past and present, or I would become another Rabbi Ben Azzai, who lost his soul in Pardes.

But as I stared into those numinous eyes, I drew the creature to *me*. I took its habits and its tricks of evolution.

And I knew then what I had to do.

###

I met Tahlmeade in the *bais medrash* after sunset: the conclusion of the Sabbath. The *bais medrash*, which means "House of Study", was a small room in the Synagogue, It had a high ceiling and long narrow windows, which let in the hazy starglow. I could see comets raining like fire through the narrow slats.

We both sat across from each other at a study table piled with ancient books and interactives that rested inches above the tables like rectangular clouds.

"I looked for you during the afternoon," Tahlmeade said, touching an interactive, which spoke and shivered into being, becoming its subject: another touch and it would transform the entire room into a mnemonic of the twentieth century mystical text *Sh'ar Hayichud* by Rabbi Dov Ber of Lubavitch. Tahlmeade withdrew his finger and the interactive dissolved into its former state. "It seems that you have become quite efficient at Jumping the Road, Rebbe."

"You are a good teacher."

"Ah, so your *Tzaddik* told you that I gave you an initial push to get you started."

"He did," I said.

"Then you believe?"

"Only after you pulled the entire congregation into your dream this afternoon."

"But you were not pulled into our dream," Tahlmeade said. "Why?"

"Do you think that I have some great strength that I was not sucked into your dream?" I asked. "I could see into your dream, and it frightened me. But then I am not a courageous man. No, Rebbe, I simply dreamed my own dream. The Valley of Creation drew me to itself, the souls of your martyrs — of our martyrs — drew me to them. It was the power of the dead. They snatched me into their dream before you could carry me into yours."

"So you chose death."

"It wasn't a matter of choice, Rebbe." I paused, and then said, "But I know what you have done."

Tahlmeade looked at me intently and nodded his head slightly as he read my thoughts, my memories. "So you know the N'már. You have seen the tigers."

I nodded

"And you have spoken to the dead."

"I heard voices," I said. "Perhaps I heard the tigers, perhaps they've absorbed —"

"You are a strange creature, Rebbe," Tahlmeade said. "You disbelieve your own senses because they conflict with your preconceptions. You spoke to the dead. You spoke to the tigers. Now you know."

"And you know what I must do."

"You wish to give us up, to reveal us to the world."

"You have not only hidden yourselves," I said. "You have taken the Gentiles' souls from them; you have taken their religion, their spirit."

"We simply concealed ourselves," Tahlmeade said.

"No, you did *more* than that. You stole from them. You took revenge. You've —" I paused, searching for words. "It's very much like murder."

"No, Rebbe, it was *they* who murdered us. We have blinded them, perhaps, but no more than that."

"And would you blind them unto the fourth generation?" I asked. "Until they became machines? When would you stop? When would you stop being afraid? When there were no more Gentiles left alive . . .?" Tahlmeade did not answer, so I continued; after all, I have a reputation for stuffing my feet into my mouth, for speaking when listening would be a *mitzvah*, a judicious act of kindness. "You have robbed them," I said, quoting *Tosefta Baba Kamma*: "It's a more heinous crime for a Jew to rob a Gentile than a Jew, for such a crime involves the desecration of the Name. And does not the *Sefer Hasidim* say, 'If a Jew attempts to kill a Gentile, help the Gentile'? You must stop dreaming their souls away, Tahlmeade. You must return to the world."

"You, who believes that the Holocaust has rendered all traditional doctrine absurd ... you are quoting *Tosefta Baba Kamma* and *Sefer Hasidim* to me? You, who cannot even find his own faith, you would preach to me in the words of the sages?"

Tahlmeade smiled at me, showing small, even teeth: an expression of pure hatred. "The Gentiles will only kill us again," he said in a soft voice, as if he were teaching a child.

"You are killing *yourselves* by robbing *them*. My hypocrisy or lack of faith will not change that."

"We will not submit to them," Tahlmeade said. "We will not allow another Holocaust, another Valley of Creation."

I pushed myself away from the table and stood up.

"I cannot let you leave, Rebbe."

"You cannot stop me," I said; and I allowed myself to dream the beast, the tiger, the *N'már*. I would jump the road. I would leave this place in the time it takes a hummingbird to flap its wings. And Tahlmeade would not find me, just as he had not been able to find me when I was in the Valley of Creation. I had learned from the beasts . . . just as Tahlmeade had, and as his father before him.

I could be as invisible as the Jews of *Ulim*.

I slipped into a dream, a dream of glowing tigers, and I imagined myself . . . away. But I was lead. I was all mass, as heavy as any body without its root, without its soul.

And Tahlmeade could see me, as I could see him. We could not disappear from each other's sight. We could not escape each other's grasp. Tahlmeade stared into me like fire, for he was fire. He was the tiger, the beast.

And the *bais medrash* began to burn with a cold light.

As stars fell by outside the windows.

###

Tahlmeade and I were locked claw to claw, eye to eye, in mortal combat.

Whosoever would let go — let down his guard — would suffer. We two were tigers fighting in a dream — *N'már* — each caught in the grip of the other. Our eyes were our weapons, for they are the mirrors of the soul. Tahlmeade and I fought and burned. I tried to pull away, to disappear, to jump the road, to escape. But Tahlmeade was like my own thought, my own volition, myself.

It was a stalemate.

I remembered being in the Valley of Creation and staring at the tiger. As he gazed at me, so had I gazed at *him*; and he tried to draw my essence into his burning eyes. Eyes of fire, of sleep, of dream, of loss, of perdition. So it was now, except Tahlmeade was no *N'már*. He was much, much stronger.

He drew me into his eyes, into his dream . . .

As I drew him into mine.

And yet, for all this wrestling of souls and minds, we were sitting quietly at the study table in the *bais medrash*: two Jews staring each other down. Two Jews trying to jump the road, trying to escape each other by any means possible.

But we found ourselves jumping the road together, as if we had but one will . . . as if our two dreams had suddenly merged into one, and the one became a chariot, the same chariot that Ezekiel had seen in a vision. In just such a chariot had the four sages — Ben Azzai, Ben Zoma, Ben Abuyah, and Akiba — entered Paradise.

We were hurled like a meteor into the darkness.

And a voice said, "How dare you disgrace yourselves before this court! Stop fighting!

Immediately!"

It sounded like my *Tzaddik.*

I was not surprised to find that it was.

Tahlmeade stood beside me; before us were the *Tzaddik* and two other men.

I had been here before when I jumped the road and met the *Tzaddik.* We were in the courtyard of a ruined temple, a synagogue. The air was warm and full of moisture, and the sun was high in the sky. I thought I was back in the *Tzaddik*'s dream, in Philadelphia, but he corrected my thoughts and revealed that we were not in our own time, or place. We were in Judea, in a place called *Benei Berak*, and we were standing before the judges of a *Bais Din*: a Rabbinical Court. The *Tzaddik* and two other men who were as old as me — as old as the sand itself — sat upon cushions, which faced east, the direction of prayer. They sat, and we stood, upon cracked and crumbling stone. Although I did not know the other two men, I knew the seating arrangements for a *Bais Din*: the one who sat in the center — who leaned forward — as if to hear every word, even when nothing was being said, was the *Nasi*, the big shot: the president of the Court. The *Tzaddik* and the other rabbi were his deputies.

They were certainly all *Tzaddiks*, all saints. They all clucked their tongues and shook their heads as we stood before them.

"You should be ashamed," the *Nasi* said to us. "You are learned men, not brawlers."

"To be one is to be the other," I said, but the *Tzaddiks* were not receptive to my wit.

Tahlmeade began to speak, but the *Nasi* interrupted him and said, "All has been decided. You will do as Rebbe Isaac ibn Chabib asks. We sent him to you. You received him. Now let him liberate you."

"*Avol* —" Tahlmeade began to say, which was "but" in Hebrew.

"There is no argument, Rebbe," the *Nasi* said to Tahlmeade.

Tahlmeade stood rigid as a bar mitzvah boy saying the blessings in front of an entire congregation. He smiled, but would not go against the decision of a *Bais Din.*

Perhaps the *Tzaddiks* misunderstood his expression of hatred and frustration and anger, for they smiled back at him.

On second thought, perhaps they did understand.

###

So even if Jumping the Road wasn't a dream but a form of revelation, we would dream ourselves back to *Ulim* in a fiery chariot. (After all, rabbis are naturally a grandiloquent and flamboyant lot.)

But before I departed, I asked the *Nasi* one question: "Who are you Rebbe?"

"Elazar ben Azaryah Akiba," he said, leaning toward me.

Rabbi Akiba . . . ?

"But don't worry, Isaac," he said. "You're not in Paradise."

###

So now . . . we shall see what we shall see.

The Ulimite Gentiles will soon be able to remember . . . to hear the voices of their Gods and consciences again. What will their voices tell them to do?

Who can know? (Well, perhaps Rabbi Akiba knows, but the rest of us *potzers* — those of us who barely manage to get by — we'll just have to take our chances.) Even if we are to be slaughtered in the next generation, even if we will have to become invisible again, even if we have to fight like animals, we will live *today*. We *will* endure.

And as for myself —

I decided to stay right here and see this thing through.

So do I believe in miracles?

Do I believe in God?

Perhaps it is enough to say that I believe in *Shabbos*. I believe in its bready tastes, its music and spicy smells. When the candles flicker and gutter like life itself, when the *kiddish* cups glisten and the stars fall into the night like fireworks, I can feel *something* . . . the Queen Bride of the Sabbath . . . the *Shekhinah*, which is the holy presence, the second soul we are given for but one day a week. And then I, too, can taste *Pardes* . . . Paradise.

And after all, if *I* can be a *Tzaddik*, then who am I to doubt the Creator?

-=-

Jack Dann is a multiple-award-winning author who has written or edited over 75 books, including the international bestseller *The Memory Cathedral*, which was #1 on *The Age* Bestseller list, and *Wandering Stars*, a 1974 pathbreaking anthology of science fiction short stories about Jewish people in the cosmos. His other short story collections include *Timetipping*, *Visitations*, *The Fiction Factory*, and *Jubilee*. Satalyte Publishers has just released a new 'unexpurgated' edition of his novel *The Rebel* entitled *The Rebel: Second Chance*. He is the co-editor, with Janeen Webb, of *Dreaming Down-Under*, which won the World Fantasy Award, and his anthology *Ghosts by Gaslight*, co-edited with Nick Gevers, won the Shirley Jackson Award and the Aurealis Award. A collection of Dann's Holocaust stories entitled *Concentration* is forthcoming. In an introduction to the volume, critic and scholar Marleen Barr writes: "Dann is a Faulkner and a Márquez for Jews. His fantastic retellings of the horror stories Nazis made real are more truth than fantasy." Also forthcoming is a showcase anthology entitled *Dreaming in the Dark*, which will launch the new imprint PS Australia, of which Dann is the publishing director; a collection of poetry entitled *Poems From a White Heart*; and a new novel (which is still under wraps). Dann lives in Australia on a farm overlooking the sea. You can visit his website at http://www.jackdann.com and follow him on Twitter @jackmdann.